REVPAC

REVENUE PARTICIPATION CAPITAL

BONDS

The New Revolutionary Financial Instrument

The new and revolutionary Financial Instrument – REVPAC BONDS - is the missing tool sought after by Bankers and Entrepreneurs that have experienced the struggle and anguish of underwriting emerging commercial enterprises - in the face of Today's EQUITY MARKETS' inability to yield "meaningful" funding solutions to worthwhile Venture Capital Opportunities.

The innovative key feature of the new Financial Instrument is the potent combination of "fractionalizing" future gross receipts of commerce and venture enterprises - coupled with an Investment Redemption Guaranty! Combining investment risk-insurance with multiple Return-on-Investment potential creates a cogent capital floodgate opener in the hands of Investment Bankers and Underwriters.

This potential flood of fresh investment capital may well be swift in coming... and 'once arrived' can create the Renaissance that many fund raising managers are seeking.

The REVPAC BOND offers the Investment-Finance World the opportunity for its first TRUE paradigm shift in recent memory...

The "paradigm shift" redirects the focus onto "fair and reasonable revenue sharing", through which to distribute "meaningful" rewards to risk takers of successful ventures - rather than the expectation of "equity appreciation" (trading stock market values) as is the present-day practice.

The REVPAC BOND "paradigm shift" is a much-needed solution for venture capital underwritings. The integration of investment-risk-insurance coverage brings together insurance-underwriters and investment-bankers into a working relationship - with the potential to foster new methods and products, radically different from anything we have hitherto seen - to fund emerging business ventures and small business enterprises.

Investment Bankers, that embrace the REVPAC BOND ... in its early stage ... will become the giants of Venture Capital. They will experience phenomenal growth - similar to that experienced by DREXEL BURNHAM and SOLOMON BROTHERS - and their investment syndicates - via their advent of the JUNK BOND and MORTGAGE BACKED GUARANTY - respectfully.

This is the most important book you will ever read for your financial future. *A must for the serious investor's reference library.* The whys and hows of financing and investing with the remarkable REVPAC financial instrument imminently to appear in your investment portfolio.

☆☆☆☆☆ **Finally, someone has written a comprehensive guide on what makes venture capital tick!**
Reviewer: **Peter Shouffle, Financial Advisor** from New York.
Ever wonder how mavens such as Gates, Pickens and Soros ensnare billion dollar ideas for a fraction of a penny on the dollar? Now you will be able to understand the dynamics of venture-capital *revenue participation* strategies that have here-to-fore been the province of wall-street mavericks and angel investors. After studying this publication, I am convinced that REVPAC democratizes venture-capital finance and *for the first time* brings the extraordinary revenue opportunities within reach of the common investor. Business Finance book of the year!

☆☆☆☆☆ **REVPAC to impact emerging nations – especially Latin America!**
Reviewer: **Tomas Bolivar-Greco, Economist-Journalist, Daily Economist and Financial Press – "Reporte Diario de la Economia" (Latin America's Financial Daily)** from Caracas.
REVPAC fills the vacuum for bankers of emerging nations, especially Latin American nations. Investors from Mexico to Argentina have never been receptive to equity financing and are suspicious of debt funding – thusly, there exists a critical dearth of regional investment capital to incubate new business ideas.

REVPAC removes all obstacles for investment bankers to underwrite emerging issues – using one of the only remaining vehicles that Latin investors trust – the "fidecomiso"(trust) that can now be based in the only accounting principle that regional investors understand – gross revenue sharing!

The REVPAC Handbook and Guide might as well have been entitled – Blueprint for Economic Launch of the Americas!

REVPAC

REVENUE PARTICIPATION CAPITAL

BONDS

The New Revolutionary Financial Instrument

Changing the Way We Fund New Ideas

EMINEM L'ÉCONOMISTE

First Printing October 2017
10 9 8 7 6 5 4 3 2 1

ISBN 978-0-692-93734-1
Library of Congress Control Number 5757532499
Eminem L'économiste
REVPAC BONDS-1st ed.

Eminem L'économiste
  REVPAC - *Revenue Participation Capital* - BONDS - The New Revolutionary Financial Instrument for Venture Capital /
 Eminem L'économiste
  ISBN 978-0-692-93734-1
    1. Venture capital-United States - Handbooks, manuals, etc. 2. Angels (Investors)United States-Handbooks, manuals, etc. 3. Investments-United States-Handbooks, manuals, etc. I. Eminem L'économiste II. Title.

Published by REVPAC BONDS.

This book is available for special purchases in bulk by organizations and institutions, not for resale, at special discounts. Please direct your inquiries to the REVPAC BONDS press@revpacbonds.com

Please address inquiries about electronic licensing of the content, for use on a network to the REVPAC BONDS at

http://www.revpacbonds.com/

For my children: Natasha and Christian…
and to all of you who foster Creative Genius.

CONTENTS

For my children: Natasha and Christian…
and to all of you who foster Creative Genius.

CONTENTS

REVPAC in Action

Impact of Art REVPAC

Securities Analysts' View of REVPAC

Capital Markets Seeking REVPAC Solutions

Entrepreneurism & REVPAC

REVPAC Variations

REVPAC in Review

Guide for the Innovator/Developer

Guide for the Investor

Guide for the Investment Banker

Role of Media in REVPAC

REVPAC FAQ

REVPAC White Papers

Actuarial Analysis

Table of Authorities

Glossary

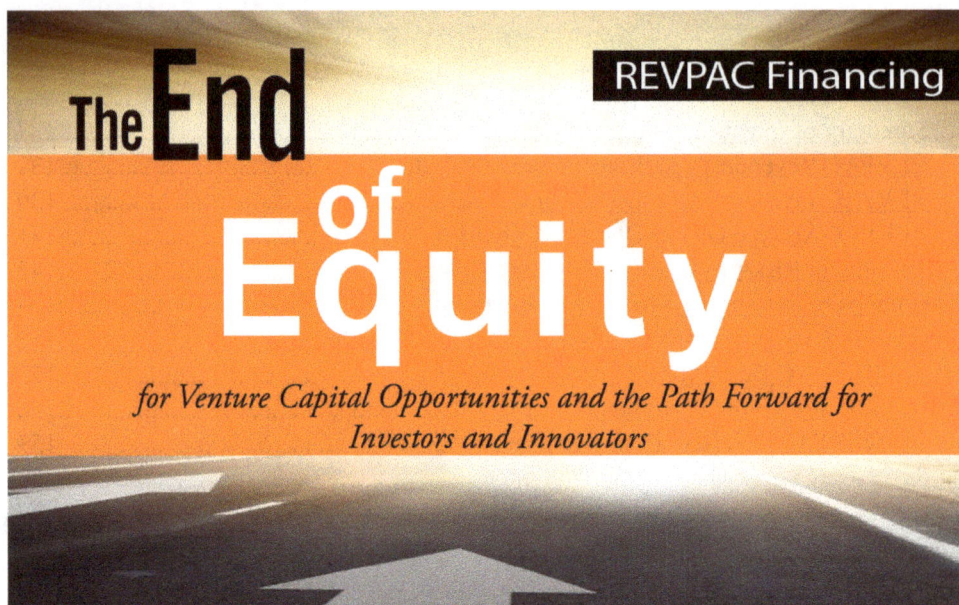

The **End** of **Equity**

REVPAC Financing

for Venture Capital Opportunities and the Path Forward for Investors and Innovators

PROLOGUE

Investors and Innovators are clamoring for dramatic changes in the ways that firms with great ideas finance themselves. Today's capital markets present a limited set of financing choices that are predominantly limited to debt or equity participation. These choices offer the investor a set percentage yield on principal (with no meaningful guarantee of repayment) /or/ a dilutable percentage ownership in the firm – with little to no yield.

Today's Equity Investment Opportunities, offering minority ownership in a firm that is emerging into the marketplace – with a New Idea – are, in effect, offering common shares that:

> • Have little or no yield entitlements – even if the firm realizes significant success in the marketplace;
>
> • Are dilutable, to substantially less equity ownership – or to *almost zero* – at the whim of majority shareholders that have made little or no capital contribution;
>
> • Wield no meaningful influence in the management of the company;
>
> • Offer little or no liquidity for divestiture.

Common Shares of Capital Stock are experiencing continuous deterioration in relevance to investors' commitment decisions and have become almost useless in venture capital market funding of New and Emerging Ideas!

The modern Venture Capital Investor does NOT trust Equity.

In the absence of accessible *trustworthy* financial instruments, to invest in Venture Capital opportunities - there is a critical shortage of fresh capital entering the marketplace and a resultant dearth of accessible financing for the rapidly widening number of Small Business Enterprises and Innovators seeking funding. In fact, a vast majority of fund raising attempts fail - virtually incapacitating many worthwhile ventures and squelching the creative genius that fostered them.

Prior to the 1930's, it was not uncommon for entrepreneurial firms with great ideas to distribute over 50 percent of their profits to investors. Today, however, no financial model exists that offers investors a meaningful percentage of revenues with the opportunity of earning multiple returns-on-investment — even ten times their investment — within a relatively short-term — five to seven years.

In this publication, beyond simply identifying the problem, this report offers a solution — Revenue Participation Capital (REVPAC) Bonds — and demonstrates its utility in key business sectors. Example: If an Investor is considering backing the expansion of a chain of "Starbuck-type" retail locations in a geographical territory - Which of the following two scenarios is preferable? 10% of the equity /or/ 10% of the gross sales revenues of the retail chain?

This publication presents a new way of thinking and evaluating indicators that identify and validate an innovation's true potential value, creating a barometer for a more up-to-date approach to critical Venture Capital investment decision-making.

REVPAC BONDS manifest the new revolutionary Financial Instrument that democratizes venture-capital economics. It brings forward, extraordinary revenue opportunities to the common investor and securitizes future revenues — minimizing the risk from investing in a new idea.

REVPAC BONDS combine the best of what Risk Insurance has to offer with the best of what Venture Capital Investments should be all about...the sharing of risk in return for the potential of extraordinary yields from successful ventures. REVPAC BONDS hold the promise of becoming the standard for global venture-capital markets — funding today's innovators into the next generation's renaissance.

Introduction

The Truth About Wall Street

Why, in this age of unprecedented prosperity and economic growth, are investors not realizing windfall returns on their investments in successful ventures?

Further, why are innovators and venture developers unable to access the capital they need to bring promising innovations to a global consumer market clamoring for new products and services?

Certainly, there is no shortage of capital — stock market indexes were, until recently, at an all-time high. Investors are continually being steered toward highly touted Initial Public Offerings (IPOs), many of which are highly speculative issues, by the promise of extraordinary returns in the secondary trading market. The abundance of available investment dollars has glutted the trading markets, driving market capitalizations of these "sweetheart" stocks to hundreds of times the value of the issuing companies themselves.

Yet even with these phenomenal overvaluations of seemingly successful ventures, investors are realizing little or no participation in the financial business success of the companies they are underwriting.

Pick up today's *Wall Street Journal*. Read the dividend column of the stock listings and compute the percentage of Return on Investment.

The average Blue Chip investment pays a dividend yield that is less than 2 percent of the stock price! In fact, since 1928, the dividend yield of Standard & Poor's "500" stock index, the most widely used benchmark of U.S. equity performance, has floated between 3 percent and 6 percent.

Do these percentages represent pieces of the action or a desirable return on investment to you? You can receive larger returns on your money from a Certificate of Deposit at your local bank while resting assured your principal will be returned in full!

Wall Street insiders would prefer that investors not look too closely at the lack of long-term yields from the stocks they promote. Instead, investors are compelled to risk their capital in anticipation of selling their holdings to other buyers in the "trading casinos" of the modern stock markets. The fickle focus of the forces behind the listed stocks direct the public's next move entirely apart from the "real-time" performance of the business of those companies bought and sold.

Today's stock markets are performing at extraordinary levels - even after the recent corrections from an all-time high, for there is more money than ever invested into our equity markets. There is so much capital activity engaged in playing the stock markets, the sheer volume is propelling most market indexes, once again, toward there record highs.

The fact remains, however, regardless of the performance of stocks, that today's stockholders are receiving miserable yields on their holdings.

In the absence of meaningful yields on investment from the success of a venture, investors must wager on what future investors will pay for a share of stock, not on what a company will distribute in profit-sharing dividends.

Worse, investors must engage in the most frustrating of conjecture in an attempt to predict a stock's future performance. The true process by which stock prices rise and fall is a complicated and closely guarded conspiracy of machinations of which the average stockholder is woefully unaware.

What makes stock prices escalate? What is the behind-the-scenes story of today's capital markets' extraordinary gains? And what is the real reason investors are not realizing the yields they deserve for financing successful ventures, while insiders reap astronomical returns? The answers are revealed in the following pages and they are sure to challenge your perspective.

Where Is the Capital for New Ventures?

In addition to precluding *good-faith* individual investors from realizing meaningful yields in return for the use of their money, traditional public issues of stocks and bonds generally exclude the entrepreneurial innovator by limiting access to expansion and marketing capital to only those sweetheart deals with high IPO appeal — and in which the underwriter and other market forces have considerable financial interest.

No matter the consumer market potential of a venture, it is extremely difficult to emerge into the marketplace with sufficient capital to meet the venture's potential through traditional funding vehicles available to develop new innovations.

In fact, analysts estimate that over 70 percent of emerging private and public offerings fail to garner sufficient financial backing to successfully develop their business plans, virtually incapacitating many worthwhile ventures and squelching the creative genius that fostered them. More often, industrial giants appropriate or otherwise subsume a promising idea at the point at which the innovator is most vulnerable to a takeover. After absorbing all of the research and development costs and investing countless hours in sweat equity to nurture an idea to fruition, most innovators and venture developers have exhausted their capital resources and are unable to finance a marketing campaign.

The large corporation with greater accessibility to capital can easily take advantage of the innovator's need, fund the venture through the marketing phase, and leave the innovator with little or no participation in the consumer success of their brainchild.

Unwilling to witness the stillbirth of a promising consumer venture, many developers accept a seemingly attractive buy-out offer and instead witness the results of their concept and dedicated efforts turned into a moneymaking machine for someone else.

Can there be a change in the way worthy innovations find their way to market? Imagine the wealth of new product choices and technology breakthroughs available to consumers in a truly stimulated competitive capital environment.

Imagine that you can design the perfect Financial Instrument for new ventures!

Now, imagine that you can design the perfect investment and funding vehicle to solve these concerns. An instrument that could access much-needed funding for entrepreneurial innovators to bring worthy ventures to market. An instrument that, at the same time, could reward loyal investors with returns truly reflective of the success of those ventures in which they invest wrapped in a liquid, tradable financial instrument that even includes the option of zero risk to the original investment.

What would it comprise? How would you structure such an investment instrument from the ground up?

1 Of course, you would want it to provide meaningful yields — with the potential for windfalls — a true piece of the action based on revenue yields that flow from point-of-sale locations to investors without management interference or deductions. You would want to be justly rewarded for your demonstrated confidence — for your "grubstake" in the venture.

You would want to be able to track the performance of your investment as the developing venture emerges into the marketplace and estimate the value of your holdings based on real-time consumer response to the venture.

REVPAC is the only financial instrument based on Gross Revenues. The investor receives a portion of each and every sales dollar realized by the venture. Investors have constant, real-time access, via the Internet, to management reports on the venture as it emerges, and to financial information from the very first transaction.

2 In designing your perfect invest-ment vehicle, you would want optimal liquidity in a secondary market, the opportunity to speculate on the future value of your holdings based on market information and the progress of the developing venture.

REVPAC holders enjoy the ability to trade their holdings in secondary trading markets at any time prior to the expiration of the REVPAC and the cessation of their revenue-sharing rights. These secondary markets for REVPACs provide investors with liquidity and the ability to participate in the success of ongoing ventures in which they are interested.

3 Of course, your perfect investment vehicle would provide a significant hedge against risking your initial investment. Were it possible, you would integrate a *guarantee* of the return of your principal so you could feel comfortable to invest, even your most precious resources, such as your retirement fund or money set aside for your children's education.

REVPAC is the only investment instrument with an optional Full Redemption Guaranty. For more conservative investors, this means you will never lose a penny of your investment, no matter what the consumer response to the venture — even if the venture is a complete failure.

4 Your ideal financial instrument would afford innovators the possibility of accessing funding without incurring debt or dilution of ownership in their enterprise. The only responsibility of the innovator should be the sharing of wealth — *not* encumbering the control of one's own destiny.

REVPAC provides venture innovators and developers access to much-needed capital without amassing debt or relinquishing equity interest in their enterprise. The sole fiscal obligation of the innovator/developer is to provide revenue participation to investors while maintaining 100 percent management control of the venture during the term of the REVPAC. At the end of the term, once investors have realized their revenue participation, the innovator/developer retains 100 percent ownership rights to the venture.

> REVPAC is the revolutionary financial instrument that will put the power — and the payout — back in the hands of the investors and innovators who deserve to reap the rewards of the successful ventures they foster in good faith.

5 Finally, you would design a fail safe system of checks and balances to assure yourself — *risking your hard-earned capital* — that all of the investment proceeds would go directly into developing the venture — *in which you're pinning your expectations for financial rewards* — and that all future gross revenues are accountable. After all, you want to be certain that if the venture is a success, you will receive your fair portion of the gross revenues. *The REVPAC Financial Model is structured to provide a bonded Business Manager who is responsible for the development of the venture project. The Business Manager is supervised during each and every step of the venture development by a Trust Administrator. The Trust Administrator is an accredited financial institution, insured against errors and omissions, responsible to allocate your investment proceeds to the Business Manager. Also, the Trust Administrator is your watchdog and is mandated to administer the gross revenues flow of the venture and to disburse your portion to you without deductions of any kind. This means you never need to worry about someone interfering with your yields.*

Within these pages, we have dissected every traditional funding and investment medium and identified the inherent flaws in each. Over 20 years of research and testing have been dedicated to developing the solution to the imminent venture-capital crises being wrought by the absence of a modern financing and investment instrument to fund new innovations. This solution is the REVPAC Investment Model.

It is time to reclaim investment capital from the secondary markets for venture-capital IPOs, and arrest the consumption of new ventures by institutional investment behemoths who are creating empires of wealth from the sweat of the innovators striving to realize the dream of a better future.

You have in your hands the tool to do just that.

* * *

Historic Highlights of Economics and Finance

1750
London Stock Exchange
(first in the modern world)

1760
Amsterdam Stock Exchange
Celebrates 50-year trading anniversary of
East India Company (First IPO and first
traded equity in modern world)

1770
Adam Smith
(Father of Economics)
Publishes: *Wealth of Nations*

1860
Karl Marx
Publishes: *Das Kapital*

1880
First Mutual Fund
Emerges in Great Britain

Scottish American Investment Company
founded by Robert Fleming (Grandfather
to Ian Fleming, Creator of Agent 007 and
Author of James Bond Novels)

007

1938
Capital Asset Pricing
Model

Changes
Equity
Investing

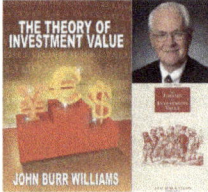

THE THEORY OF
INVESTMENT VALUE
JOHN BURR WILLIAMS

1940
John M. Keynes
Publishes:
General Theory of Interest and Money

1960
John Galbraith
Publishes: *New
Industrial State*

1990
CMA Patent issued to
Merrill Lynch
(First financial instrument patented)

Junk Bonds and LBOs
emerge

2000
DotCom Bubble / Enron /
Arthur Andersen & Worldcom

ENRON
WORLDCOM
ARTHUR
ANDERSEN

NOW! REVPAC
First Venture Capital Revenue–Powered Unit Trust Bond

1790
New York Stock Exchange
Established

1810
Limited Partnership Entity
Emerges in Great Britain

1850
Industrial Revolution begins

1890
Alfred Marshall

PRINCIPLES OF
ECONOMICS

1924
First Mutual Fund
Emerges in America

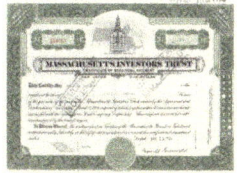

1929
Great Depression

1970
U.S. Dollar

Exits gold
standard

1980
Arthur Laffer

Publishes:
Private Short Term Capital Flow

2008
Global Financial Crises

2016
Chinese Stock Market Crash / Brexit

EMERGES INTO GLOBAL MARKET

Highlights of Our Economic Landscape

Debt Financing

History
Debt financing is the oldest mechanism for leveraging other people's money to finance emerging ventures or access capital for asset-rich but cash-poor enterprises.

Consumers and investors are comfortable with the concept of borrowing against future income. In fact, by volume, the second most widely used form of financial instrument in the past 50 years is the home mortgage. In 1996 the value of outstanding mortgages was over $3.6 trillion, 2.5 times more than the value of outstanding corporate bonds.

Bonds are currently the only publicly traded security with any assurance of a return of capital invested. This doesn't mean bonds are guaranteed or that there is no downside to buying even AAA- rated issues.

For the investor, highly rated bonds offer a long-term, relatively secure income vehicle — but never do they provide windfall returns. Secondary markets for debt instruments are as volatile as the stock markets, and more subject to the crests and ebbs of inflation.

Issuers who qualify for debt financing through bank loans, bond issues, or other underwriting sources may be well- advised to proceed with caution.

Corporations seldom envision the lean years in which they will continue to accumulate, and must pay, the interest incurred via debt financing. One failed venture can wipe out years of strong revenue achievement, leaving the liability on the books.

Insiders of companies heavily burdened with debt may also experience a sobering realization as they witness the gradual reduction in value of their equity ownership in a troubled company, making liquidation virtually impossible.

Why isn't debt financing the answer?
Debt financing limits the investor to a fixed rate of return in an instrument with limited secondary market upside and little to no inflation hedge.

The lack of adjustment for inflation or recession works against both the issuer and the investor. Interest rates can fall substantially below those at which the bonds were issued, increasing the liability of the issuer when the bonds mature.

For investors, the risk is great when in- terest rates rise above that at which they purchased the bond, tying up their capital with few options for liquidity at a break-even price.

"Besides compensating a buyer for the use of this money and for the issuers' credit risk, a bond's interest rate has to fully compensate for future inflation — otherwise the bond buyer's investment will shrink by the year." Charles R. Morris in **Money, Risk and Greed**

Today's corporations are swimming in debt. The venture-capital industry is in dire need of a mechanism to produce the capital to fund new ideas and further current growth, while easing the debt burden of the enterprises that bring those innovations to market.

Many corporations, and especially start-up enterprises, are simply not "debt-qualified" (or qualifiable). With no history of revenues, a company will encounter tremendous difficulty accessing the capital needed to emerge into the marketplace through bond offerings or lending institutions.

If a company is able to secure debt financing at a reasonable interest rate, any ensuing lean revenue years can send the balance sheet into a nosedive as heavy debt obligations erode even a substantial asset base. Debt obligations do not go away. Even bankruptcy protection cannot ensure the retention of any assets to revitalize a failed or failing venture.

The value of any fixed-rate, long-term instrument is very susceptible to fluctuations in interest rates. A 30-year AAA and fixed-rate long-term bond purchased for $1,000 at 5 percent

interest per annum becomes virtually worthless (at maturity) assuming even a 3 percent average inflation over the 30 years. The value of the bond is determined almost entirely by the stream of interest payments.

If interest payments rise to 10 percent, and newly issued bonds return $100 per year for every $1,000 invested, the market value of a bond that returns only 5 percent per year would drop to about $500. As little as a 1 percent rise in interest rates causes roughly a 10 percent loss in the value of the bond.

Bonds will always have a conservative investor appeal for those AAA-rated corporations with a history of increasing annual financial performance. Savvy investors, seeking potentially unlimited returns and an option of zero risk, will not allow themselves to be duped by the fallacy that bonds are the only stable investment instrument.

Partnership Financing
Limited partnerships are another form of funding doomed to be relegated in the coming years to family businesses and select long-term ventures. A partnership structure is, by nature, high-risk to the partners — with little to no guarantee of

return on investment and great liability for debt incurred by the venture.

No regulatory body exists to protect partnership investors, and there are limited reporting requirements for partnership ventures. This lack of regulation, combined with the potentially severe liability of partnerships, leaves investors with little recourse in incidents of failure of the general partners (venture managers) to perform to the objectives set for the venture.

General partners usually glean a percentage of net revenues from successful partnership-financed ventures — sometimes as much as 40 percent — with no risk-capital participation.

Overview and History
The limited partnership model is a product of 18th-century Britain. For over 200 years, it remained the most widely chosen option to marry venture capital to new business development.

In the United States, partnerships came into vogue in the tax-shelter years of the 1960s and '70s but proved to be woefully inadequate sources of meaningful investor returns. In recent decades, the elimination of previous tax benefits and the inherent flaws in the partnership structure have driven investors to seek higher, and often more secure, yields elsewhere.

Partnership financing retains a certain appeal in some business sectors, offering the opportunity to spread the financial risk among the partners and lessen the impact of venture failures.

Like all traditional forms of venture capital, competition for partnership

financing is fierce and remains out of reach for many worthy endeavors.

Future
Partnerships offer zero opportunity for liquidity. There exists no secondary trading market for partnership instruments. This lack of liquidity, combined with potentially high liability and no assurance of return on investment (or even return of investment), will continue to erode the appeal of partnership financing.

Equity Financing: Wall Street's Rube Goldberg Apparatus
Once upon a time, investors bought stocks with the good faith that a company would return a portion of its earnings to its shareholders in the form of substantial dividends. That tale seems almost preposterous to consider in this electronic age in which it is rare that an investor ever sees an actual stock certificate, let alone retains a position in a stock long enough to earn any dividend that might be distributed.

In fact, before the infamous U.S. stock market crash of 1929, American investors were rewarded with meaningful yields via generous dividends based on the financial success of the businesses in which they invested.

Prior to 1929, investors were true partners in business with the companies with which they entrusted their funds. The money pioneering an undertaking was afforded the same level of monetary consideration as the talent producing the venture and the sales effort promoting the product or service in the marketplace. When it was time to divvy up the spoils, those who had funded the venture could count on an equitable share of revenues generated in the marketplace. It was not uncommon for pre-1929 corporations to issue dividends to stockholders representing 30 percent or more of their net revenues.
Many corporations issued dividends ranging from 50 percent to 90 percent of net revenues!

After the Crash, government and industry — jointly and severally — strove to implement mechanisms to prevent the calamity from recurring, and adopted measures and practices that dramatically changed the investor-reward landscape.

In 1934, the U.S. government chartered the Securities and Exchange Commission and charged it with the onerous task of policing the securities industry and regulating issuers of investment vehicles. This was done to "protect" the investing public from the potential pitfalls of an unstable market. Concurrently, the advent of the Internal Revenue Service was in process — with one key aspect of their charter being to enforce the collection of taxes on corporate net revenues and investor dividends.

In 1938, economists adopted a new Equity Investment Model — devised at Harvard University — known as the Equity Capital Asset Pricing Theory.
This theory postulates that a company can retain the majority of *Net Revenues* to reinvest into corporate growth and issue minor arbitrary increments of *Net Revenues* to shareholders as dividends. The result of this marked philosophical change is that investors are now forced to rely on the appreciation of share holdings in secondary markets to compensate them for their demonstrated faith in backing new ventures.

This theory was based on the presumption that a company could hold back earnings and opt not to pay dividends — instead reinvesting in expansion programs and/or the buy-back of their own stock on the open market — to produce the net effect of an increase in the stock price. In tandem with this, the company would exhibit improved performance and more impressive balance sheets, thereby increasing the value of investors' shares. This paved the way for the current market mindset — which was accepted with appalling ease — that companies have little or no obligation to "share the wealth" generated from successful ventures with the investors that made that very success possible. The investing public was given no alternative but to gamble on the future price of stocks of even the most historically outstanding revenue performers.

The model fails mightily to fulfill its intent. For the investing public, it actually *increases* risk. Regardless of the business success of a company, market manipulations and inevitable market corrections can send the value of even Blue Chip holdings into a downward spiral, leaving investors with grievously undervalued holdings.

The model, in practice, also serves to prevent many worthy endeavors from ever seeing the light of day. Investors are often wary of promising innovations not backed by industrial giants with the substantial assets necessary to support market emergence.

Each year, over 70 percent of new offerings fail to achieve adequate capitalization for market emergence. We cannot begin to estimate the number of potential market blockbusters that fall just short of that threshold.

The Equity Capital Asset Pricing Theory is a barrier erected and diligently maintained by the investment banking community that prevents innovative genius from accessing the much-needed funding to bring the fruits of that genius to the consumer market.

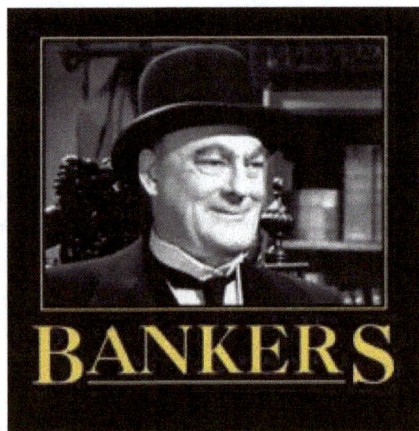

BANKERS

Best-Kept Secret on Wall Street
The investment community is dominated by institutional investors (funds, insurance companies, banks, etc.) that control over 85 percent (by market value) of all capital activity engaged in the equity and bond markets. This consortium of institutions would like the small investor

to buy into the popular belief that stock market prices fluctuate on the basis of supply and demand.

If the demand for a stock outstrips the number of shareholders willing to sell their shares at a certain price, the stock price will increase in value until shareholders are willing to sell enough shares to meet the demand. This is what causes Price-Earnings (P/E) Ratios to increase until, theoretically, the price of the stock is overvalued and buyers back away from overpaying.

In reality, supply and demand is but a small component of a much larger picture — replete with intricate and covert influences at work to control the trading performance of a stock. There are "short-sellers" (stock traders working *against* the company's stockholders) and "long buyers" (traders working *for* the company's stockholders) all trying, through complex machinations, to send the prices of shares up or down. There are option traders, program traders, and market makers artificially bolstering or driving down the price of a stock through esoteric maneuvers, and a host of other factors that affect the stock performance — none bearing any relation to the business performance of the venture!

Stockbrokers and investment bankers argue that the Equity Investment Model is sound because public companies reinvest their earnings, thereby increasing the value of the assets, earning potential, and the overall stockholders' equity.

This sounds reasonable. However, historically very few companies completing a stock offering for a new venture realize more than three successive years of increased earnings during the first 10 years following the Initial Public Offering (IPO).

Consequently, in a capital environment that practices the Equity Investment Model, there are no real rewards (dividends) for equity participation in an emerging venture, and investors are forced to rely on future trading value appreciation of their holdings. Those shareholders who back new ventures in anticipation of long-term gains rarely realize an appreciable Return on Investment.

Future of the Equity Investment Model

It would seem, with this bleak snapshot of the antiquated Equity Investment Model, that the investment banking community would be clamoring for restructure to prevent the imminent crisis as investors wise up and redirect the flow of capital away from *micro-cap* or thinly capitalized emerging ventures.

On the contrary, even as the micro-cap venture-capital pool shrinks (see chart, page 1) and competition for that capital intensifies, there exists no exigent demand for change in the investment banking community.

The majority of the capital invested in the stock markets today is managed by performance-driven, market-sector specialists who have little interest in the dwindling demand by individual investors for innovative micro-cap IPOs. Institutional investors have not abandoned the underwriting of *select* IPOs. Insiders and market makers are still reaping huge windfalls from those favored issues in the secondary trading markets as institutions trade securities among themselves.

Historically, it is the independent investor — *not the institutional investor* — who contributes most of the capital funding for pioneering-concept IPOs. In the absence of significant dividend yields, and with a highly manipulated secondary trading market, where is the payoff for the individual investor who identifies and backs a market rainmaker?

Change and innovation in the financial community are instituted first at the venture-capital investment-banking stage. Because there has been no outcry from the individual investors who make up the venture-capital community, and as there has been no viable new financial instrument on the scene, no revolutionary change has occurred since the advent and worldwide embrace of the Equity Capital Asset Pricing Theory— in 1938!

Due to the increasingly myopic concentration on short-term trading profits, the investment-banking community has abetted, however unwittingly, the dwindling of the venture-capital pool available to cultivate creative genius.

Because so many worthy ventures are unable to access much-needed capital, creative innovations are prevented from emerging into the consumer marketplace in this, the most enduring economic boom in the history of the industrialized nations.

A Change in the Wind

The emergence of Silicon Valley's "angel investors" is a recent example of the impetus to change to which the investment community reacts. Thousands of new millionaires and billionaires are investing heavily in ventures they predict will have broad — and deep — consumer market appeal.

These pennies from heaven don't come cheap. Angel investors take hefty equity positions in the ventures they back. These are typically high-technology, high-risk endeavors that, when successful, pay out big — both to the angel investor and to insiders — leaving the historically all-powerful investment-banking community and the private investor completely out of the loop.

Private investors are becoming leery of IPOs, especially micro-cap issues — the cradle for new and emerging business ventures. They are tired of backing winning concepts and receiving no meaningful return on their investments. The resilience of secondary markets has become the sole reason to buy any stock.

The probability of trading shares at a profit is the only consideration investors weigh. The days of holding stocks and anticipating long-term yields are gone. Investors no longer expect windfall yields from their stakes in new ventures.

This expectation of a rich secondary market seemed reasonable in yesterday's bull market. However, the "take-out" (selling price at which a profit is realized) rarely develops to a degree commensurate with the risk. Secondary trading markets for new micro-cap ventures are not active or deep enough to sustain steady increases for large volumes of shareholders attempting to extract profits when those takeout prices are pegged.

Why should investors not receive a meaningful percentage of the success of a venture funded with their money? It is not only fair play, but will serve to stimulate secondary markets as well, to reward investors with yields derived directly from the consumer success— the *revenue generation* — of a venture.

With the REVPAC Venture Capital Unit Trust Bond, we accelerate into the future — using the best ideas from the past, scrapping some of the current thinking, and coupling it together with new ideas.

The time for REVPAC has come.

*　　*　　*

Why Traditional Investment Mediums Fail to Produce Meaningful Returns

Management "appropriates" revenues

Why do insiders think in terms of multiples (50x-plus) when they envision Returns on Investment (ROI) for themselves, but think in terms of mere "percentages" (10-15 percent) when they plan ROI for their faithful investors? Where is the reward for the money that brings the venture to market?

Let's face facts. No one savvy in the ways of the business world will invest acquired knowledge, experience, time and effort into an enterprise for anything less than extraordinary returns. Entrepreneurs dream of the multimillion-dollar rewards of "going public," using leverage and enhancement strategies and OPM (Other People's Money) — yours!

Revenue Participation has been a foreign concept since the crash of 1929, when those who grubstaked a venture were true partners and reaped the rewards — *in the form of meaningful yields* —
of the successful ventures they backed.

Today's business start-up is structured along lines more favorable to the insiders. Let's look at an example of the typical thinking behind a new business venture.

Company A needs $10 million to finance the marketing phase of its latest innovation, and it projects $10 million to $50 million in sales for Year 1. Cost of sales should run 35 percent of wholesale receipts, and operating expenses an additional 40 percent, leaving 25 percent of gross receipts (or $2.5 million at the low end) of net earnings before taxes.

Through an IPO, Company A offers one-third of the company's equity (common shares) to investors for $10 million. If the company distributes 10 percent of net revenues as a dividend, on sales of $10 million (net being 25 percent less taxes of 35 percent), the result is an after-tax net of 16 percent. Company A's 10 percent dividend payout will be equivalent to 1.6 percent of gross sales, providing stockholders $160,000 in dividends and leaving $1.44 million in earnings for the company.

If Company A sells 10 million shares at $1 per share and allocates 20 million shares for insiders, the company will realize a per-share earnings of 16 cents on gross sales of $10 million ($4.88 million in after-tax earnings divided by 30 million shares). If Company A's shares trade at only a 15-to-1 Price-Earnings Ratio, the stock will trade at $2.45 per share.

If the company realizes its goal of $10 million in sales, investors receive a dividend of 1.6 cents per share (10 percent of earnings), plus a trading-price for their shares of almost 2.5 times the IPO price.

Sounds great, doesn't it?

Let's look at how this scenario truly plays out in the stock markets.

The investors, who assumed all the financial risk, receive a yield of 1.6 cents per share (1.6 percent ROI). Their shares are projected to a trading value of $2.50 in secondary markets. Of course, that value is dependent upon sufficient interest in the secondary market for the company's shares, enough depth and volume of trading to assure a 15-to-1 price-earnings ratio — *and* the ability of the market interest to sustain that ratio as investors sell into the market to reap the rewards of their demonstrated confidence in the venture.

In the highly competitive real world of stock trading, once the Initial Public Offering is completed, the retail brokers who sold the stock abandon the offering and move on to the next great underwriting effort.

The wholesale trading brokers take over the trading market with the sole interest of earning the difference between the *bid price* (the price at which the trader will buy the shares from a seller) and the *ask price* (the price at which the trader will sell the shares to a buyer).

If there are more sellers than buyers, the wholesale traders will bid lower and lower prices, discouraging sellers, while moving the ask price lower in tandem with the bid price to encourage buying.

If interest is not generated among new stock buyers for the company's shares, the wholesalers will not take a "long position" (buy stock for the brokerage firm's own account), anticipating future buyers to whom the shares can be sold.

A sale of a block of 100,000 shares of stock can cause the price of shares in a thinly traded stock to fall from $2.50 per share to $1 per share or less. The investors who backed Company A's market emergence may well find themselves holding nearly worthless paper, waiting for their measly 1.6 percent ROI through dividends.

All the while the insiders, one year after the IPO and leveraging the investors' money, have collected ample salaries plus $320,000 in dividends — and retain control of a company with retained earnings of $4.4 million.

Not a bad Year 1 for the insiders.

If Company A can repeat its inaugural success in subsequent years, and can successfully compete — having created a competitive market for its products — a second year of increased sales may indeed sustain the 1.6 percent ROI for the IPO investors.

The truth of the matter is, very few companies in niche markets return for a second banner year. The odds are the company will *never* repeat the success it enjoyed in Year 1, and will experience a series of losing years while searching for its next breakthrough sales winner.

Despite the dismal future likely for Company A, *some people* got wealthy as a result of the successful Year 1. Why was it not the investors who assumed all the financial risk to achieve that profitable year?

If the entrepreneur of Company A had brought his venture to market in the pre-1929 era — before the adoption of the Equity Investment Model — company IPO shareholders would have realized a ROI between 8 and 15 percent *(50 to 90 percent, respectively,* of earnings distributed as a dividend), instead of the paltry 1.6 percent. The "insiders" would *still* have netted $1 million!

Imminent Crisis in the Capital Marketplace

The coming venture-capital crisis is undeniable. Innovators have severely limited opportunities to emerge into the marketplace. In seeking much-needed capital, entrepreneurs often are forced to relinquish management and equity control to venture capitalists or behemoth corporate entities.

This lack of independence in the competitive arena is eroding the essence of capitalism from its core outward. A few industrial giants have put a stranglehold on innovation, keeping from market new technologies, entertainment, art, healthcare products, and other breakthrough innovations that in an environment of true consumer choice could revolutionize the marketplace.

Capital for new, independent enterprises is at such a premium that venture capitalists and angel investors can take huge percentages of earnings — virtually raiding the coffers of creative genius, venture developers, and investors.

As consumers, investors, and innovators become aware of the extent to which a core conglomerate dictates the availability of resources, in what is lauded as the laissez faire philosophy at the heart of capitalism, the pendulum is beginning to swing back to the days of meaningful rewards for participation in independent ventures.

REVPAC
UNIT TRUST BONDS
level the playing field for developer-innovators, and removes the obstacles to opportunity that are integral — by design — in today's traditional financing theories and practices.

REVPAC TRUST BOND

REVPAC (Revenue Investment Trust Bond) is the culmination of over 20 years of development toward perfecting an investment instrument capable of solving the multitude of problems inherent in every major form of financing. *The architects of REVPAC looked "forward to the past" when investors were truly partners and shared in consumer success through meaningful revenue participation yields, distributed directly from the marketplace without middle-management interference.* The REVPAC instrument represents the amalgamation of the best of the most viable investment vehicles — with some revolutionary innovations to set a new world standard for funding ventures. REVPAC is simple to understand, straightforward to administer, and consistent in its application throughout every venture in which it is applied.

Anatomy of a REVPAC

Imagine a "gross" Revenue Participation Share, Zero Risk Redemption Guaranty, Windfall Warrant, and Surety Risk Insurance Wrap bundled together into an easy-to-use Financial Instrument. Voila! You have REVPAC.

REVPAC embodies four component parts wrapped into an Investment Trust that provides unerring accountability — real-time performance reporting — extraordinary revenue yield potential and Surety Risk Insurance Wrap where *investors never lose a dollar of their investment!*

REVPAC is comprised of a Revenue Trust Bond with attached yield coupons, Full Redemption Guaranty, Future Participation Warrant and built-in Risk Insurance Coverage Package.

REVPAC INVESTMENT TRUST BOND

Holder receives yields based on "gross" revenues of business venture received by Investment Trust.

Revenue Yield Coupons mature 36, 48, 60, 72 and 84 months following IPO of the Investment Trust.

Holder is guaranteed to recover 100% of original investment at full term.

Holder can purchase future REVPAC issue for ensuing term of Investment Trust.

REVENUE SHARE

The REVENUE SAHRE is the "REVENUE ENGINE" that drives the REVPAC TRUST BOND.

REVPAC accesses funding capital to launch Commercial Ventures – without encumbering "Recourse Debt" or causing "Equity Dilution" upon the Innovator /and/ "secures" extraordinary Return-on-Investment (ROI) potential for Investors.

REVENUE SHARE CERTIFICATE

For Example: If a venture grosses $50 million and the REVPAC Trust Unit Bond holders own a 10 percent Revenue Participation Entitlement, the Certificate yield $5 million.

How it Works

The REVPAC "bundles" Investment Capital into a "Debt Obligation" – through the Subordinated Debenture Wrap – together with the "Intellectual Properties" and the "Capital Assets" of the Venture. The SURETY Wrap – known as the Collateralized Yield Obligation – WARRANTIES and SECURITIZES the Revenue Entitlements of the Investors.

The Revenue Share allows investors to share in each and every dollar derived from the marketplace. No more guesswork about yields: The revenues flow directly from the marketplace to the investors; no middle management interference or deductions.

Key Features

For Investors:

•   100% Revenue Entitlement Yields. Revenue Entitlement – *Future Gross Revenue Yields* – "flow" from the Commercial Venture to Investors, as "Debt" disbursal. This allows full "pass through" of Revenue Entitlements without TAX or YIELD Interference, Interruption or Deduction, of any kind.

•   No "Cap" on ROI Yields. Revenue Entitlements are directly "linked" to gross revenue receipts of the Commercial Venture. There exists no "maximum" amount of yield that the Investors may receive.

•   Ultimate Hedge against Inflation. Since the Revenue Entitlements flow to investors from the Point-of-Sale level /and/ Prices at the Point-of-Sale level, adjust to market and currency conditions - quicker than at any other level of the economy – Investor Yields ride the tide of inflation like a floating cork.

For Innovators:

•   No Personal Liability. Investment Capital is accounted for as NOT-RE-COURSE DEBT. In the event the Venture gross revenue receipts are insufficient to repay the "Non-Recourse Loan" – in the event that the Commercial Venture fails to generate sufficient revenues, Innovator is NOT liable to repay Principal or Interest remaining on unpaid balance.

•   Does Not Encumber Credit. Non-Recourse Debt is an "Off-Balance-Sheet Entry" – for accounting purposes. REVPAC funding does NOT encumber "Credit Worthiness" of Innovator or the Commercial Venture (as would be the case with traditional debt financing).

•   100% Equity Ownership. REVPAC Funding does NOT dilute EQUITY INTEREST in the Commercial Venture. Innovator retains entitlement to own 100% interest in the Commercial Venture, at full term of the REVPAC TRUST BOND.

REVENUE YIELD DISTRIBUTIONS (COUPON vs SMART CARD)

REVENUE YIELD COUPONS
REVPAC Bonds Eligible to be publicly traded

The REVPAC Trust Bond, if registered to be traded on a secondary trading market, will have Revenue Yield Coupons, attached to the Bond Certificate. The Revenue Yield Coupons entitle the holder to receive revenue yield distributions, based on an established percentage of the gross revenues, derived from the venture during the term of the REVPAC. The term may be for five, six, seven, or more years, depending upon the life cycle of the venture's emergence into the marketplace.

For example, a seven year REVPAC Trust Bond will have five Revenue Yield Coupons. All revenue yields accumulate in the Investor's trust account, until distributed. Distribution commences with the redemption of Coupon #1, on the third anniversary of the completion of the Bond's Initial Offering. Distribution of yields continues each year, thereafter.

Coupon No. 1	After 36 months: first distribution of gross revenue yields	
Coupon No. 2	After 48 months: second distribution of gross revenue yields	
Coupon No. 3	After 60 months: third distribution of gross revenue yields	
Coupon No. 4	After 72 months: fourth distribution of gross revenue yields	
Coupon No. 5	After 84 months: fifth distribution of gross revenue yields	

When all Revenue Yield Coupons have been redeemed, the REVPAC has expired and all revenue participation entitlements of the holder cease.

REVPAC SMART CARD
REVPAC Bonds Ineligible to be publicly traded

The REVPAC Trust Bond, not eligible to be traded on a secondary trading market, may opt to include Revenue Yield Coupons, attached to the Bond Certificate /or/ in lieu of the Coupons, issue an electronic smart card to the holders of the Trust Bonds.

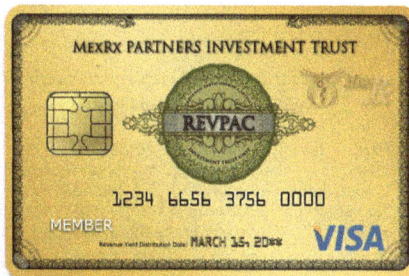

Revenue Yield Entitlements accumulate in the Investor's trust account, until distributed. Yields are streamed to the REVPAC Holder Smart Cards, daily, monthly, quarterly or as otherwise provided for in the Investment Trust Administrator Agreement.

When the REVPAC has expired, all revenue participation entitlements of the holder cease.

How it Works

All Revenue of the Commercial Venture is deposited into an "Electronic Lockbox" at the Depository Banking Institution, serving the Commercial Venture. The Trust Administrator for REVPAC Holders monitors all deposits.

Cash Deposits – for Point-of-Sale Cash Receipts are made at the end of each Business Day. *Digital Deposits* – for Point-of-Sale Debit/Credit Card /or/ "Electronic Receipts" are made as they occur.

All "apportioned" Revenue Entitlements are instantaneously segregated from deposited Revenues and electronically transferred to Trust Account for further distribution to REVPAC Holders' Smart Cards.

The "Seamless and Simultaneous" Banking Transaction of *Digital Deposits*: provide REVENUE YIELD ENTITLEMENTS to be transmitted and credited to the accounts of REVPAC Holders – *within milliseconds of the receipt-of-revenue at the Point-of-Sale.*

Key Features

•   Real-Time Revenue Entitlement. The REVPAC Holder with Revenue Yield Coupons has immediate yields (credited for future distribution) that enhance the valuation of the REVPAC Trust Bond in the secondary trading market /and/ the REVPAC Holder with electronic smart card has instant access to REAL-TIME Revenue Yields.

•   Ultimate Transparency. No more GUESSWORK of How a Commercial Venture is faring in the market. REVPAC Real-Time Yields represent the Ultimate Investment Tracker with market response that is IMMEDIATE, TANGIBLE and INFALLIBLE.

FULL REDEMPTION GUARANTY

The Full Redemption Guaranty is a "unified" Investment Risk Insurance coverage – comprised of a composite of risk-insurance policies – guaranteeing the original investment price of the REVPAC TRUST BOND.

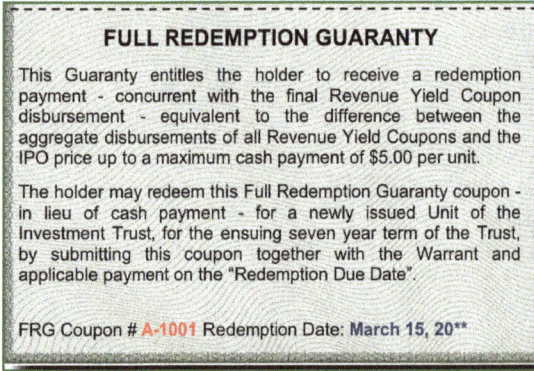

FULL REDEMPTION GUARANTY

This Guaranty entitles the holder to receive a redemption payment - concurrent with the final Revenue Yield Coupon disbursement - equivalent to the difference between the aggregate disbursements of all Revenue Yield Coupons and the IPO price up to a maximum cash payment of $5.00 per unit.

The holder may redeem this Full Redemption Guaranty coupon - in lieu of cash payment - for a newly issued Unit of the Investment Trust, for the ensuing seven year term of the Trust, by submitting this coupon together with the Warrant and applicable payment on the "Redemption Due Date".

FRG Coupon # A-1001 Redemption Date: March 15, 20**

How it Works

The GUARANTY – SURETY Coverage guarantees that future Revenue Yields – disbursed through the Revenue Yield Coupons – will equal to /or/ be greater than the Initial Offering price of the REVPAC TRUST BOND.

In the event, the Commercial Venture YIELDS – disbursed to the REVPAC Holders – are less than the original investment price – at full term – the Full Redemption Guaranty pays the "shortfall" (difference between the original investment price and the yielded revenue share entitlements).

Key Features

For Investors:

•   The Full Redemption Guaranty Coverage affords Investors the opportunity to set-aside the consideration of risk for their Investment Capital.

For Innovators:

•   The FULL RISK GUARANTY Coverage is a composite Surety Risk Insurance Wrap that bonds and warranties the commercial venture, as well as the Investors. The Insurance Wrap serves to provide the assurance for the Innovator's "support team"– Management, Equity Partners, Vendors, Associates and all other parties – with an interest in the enterprise – that the Commercial Venture will emerge INTO THE MARKETPLACE.

•   The Insurance Underwriters' bonding and warranty of the venture's capability to emerge into the marketplace, significantly enhances the Innovator's ability to structure strategic alliances, which increases the opportunities of the commercial venture's potential to achieve Revenues and Success.

FUTURE PARTICIPATION WARRANT

Entitles the REVPAC holder to purchase one REVPAC Bond in the same venture for an additional term, or in a future commercial venture, developed by the same Innovator and managed by the identical Business Manager of the REVPAC Bond, to which the warrant is attached.

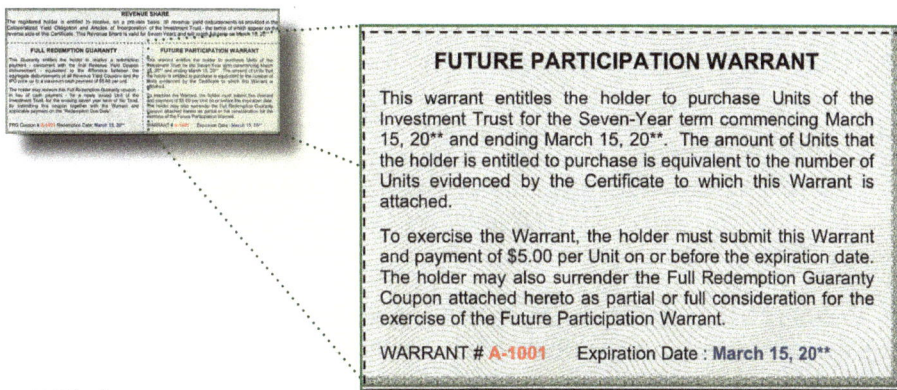

FUTURE PARTICIPATION WARRANT

This warrant entitles the holder to purchase Units of the Investment Trust for the Seven-Year term commencing March 15, 20** and ending March 15, 20**. The amount of Units that the holder is entitled to purchase is equivalent to the number of Units evidenced by the Certificate to which this Warrant is attached.

To exercise the Warrant, the holder must submit this Warrant and payment of $5.00 per Unit on or before the expiration date. The holder may also surrender the Full Redemption Guaranty Coupon attached hereto as partial or full consideration for the exercise of the Future Participation Warrant.

WARRANT # A-1001   Expiration Date : March 15, 20**

How it Works

Each Warrant entitles the Investor to purchase a new REVPAC Bond for the ensuing term of the Investment Trust. The purchase price is the identical Initial Offering Price of the instant REVPAC Bond (usually, $5.00 per Bond Unit). The Revenue Share entitlements for the next term are the identical percentage of gross revenues as the REVPAC Bond, to which the Warrant is attached plus additional revenue sharing entitlements that the Trust Administrator may declare.

In the event that the REVPAC holder elects to exercise the warrant, an IDENTICAL REVPAC BOND is issued for the succeeding term of the Investment Trust. As a general practice, REVPAC Bonds – purchased via the Future Participation Warrant – are issued without brokerage expenses.

In the event that the REVPAC holder elects NOT to exercise the Future Participation Warrant, the instant REVPAC Bond continues in full effect – however, the Future Participation Warrant portion is deemed as "expired" and ceases to be "effective" for purposes of purchasing future REVPAC Bond entitlements for succeeding commercial ventures.

Key Features

For Investors:

• The Future Participation Warrant ensures that the Investor can financially benefit from the "enhanced maturity value" of the overall Innovator/Business Manager "team" – attributable to the first term of the Investment Trust – funded by the Investor.

For Innovators:

• The Future Participation Warrant provides the Innovator with a viable source of capital resources for the development of future commercial ventures.

Built-In Risk Insurance Package Wrap LLOYD'S ZURICH AIG
LLOYD'S OF LONDON

The Venture will be wrapped with a complete Surety Risk Insurance Package of Policies. This "package" entails Ten (10) insurance, bond, guaranty, surety and warranty "wraps" that guarantee the performance of the Business Manager to get the Commercial Venture to the marketplace and ensure fiduciary accountability for all revenues.

The package of Risk Insurance Coverage is integrated into both the REVENUE SHARE and the FULL REDEMPTION GUARANTY for the REVPAC BOND Investors - which guarantee the Investors 100% Return-of-Original-Investment as well as any other guaranteed yield covenants contained in the REVPAC Funding Program. The Risk Insurance Wrap includes the following package of Risk Investment Surety policies:

1. *PERFORMANCE COMPLETION BOND* - Guaranty provides the Surety that the Innovator and Business Manager will fully develop the Commercial Venture and emerge into the marketplace within the Time-Line covenant promised to the Investors. In other words: this policy guarantees the Investors that their expectation of return-on-investment - which is wholly dependent on the capability of the Venture to generate revenues, in the marketplace - will have the opportunity to succeed.

2. *CREDIT/RECEIVABLE INSURANCE* - Guaranteeing the payment by customers for the Product/Services that are the underlying foundation of the Commercial Venture. In the event the customer is delinquent or incapable of fulfilling the payment - the Insurance coverage will pay the order in full. In this manner, the Commercial Venture and Venture Developers (including Investors) are not at risk of customer default.

3. *BUSINESS LIABILITY INSURANCE* - Fully inclusive risk coverage for product/ services of the Commercial Venture. This Insurance safeguards the Commercial Venture, Innovator/Business Manager and Investors from any and all claims from end-users or others arising from the emergence of the Commercial Venture into the marketplace.

4. *KEY MAN INSURANCE* - Coverage for the Commercial Venture and the Venture Developer. Insurance for Financial Recompense, in the event a "key" person that is integral to the development and emergence of the Venture is unable to fulfill the obligations requisite for full fruition of the Business Venture - and on which the success of the Venture is dependent in whole or part.

5. *FRAUD PROTECTION INSURANCE* - Risk coverage of any Claims or Losses that result from fraudulent acts or practices by any member of the management team, responsible for the development of the **Commercial Venture.**

6. *BUSINESS INTERRUPTION INSURANCE* - Protects the Commercial Venture from any Claims or Losses that result from the interruption of the development and emergence of the Venture, whether by labor strife, force majeure or any other occurrence.

7. *POLITICAL INSTABILITY INSURANCE* - Risk coverage to protect against Claims and Losses that result from any national conflict, embargo, civil unrest or any other interruption of the development and emergence of the Business venture due to political instability - whether domestic or foreign.

8. *CURRENCY CALAMITY INSURANCE* - Risk coverage to protect against the loss of value for revenues denominated in U.S. Dollars /or/ other approved national currencies. If Business Revenues lose in excess of 10% of their value, as a result, of devaluation, re-evaluation, currency control measures or any other mal-adjustment - to the deficit of the Commercial Venture - the Risk Insurance coverage guarantees restitution payment to correct the loss.

9. *DIRECTORS ERRORS & OMISSIONS INSURANCE* - Insurance that covers any Claims or Losses incurred by the Commercial Venture, as a result, of any actions by management of the Innovator/Business Manager or other integral entities responsible for the development of the venture.

10. *PROFESSIONAL SERVICES ERRORS & OMISSIONS INSURANCE* - Insurance that covers any Claims or Losses incurred by the Commercial Venture or the Venture Developer as a result, of any legal and accounting services rendered by the professional service providers responsible to the Venture and the Venture Developer.

*　　*　　*

The afore-stated Risk Insurance coverage is wrapped into the FULL REDEMPTION GUARANTY for the Investors. In effect: Investors are guaranteed to never be at risk of realizing any less than the Face Value of the REVPAC Bond.

The FULL REDEMPTION GUARANTY guarantees the Investors that the Revenue Participation Yields will equal certain minimum standards. These standards vary, depending upon the guaranteed yield provisions provided by the REVPAC BOND.. In all cases, the standard includes 100% Return of Original Investment.

This Guaranty provides: in event of Commercial Venture failure, for whatever reason, to yield revenue participation distributions to the Investors - sufficient to fulfill the guaranteed yield provisions contained in the REVPAC BOND - the Surety Risk Insurance Coverage will effect payments equal to the difference between revenue participation yields received (if any) and guaranteed yield provisions.

Key Features

For Risk Insurance Underwriters:

•　　　Risk Insurance Underwriters are afforded opportunity to participate in the business of insuring inherent uncertainties of commercial development, market conditions and future revenues for the Venture Capital Investment Banking Sector – in return for a participating share of the potential Gross Revenues of the underwritten Commercial Venture.

How REVPAC Works

A uniquely structured Investment Trust finances 100 percent of a business venture and takes, in return for its capital investment, "gross revenue-sharing rights." The Investment Trust receives a percentage of all revenues generated by the venture and issues a predetermined number of REVPAC Revenue Share Units to investors in an IPO.

The REVPAC IPO price is standardized at $5.00 per unit to simplify the formulas used to arrive at the optimum number of REVPACs to be issued.

The capital assets and proprietary claims (i.e., patents, trademarks, copyrights) of the venture, purchased with proceeds of the IPO, are held as chattel by the Investment Trust as collateral to secure the revenue-sharing rights.

The percentage of revenue- sharing rights to be allocated to the Investment Trust, and subsequently to REVPAC investors, is based on several factors — including the relative risk of the investment and the projected revenue generation of the venture.

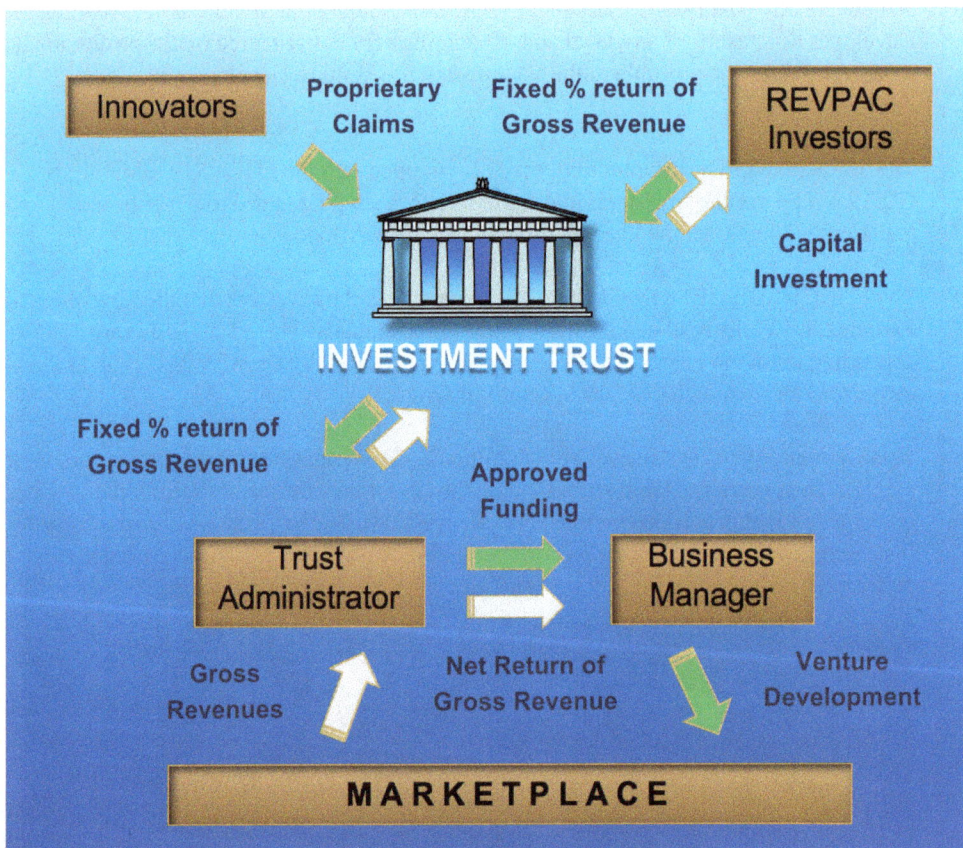

Innovators — Proprietary Claims — Fixed % return of Gross Revenue — REVPAC Investors

Capital Investment

INVESTMENT TRUST

Fixed % return of Gross Revenue

Approved Funding

Trust Administrator — Business Manager

Gross Revenues — Net Return of Gross Revenue — Venture Development

MARKETPLACE

The Investment Trust — through a Trust Administrator — collects proceeds from the IPO and allocates those proceeds to a Business Manager — the corporate entity that will direct the emergence of the venture into the consumer marketplace and manage daily operations toward revenue-producing goals.

All revenues generated from the venture are funneled through the Trust Administrator. Revenues are segregated by the Trust Administrator for allocation to the Business Manager and also to accumulate as yields to REVPAC investors.

During the first three years following the IPO, yields accumulate in an interest-bearing account. Yield distributions begin on the third anniversary following completion of the offering and occur annually thereafter through the term of the REVPAC.

The reason for the 36-month period between the IPO and the initial revenue yield (Coupon No. 1) is to provide sufficient time for the venture to mature in the marketplace and to give speculators the opportunity to trade in the secondary markets, potentially increasing the value of investors' holdings as the venture emerges.

Each REVPAC Investment Trust is structured independently — and specifically — to meet the needs of the venture to be funded, while providing optimal ROI to investors. The term of a REVPAC Investment Trust extends for five, six, seven, or more years, depending on the venture's projected revenues over time.

The term of the REVPAC is optimized to produce a minimum ROI of five to seven times the IPO price.

Management reporting is requisite throughout the emergence of a venture and for the life of the revenue-sharing rights of the REVPAC participants. Access to information is instantaneous for the investor through the Internet. Sales revenues are reported in real time.

REVPAC Business Managers are chartered with the singular goal of generating maximum revenues and performance bonded to ensure that the venture is not compromised by any substantial failure of management in the development of the venture.

REVPAC Investment Trust Administrators maintain absolute accountability for distribution of revenue yields — first into trust for revenue-sharing distribution to REVPAC participants, then to the Business Manager from which to derive operational capital and profit.

REVPACs trade on select public securities markets. As the venture is emerging into the marketplace, investors can speculate both on future revenues from the venture and future trading prices of the REVPAC Bond Units.

Only with REVPAC can investors be offered extraordinary short-term yield potential, long-term revenue participation, a built-in Risk Insurance Package Wrap, and the guaranty of zero-risk to their investment capital — all bundled in a simple-to-understand, and easy-to-use, publicly tradable investment instrument.

Why REVPAC Is Superior to Today's Other Venture-Capital Options

REVPAC makes possible extraordinary returns to the investor. The ROI potential is limited only by the consumer market share the venture can capture, and the revenue- share percentage is guaranteed the REVPAC holder. *There is no option for middle management to change accounting tactics and reinvest the revenue percentage accumulated to pay REVPAC yields. REVPAC holders are paid* first.

Additionally, REVPAC makes access to capital easier for the venture developer. No longer are options limited to debt, equity, or other severely limiting forms of financing. No debt is incurred and no equity is sacrificed. Instead, the venture is financed by investors who believe in the revenue potential of the enterprise.

COMPARING COMMON SHARES AND PARTNERSHIP INTERESTS WITH THE REVPAC INVESTMENT TRUST BOND

	COMMON SHARES	LIMITED PARTNERSHIPS	REVPAC TRUST BONDS
Use of proceeds: 100% of IPO proceeds (Must be allocated to develop the venture?)	NO	NO	YES
Are investors protected by performance bonding of the Business Manager responsible to develop the venture?	NO	NO	YES
Do ownership rights to the proprietary claims — protecting the venture — collateralize management obligations?	NO	NO	YES
Is IPO investment guaranteed to be returned to investors?	NO	NO	YES
Are investors assured of receiving yields if the venture realizes revenues?	NO	YES	YES
What are investors' yields based upon?	Net Earnings	Net Revenues	**Gross Revenues**
Do yield obligations for investors take precedence over all other management fiscal obligations?	NO	NO	YES
Are investors' earned (but not yet distributed) yields protected from erosion by currency calamities?	NO	NO	YES
Liquidity: Are securities tradable on a public securities market?	YES	NO	YES

First Guaranteed Return of Investment in a Tradable Venture-Capital Security

REVPAC is the first instrument to offer optimal liquidity *and* a guaranteed return-of-investment capital with an inflationary hedge to investors within the venture-capital investment sector.

REVPAC BONDs trade just like any stock or bond. Trading prices directly reflect the investment community's confidence in the emerging and maturing venture to achieve revenue projections.

What happens if a REVPAC venture is a complete failure in the marketplace? Even if it loses money, investors who have elected the exclusive Full Redemption Guarantee coverage will receive 100 percent of their investment returned to them at the end of the revenue-sharing term.

By providing risk-free capital access for venture-capital development — wherein the investor is rewarded directly from the end-user marketplace without middle-management interference with the yields — a clear and lucid performance reporting method is established. This will enhance institutional investment participation in pioneering new developments.

The venture synergism created by REVPAC promises to create a surge of interest and confidence from the investment community in taking an idea and cashing in, which can pave the way into a new era for the relationship between capital and innovative resources.

Setting a Global Standard

REVPAC has the potential to be the fastest expanding financial instrument in the world. Combining the most powerful elements of traditional financial instruments, REVPAC affords investors opportunities for extraordinary yields, while protecting their investment capital against loss and inflation.

After the IPO, REVPAC BONDs are eligible to be listed on securities exchanges around the world, providing investors with a liquid market. Investors, secondary trading speculators, and arbitrageurs will enter the market as ventures emerge, as less successful ventures reach expiration, and when Future Participation Warrants are activated by the Business Manager. Opportunities to invest in an emerging global consumer venture, the inherent currency-devaluation hedge of the Risk Insurance Package Wrap, and the guaranteed return of the Full Redemption Guaranty election will compel speculators — further enriching the trading markets at every stage of the REVPAC life cycle.

By establishing a universally accepted financial instrument with the solubility to be liquidated in secondary trading markets, venture developers are afforded an instrument that can be utilized for financial transactions between themselves and varying levels of subcontract service providers. This allows the developer to transfer to foreign service providers a participating interest in the venture development and the future success of the international market response — dissolving international borders as global venture developers and service providers unite behind a single REVPAC denominated business venture.

Ventures Ideally Suited for REVPAC

Requirements

The optimal REVPAC venture must meet a few tightly defined parameters to achieve success for the investor and the venture developer.

1. Revenues likely within 12 months

Most importantly, REVPAC ventures *must* be projected to produce revenues within a year of the Initial Public Offering.

If a venture is not ready to emerge to market and begin making money at once, a REVPAC offering will not generate investor interest because it cannot generate meaningful investor returns within its revenue-participation term.

A venture proven to be at the threshold of significant revenue generation will readily attract REVPAC financing.

2. High Gross Margins

Gross margins (the difference between the gross revenues and the costs of bringing a product or service to market — including production, marketing, and sales) must be sufficient to defray the allocation of the revenue sharing rights to the REVPAC holders, while leaving sufficient capital for the operation and profit of the Business Manager.

3. Competitive edge in a niche market

The unique product or service must be projected to enjoy a lucrative and highly competitive edge in a largely untapped, but viable, market.

4. Proprietary rights

Due to the structure of the REVPAC Investment Trust, there must be proprietary rights inherent in the venture — such as copyrights, patents, or other intellectual property — to be held as chattel by the Investment Trust during the term of investors' revenue participation.

5. Integrity of Business Manager and Trust Administrator

The REVPAC Financial Model is the ultimate business structure for venture-capital development. However, the Financial Model can succeed only if the professionals managing the underlying business interests of the Financial Model are successful. Success depends on the integrity of management resources.

The Business Manager and Trust Administrator of a REVPAC denominated venture *must* be seasoned veterans in emerging ventures. They must possess a historical record of knowledge and experience and are required to be bondable (in the case of the Business Manager) and be covered by Errors and Omissions insurance (in the case of the Trust Administrator). This requisite instills confidence and a fail safe recourse to ensure business integrity.

Ventures Not Suited for REVPAC

We have outlined the ways in which REVPAC outperforms traditional forms of financing for innovative ventures and myriad other enterprises, for both the innovator and the investor. But REVPACs aren't for every venture. The unique composite of its component parts makes REVPAC highly desirable for those business opportunities in which revenue is, if not a certainty, at least highly likely. Optimal feasible revenues must afford the REVPAC holders a minimum return of five to seven times their investment (500 percent to 700 percent ROI).

In many cases a debt-qualified company can access cheaper money elsewhere, through bond offerings or traditional lenders. An established and highly rated company can probably finance a project into the marketplace for less in interest payments than would be allocated to investors through a REVPAC offering.

Equity or partnership financing is usually better for research and development projects or ventures that will not produce revenues in the short-term. By definition, the long ramp-up and maturation stages of ventures such as medical and defense research programs fundamentally cripple the appeal of the REVPAC model to investors and severely limit any affinity draw.

Similarly, REVPACs are not for original equipment manufacturers (OEMs) and other companies that price on very small margins and depend on sales volume to sustain a positive retained earnings bottom line. Because REVPACs are based on a percentage of gross revenues, these types of enterprises would have to give away the store to attract REVPAC financing.

The strike-zone timing for REVPAC also plays a major role in the financing decision for a venture developer. Whatever the research and production stage, if revenues are significantly greater than 12 months from realization, REVPAC financing is unlikely to be desirable.

Also, REVPACs are not for innovators that are steeped in debt and are in need of retiring the obligations incurred by them during the incipient stage of development. One hundred percent of the net proceeds of a REVPAC offering *must* be allocated toward those expenses directly associated with the emergence of the venture.

Finally, REVPACs are intended to fund a well-structured Business Manager with a well-formulated Business Plan that has been reviewed by an accredited financial institution. Additionally, the Business Manager must be well organized and possess a staff with a historical record of developing successful emerging ventures that is bondable. *Innovators that lack a Business Manager with these qualifications should consider REVPAC financing — Inelegible to be Publicly Traded (discussed in this book) — or an alternative form of financing.*

REVPACs are designed for the *emerging* venture. Those innovations hovering on the precipice of revenue generation, that need only the confidence of the investor and the capital to make the profitable journey to market, are the ideal candidates for a REVPAC.

Liquidity in Secondary Trading Markets

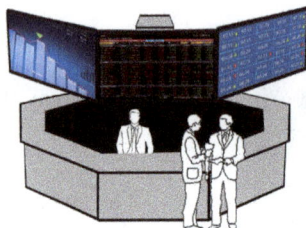

Impacts of Component Parts on Secondary Trading Performance

Broad Secondary Market Potential

The synergy of the components of the REVPAC Bond offer the investor a potent financial instrument, the value of which is influenced by myriad factors, directly and indirectly associated with the emerging venture itself.

The Revenue Sharing Venture Bond trades in a single class, Full Redemption, throughout the term of the emergence of the venture.

Newly issued REVPAC Bonds, typically trade at higher prices than the IPO price, reflecting consumer response to the current venture as it emerges into the marketplace and consumer confidence in the projection of future revenues. If consumer response is less than favorable, Full Redemption Guaranty REVPACs will reflect greater value in secondary markets as maturity of the REVPAC approaches full-term, at which time the Full Redemption Guaranty ensures the holder payment of the difference between distributed Revenue Yields and the IPO price.

The REVPAC instrument is designed to afford optimal liquidity throughout the term of the investment. Each of the component parts of the REVPAC independently and substantially impacts the value and liquidity of the instrument throughout its life cycle.

Impact of the Revenue Share

The Revenue Share's secondary market value, based in gross revenue yields, will rise and fall in direct correlation with consumer response to the venture. Investors can speculate on future revenues in consumer markets in a real-time trading market — investing while the venture is emerging.

The gross revenue yields provide an inherent inflationary hedge by adjusting with inflation. As consumer prices rise, so does the price of the products and services inherent in the venture. As a result, REVPAC values ride the tide of inflation like a cork.

Impact of the Future Participation Warrant

The windfall potential value of the warrant cannot have a value assigned at the time of the IPO. However, regardless of the success or failure of the current venture, the warrant is exercisable for future REVPACs issued by the same developer/innovator. The warrant will entice secondary buyers to bid on the REVPACs, even if most of the yields in the venture have already been distributed or the venture has failed.

The REVPAC will experience an increase in secondary market value commensurate with the value placed on next-generation emerging ventures, or the continuation of the successful current venture.

The Warrant is a powerful investment device and a key component of REVPAC, affording investors the first-ever opportunity to "franchise" innovative genius. The Warrant can significantly impact the trading price of REVPACs in secondary markets.

> *If a Warrant is activated within 100 days of full maturity of the REVPAC, REVPACs cease to trade in the secondary market for the final 10 days of the revenue-sharing term. (See "Guide for the Investment Banker," for a detailed explanation.)*

Impact of the Full Redemption Guaranty

The Guaranty provides assurance that there will always be a trading value for REVPACs. If a venture is an utter failure, 100 percent of the IPO price will be paid to holders of Full Redemption Guaranty REVPACs upon maturity. The secondary trading market value of failed REVPACs will inevitably fall below the initial public offering price but never to zero.
The market price will be determined by:

(1) the time remaining to maturity of the REVPAC, and
(2) current interest rates within world debt markets.

For ventures that fail to provide cumulative revenue-sharing yields equivalent to the IPO price of the REVPACs, the secondary trading market prices for those backed by the Full Redemption Guaranty will continue

to increase as maturity of the REVPAC approaches.

Subsequent to the failure of a venture, a new class of investors will enter the trading market to bid on failed REVPACs, providing a steadily increasing bid price until the day of redemption.

> *In most cases, the trading price for failed Full Redemption Guaranty REVPACs will top out at the IPO price. However, world interest rates and the impact of the Risk Insurance Package Wrap may further influence the secondary markets, driving trading prices higher still.*

Impact of Risk Insurance Wrap and U.S. Dollar Denominated REVPAC Bonds

The Built-in Risk Insurance Package Wrap and the value of the currency in which the REVPAC Bond is denominated, play significant roles in the secondary trading markets for REVPAC ventures – especially when applied to foreign investment participation.

If foreign currency values, tied to the gross revenue flow of the Commercial Venture, de-escalate, against the currency – in which the REVPAC Bond is denominated (usually the U.S. Dollar) – the Risk Insurance Wrap will "kick in" and safeguard the Dollar based valuation of the REVPAC Bond.

The Risk Insurance Package Wrap sustains the interest of foreign currency speculators and holds the value of the REVPAC Bond, above that which an uninsured financial instrument might experience.

Changing the Way We Invest in New Ideas

World Financial Markets have long awaited the emergence of a new Financial Instrument that is revenue-powered, not equity- or debt-driven. REVPAC is a financial instrument designed to fuel the cutting edge with the ancillary benefit of providing a risk-free investment opportunity to realize extraordinary yields.

Here is a partial listing of select business sectors — *under constant pressure to fund new concepts, products and ideas in the increasingly competitive marketplace* — most likely to opt for REVPAC as the financial instrument to fund future expansion.

Indy Screen Productions
Motion pictures (independent distribution).

Designer and Fashion
Emerging fashion/clothing accessory lines and labels.

World Entertainment
- Publishing high-promo/profile books.
- Stage productions headed for Broadway.
- Pilot launchers of new television series.
- Music industry's rising stars.

Spirit of America
Exporting U.S. franchises worldwide.

It's a Small World
High-promo/profile toys and children's products.

Phoenix of America
Revival of distressed U.S. corporations.

Age of the Consumer
High-promo/profile consumer products and services.

Jurisprudence
Purchasing plaintiff positions in civil suits.

Medical-Health
New medical-health products/services.

Funding of the Lost Fortunes
Search and salvage for lost treasures, archaeological finds and valuable artifacts.

Emerging Food/Beverage Brands
High-promo/profile food/beverage and related products.

Funding Sports Champions
- Emerging thoroughbreds.
- Professional golf, tennis athletes and Professional Boxing
- Motor Sports Racing

THE POWER OF REVENUE YIELDS LINKED TO REAL-TIME PERFORMANCE!

REVPAC is destined to become the financial instrument of choice for future generations and represents the most significant breakthrough the investment community has witnessed since the advent of the Mutual Fund Concept.

KPI

QUANTITATIVE · Output
ACTIONABLE · Leading
Scorecard · EVALUATE · Activity
Evaluate · Events · PROCESS · Marketing
Product · GOAL
Strategy · Balanced scorecard
KEY PERFORMANCE INDICATOR
MEASURE · Goals · PERFORMANCE MEASUREMENT · DIRECTIONAL
DATA · Practical · SALES

How REVPAC Performance Is Reported

Number of months since completion of Investment Trust IPO

Names of Investment Trusts listed alphabetically.

Highest and lowest trading price for the last 52 weeks.

The projected ROI multiple yield for the Investment Trust and the estimated month that the optimum yield will be realized as forecast by the Business Manager. In this case the investor will realize 10 times Return on Investment when the venture achieves gross revenue sales of $100 million – *projected at the end of 60 months.*

Revenue Share Yields derived from Venture Project and held or distributed by Trust Administrator for REVPAC holders. *Think of it this way:* The REVPAC holders have earned over two times their investment if the venture realizes no further revenues.

52 Week		Inv. Trust	Yld.	Projected Revenues	ROI YTD	Volume (00's)	Bid	Ask	Chg
High	Low								
7 1/2	5	Consumer Proc $_{21}$	10_{60}	100	$2\ 3/8_{12}$	150	5 1/2	5 1/4	- 3/4
13	5	Feature Films $_2$	20_{60}	400	--	110	13	12 3/4	-1/4
5 3/8	5	Franchise Chains $_{13}$	10_{84}	500	$1/8_{12}$	150	5 1/2	5 1/4	+1/8
6 1/2	5	Medical Services $_{12}$	10_{84}	90	$2\ 1/8_{14}$	108	6 1/4	6	+3/8
6 1/2	5	Computer Games $_5$	50_{60}	500	$-_{10}$	100	6 1/4	6	unch

The number of projected months required for the venture to mature (wherein the projected ROI multiple yield for the Investment Trust is forecast to be achieved).

Number of months that the venture has been in progress. By comparing this number with the Projected Yield Month number, you can project the "maturity" of the venture. If no number appears the venture is not yet in progress.

The sales volume for the day (10,000 units in this example).

The highest bid and the lowest ask of the day, and the net change for the day (all Ventures start trading at an ask price of $5.00).

Life Cycle of a REVPAC: Joe's Cyber Sleuth Games

To demonstrate how REVPAC work in real-time application, let's step through the process with a new business venture - in this case, a developer of computer games.

The Innovator

Research and Development

Joe has spent three years and $500,000 to develop and test an entertaining, educational multimedia tool for children called "Robber Barons." Joe has exhausted his capital reserves to bring the program through the beta testing phase successfully. "Robber Barons" is fully operational and ready for market.

Joe has done the market research to ensure that the program is consumer viable. Preliminary market testing has proven his concept and his execution. He is sure to make big money from his wondrous innovation providing he can locate the capital to wage an aggressive market-awareness and sales campaign.

Reasons to Use a REVPAC
Desire for Involvement in Venture Emergence

Joe has choices. As a respected engineer, he can pitch his product to a major software developer and hope for an attractive buy-out offer. Joe knows the

risks he runs with that approach. Time and again he has seen his associates' ideas pirated by technology giants, leaving them with no resources and little legal chance of contesting the appropriation of their intellectual property — the literal theft of genius.

An entrepreneur at heart, Joe is unwilling to see his creation subsumed by the industrial monoliths that feed on the brainchildren of innovators. He is confident in his program and in the marketability of future iterations he can produce based on the primary product. Even if Joe is well compensated for the use of his idea, by selling out he relinquishes all rights to the product, any role in the emergence of the product to market and — most appallingly — all rights to develop and market future versions based upon *his* original design — even if the purchasing company chooses not to produce or promote the product at all!

Even if a large software developer rigorously backs "Robber Barons," Joe is unlikely to realize, through royalties, rewards commensurate with his contribution of time and money to bring the game to marketing readiness.

By using REVPAC to raise marketing capital for "Robber Barons," Joe is able to retain 100 percent management control of his enterprise and all future proprietary rights to the game. He will be able to control the growth and direction of his company and the next generation of programs developed using his concepts and designs.

Protection of Proprietary Rights

With REVPAC, Joe's future rights to his creation are assured. Those rights are further protected during the REVPAC term by the cross-collateralization of the proprietary rights into the investment instrument itself through the Collateralized Yield Obligation.

Until all revenue-sharing rights of the REVPAC holders expire, all copyrights, trademarks, patents, and other intellectual property (IP) are owned by the REVPAC Investment Trust, providing the IP with an additional dimension of regulatory protection. An infringement of IP becomes an instant securities law violation, giving teeth to the enforcement of proprietary rights and protecting Joe's program from both competitors and software pirates seeking to exploit his concept.

After all revenues have been distributed to investors, and the term of the REVPAC has expired, all intellectual property reverts to the business itself — in this case, Joe's Cyber Sleuth Games.

Strike-Zone Timing for REVPACs

There is a perfect time to launch a REVPAC to fund a new undertaking. Before or after this optimum window of opportunity, REVPAC may not be the best vehicle through which to capitalize a venture.

The three preliminary tests to be applied when considering whether to REVPAC:

- Is the venture within 12 months of revenue generation?

- Does the volume of revenue projections and gross margins substantiate the revenue share to be distributed to investors? (To determine this, use the formula provided in the chapter titled: "Guide for the Innovator/Developer").

- Does the venture contain (or will IPO proceeds be used to purchase) proprietary intellectual property (i.e., copyrights, patents, trademarks) or sufficient capital assets to secure the Investment Trust?

Most often, the REVPAC Window occurs between the completion of the research and development stage and emergence of the venture into the consumer market.

In our "Robber Barons" scenario, Joe has completed his research and development stage and has filed applications for copyright protection of his software and design. He has done his test marketing and he has developed a comprehensive business and marketing plan to demonstrate the potential of the product to generate revenues within 9 to 12 months of capitalization.

His most conservative five-year sales projections for the United States alone are in the tens of millions, with a gross margin of 65 percent. Further projections indicate worldwide success for foreign-language versions of "Robber Barons."

Joe estimates that his costs of achieving and supporting those sales projections — including production, overhead expenses, and an international promotional and advertising campaign — will be $3.5 million for Year 1 and 35 percent of gross revenues for Years 2 through 5.

THE REVPAC BOND WRAP

1

VENTURE
MANAGEMENT
MANDATE / TRUST
FIDUCIARY AUTHORITY

RISK
INSURANCE
PACKAGE

5

REVPAC BOND

2

INTELLECTUAL
PROPERTY
LICENSE

COLLATERALIZED
YIELD
OBLIGATION

4

DEBENTURE
FUNDING
PACKAGE

3

Contractual Authority	Key Features(s)
1 Venture Management Appointment	Development and Management of Commercial Venture.
Trust Fiduciary Appointment	Investment Trust Fiduciary Administrator and Comptroller: • Monitors and Regulates Commercial Venture • Oversees fiduciary management and accountability of Venture • Distributes Revenue ad windfall Entitlement Yields to Bond holders • Administrates Bond holders' services.
2 Intellectual Property License	Exclusive Licensed Authority to develop Intellectual Property Rights, Title and Interest of Commercial Venture.
3 Debenture Funding Package	Capital Financing Instrument – structured as Subordinated Debenture Non-Recourse Debt – for funding Commercial Venture. Gross Revenue Entitlements of Venture are indentured to REVPAC holders for term of Bond.
4 Collateralized Yield Obligation	SURETY for REVPAC holders' entitlements – collateralizing Commercial Venture (Intellectual Properties and Capital Assets) to securitize performance obligations.
5 Risk Insurance Package	Risk Insurance Underwriters Package of bond, guaranty, surety and warranty "wraps" that guarantee the performance of the *Venture Management and Trust Fiduciary* Stewardship.

Identify an Underwriter

Joe has determined that his "Robber Barons" program is a perfect candidate for REVPAC.

His next step is to identify an underwriter to evaluate his venture and prepare a REVPAC prospectus for the initial public offering. Joe is prepared to demonstrate the feasibility of his undertaking using his well-defended business plan, his preliminary market research, and his revenue projections.

The REVPAC underwriter will contract with a reputable accounting firm to prepare a certified feasibility study accrediting Joe's business plan and the management principles on which it is based, and to assist in the preparation of an agreeable development budget and market-emergence schedule.

Using the methods detailed in the "Guide to the Innovator/Developer" the underwriter will assist Joe in determining the most favorable distribution of revenue percentages among investors and the innovator/developer, the appropriate number of REVPACs to be issued, and the optimum duration of the revenue-sharing participation period (five, six, seven, or more years). An insurance carrier will be identified to assume the risk for those Full Redemption Guaranty REVPACs elected.

The underwriter will then prepare the prospectus and make the initial public offering into the market. Further, the underwriter will register for listing the REVPACs with national and international stock exchanges to establish secondary trading markets for the REVPAC after the IPO.

The Offering

With the guidance of his underwriter, Joe determines to sell 700,000 REVPACs at $5.00 each to raise a total of $3.5 million in gross IPO proceeds.

The REVPAC holders will be allocated 20 percent of all gross revenues derived from the sales of "Robber Barons" into the consumer market — providing the investor with a potential 5.5-to-1 ROI within five years, if Joe is able to meet his sales targets.

Joe is also offering the investors an opportunity to participate in future program developments with the identical revenue-sharing rights via the Future Participation Warrant.

For purposes of this example, we have used a traditionally high-risk consumer product — a computer game. Joe must offer very high potential returns (20 percent of gross) in order to attract REVPAC investors. For lower-risk ventures, lower gross-revenue sharing rights may be sufficient. See "Guide to the Innovator/ Developer," for more details about how to determine revenue-sharing percentages.

*　　*　　*

Investment Trust

Joe, with the help of his underwriter, will establish an Investment Trust to issue REVPAC Bond Units to subscribers of the Initial Public Offering. All REVPAC proceeds will be held in the established investment trust.

The Investment Trust will fund 100% of the requisite expenses for "Robber Barons" to emerge into the consumer marketplace in return for 20% of the gross revenues.

The Trust Administrator of the Investment Trust allocates the proceeds to the Business Manager in accordance with a Use of Proceeds schedule and monitors the development, reporting the Business Manager's progress to investors.

Through a Collateralized Yield Obligation (see Table of Authorities), Joe will then assign all intellectual property — trademarks, patents, copyrights, and other proprietary claims — to the Investment Trust for the duration of the revenue-sharing rights of the REVPAC holders. Through this assignment, proprietary property can be aggressively protected through securities-law litigation in instances of infringement. Following the expiration of the REVPAC term and satisfaction of all revenue-sharing rights, all proprietary claims revert to Joe.

Joe need never relinquish control of his intellectual genius or the future application of his designs.

Business Manager

Qualifications

For Joe's program to achieve its maximum revenue potential in the marketplace, it must be carefully and aggressively directed by a manager — or management team — capable of succeeding in a highly competitive consumer environment.

With the assistance of the underwriter, Joe will identify and recruit a Business Manager with the experience and reputation to direct the venture's consumer campaign to maximum benefit. If Joe meets these qualifications, he may choose to direct the emergence of "Robber Barons" into the marketplace himself.

Joe's chosen Business Manager must have sufficient credentials to be performance-bonded by an accredited bonding agency to ensure the success of the venture is not compromised by any failure on the part of the Business Manager to deliver the venture to the marketplace. Typically, the innovator and the Business Manager are not the same person. In some cases, however, the role may be shared between them or among a team of proven successful leaders working in tandem toward the commercial success of the venture.

Responsibilities

The primary charter of the Business Manager is to produce maximum revenues from consumer response to the

venture — to realize the revenue goals outlined in the prospectus.

The Business Manager hires and oversees project contractors, directs marketing and advertising campaigns, and manages project resources toward the achievement of organizational objectives.

In our "Robber Barons" scenario, Joe is successful in recruiting a well-qualified team to act as Business Manager. "Joe's Cyber Sleuth Games," with Joe acting as Chief Executive Officer, will direct the day-to-day operations and market emergence of "Robber Barons."

Accountability
The Business Manager is entirely accountable for the accurate and timely reporting of the progress of the emergence of the venture to market and of revenues produced by consumer response to the product.

REVPAC holders can monitor performance — and accurately calculate their expected returns — with constant, real-time access to full-disclosure reporting via the Internet.

Performance Bond
If a venture fails to reach the marketing phase — through a substantial failure of the Business Manager to perform — the performance bond will be exercised, the Business Manager replaced, and the venture will continue toward the original goals set forth in the prospectus.

Egregious, even criminal, misconduct on the part of middle management is prevented from jeopardizing the revenue-producing potential of the project through the performance bond required by all REVPAC investment offerings. A bad hiring decision will not doom "Robber Barons" to market obscurity. Management will be summarily replaced,

and the venture will continue toward its revenue-producing objectives with minimal impact to progress.

Emerge Into Marketplace

Once the IPO is completed, Joe's promising "Robber Barons" game enters the marketplace with sufficient funding for promotion, administration, production and other costs associated with meeting the revenue objectives set forth in Joe's business plan.

From the first order received, a portion of the Gross Revenues is set aside for the REVPAC holders' revenue-sharing rights. In our scenario, "Robber Barons" is a huge success. Of course, not all ventures make money.

Ventures fail to produce revenues for many reasons from poor management decisions to poor timing. Later, we'll discuss what happens when a REVPAC venture fails in the marketplace.

For purposes of our example, Joe's "Robber Barons" sales were $100 million over the Five Year Term.

Each and every sale of a "Robber Barons" game in the marketplace produces a revenue percentage that is directly funneled into the REVPAC Investment Trust to accumulate for distribution to REVPAC investors upon maturity of their revenue-sharing rights.

No mechanism exists by which middle management may redirect or otherwise reallocate those accumulated yields. As opposed to an equity-financed company, no board of directors can elect to forego a dividend distribution to bolster the company's assets for a quarter. If sales are occurring, investors will reap the rewards of their good faith.

The remaining revenue is directed to the operating account of the Business Manager, who is chartered with the sole objective of generating revenues.

Trust Administrator

An accredited institution must now be identified to act as Trust Administrator to administer the proceeds from the sale of REVPACs and to distribute revenue-sharing yields, Full Redemption Guaranty Payments, and the Gold Benchmark Payments to REVPAC holders upon maturity.

The chosen institution must have a demonstrated record of success and have exhibited the ability to sustain fiduciary accountability for the duration of the Investment Trust.

The administrator must have in place comprehensive errors and omissions (E&O) insurance coverage to at least the amount of maximum anticipated revenue yields for any one coupon.

The Trust Administrator will administer and account for all proceeds from the sale of REVPACs and will allocate funds — in accordance with the approved budget and as published in the IPO prospectus — to the Business Manager for the costs of developing the venture. Revenues generated from the venture are allocated in accordance with the REVPAC terms and flow directly into segregated accounts —

one for the Business Manager and a second for the Investment Trust. These funds accumulate until maturity and distribution. Accumulated but undistributed revenue yields earn interest.

REVPAC Trust Administrators are required to provide real-time sales-revenue disclosure to the Investment Trust, which issues public disclosure via the Internet. This affords up-to-the-minute reporting to REVPAC investors and speculators eyeing emerging ventures as well as the secondary REVPAC markets.

Management reporting is fundamental, requisite, and timely. Full disclosure is incumbent upon venture developers within the term of the REVPAC. Investors can track the performance of their holdings 24 hours a day, seven days a week, via the Internet.

Revenues in excess of the REVPAC revenue-sharing and the Risk Insurance Premium percentage — 20 percent in Joe's example — flow to the Business Manager to further the development of the venture. From this 80 percent the Business Manager pays operating expenses and derives the venture's net profits.

As Revenue Share Yield Coupons become due, the Trust Administrator distributes yields to REVPAC holders. Upon maturity of each REVPAC Revenue Share, the Trust Administrator allocates final revenue yields and Full Redemption Guaranty payments. The Trust Administrator also distributes Windfall Yields when such payments are due.

The Trust Administrator also holds responsibility to administer the activation of — and election to exercise

— the Future Participation Warrant. Trust Administrator is appointed to Business Manager Board-of- Directors and is granted Veto Power for any and all corporate resolutions affecting Insurance/Financial-Banking Contracts of the Commercial Venture. Additionally, Trust Administrator is granted Oversight, Regulatory Enforcement and Arbitration powers over Business Manager and Commercial Venture.

Please see "Guide to the Investment Banker," for details of qualifications, requirements, responsibilities, and authorities of the Trust Administrator.

Trust Arbitration Association

In the event of a breach of fiduciary responsibility on the part of the Trust Administrator, a Trust Arbitration Association holds the charter and the authority to provide a remedy — including replacement of the Trust Administrator — to ensure that all financial obligations to the REVPAC holders and the Business Manager are satisfied.

The Trust — represented by a committee of the major REVPAC holders — shall act on behalf of the Trust. The Arbitration Association is responsible to arbitrate any disputes arising from the administration of the venture or the Investment Trust during the term of the REVPAC.

Full Redemption Guaranty

FULL REDEMPTION GUARANTY

This Guaranty entitles the holder to receive a redemption payment - concurrent with the final Revenue Yield Coupon disbursement - equivalent to the difference between the aggregate disbursements of all Revenue Yield Coupons and the IPO price up to a maximum cash payment of $5.00 per unit.

The holder may redeem this Full Redemption Guaranty coupon - in lieu of cash payment - for a newly issued Unit of the Investment Trust, for the ensuing seven year term of the Trust, by submitting this coupon together with the Warrant and applicable payment on the "Redemption Due Date".

FRG Coupon # A-1001 Redemption Date: March 15, 20**

Because Joe's product is a "start-up" and subject to traditional risk-factors, inherent in new ventures, the investors will be protected against loss of their investment via a FULL REDEMPTION GUARANTY.

The GUARANTY is underwritten by a composite Package of 10 insurance, Bond, Guaranty, Surety and Warranty "wraps" from world class Risk Insurance Underwriters that guarantee the Commercial Venture's full development and emergence into the marketplace plus fiduciary accountability for all revenues. In return, the Risk Insurers receive 30% of the REVPAC revenue-share, as a "Premium" Insurance allocation – in the case of the "Robber Baron" Venture: Risk Insurance Insurers receive 6% and REVPAC Bond Holders receive 14% of the gross sales. A total of 20% Revenue-Share.

The Risk Insurance Coverage guarantees the REVPAC Bond holders of 100% Return-of-Original-Investment as well as any other guaranteed yield covenants contained in the REVPAC Funding Program.

*　　　*　　　*

Distribution of Yields

There are no surprises when the time comes to distribute revenue-sharing yields to REVPAC holders. Investors have full-disclosure access to all revenue reporting and can accurately project returns. On the third anniversary of the offering, the first distribution is made based upon the revenues generated in Years 1 through 3. Yields are distributed each subsequent year for the duration of the revenue-sharing term.

Future Participation Warrant

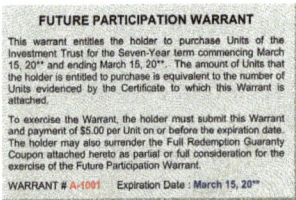

FUTURE PARTICIPATION WARRANT

This warrant entitles the holder to purchase Units of the Investment Trust for the Seven-Year term commencing March 15, 20** and ending March 15, 20**. The amount of Units that the holder is entitled to purchase is equivalent to the number of Units evidenced by the Certificate to which this Warrant is attached.

To exercise the Warrant, the holder must submit this Warrant and payment of $5.00 per Unit on or before the expiration date. The holder may also surrender the Full Redemption Guaranty Coupon attached hereto as partial or full consideration for the exercise of the Future Participation Warrant.

WARRANT # A-1001   Expiration Date : March 15, 20**

In addition to the revenue participation for the five-year term of Joe's REVPAC, REVPAC holders may elect to exercise the attached Future Participation Warrant for a subsequent offering by Joe's Cyber Sleuth Games.

No later than 100 days prior to expiration of the initial revenue-sharing term, Joe must notify REVPAC holders of his intent either to continue the "Robber Barons" revenue sharing participation for an additional five-year term, or to introduce a REVPAC program for the next Cyber Sleuth game emerging into the marketplace. If REVPAC holders elect to exercise their Warrants, they must do so within 90 days of notification that a Warrant is exercisable.

Joe is introducing a new game, "Patent Pirates" to the marketplace at the end of Year 5. He plans to capitalize on the established confidence of his loyal investors by activating the Future Participation Warrant to fund the new game's emergence into the market.

The Warrants entitle the holders to receive the same revenue-participation rights in the new software product as they enjoyed in the successful consumer hit, "Robber Barons" (20 percent of gross revenues).

Joe's market projections indicate that "Patent Pirates" will generate over the first five years $20 million, $31.5 million, $37 million, $22 million, and $13 million, respectively.

Warrants may be activated by the Business Manager at any time, but not later than 100 days prior to the expiration of the initial REVPAC term. This allows all REVPAC holders 90 days to elect whether to exercise their Warrants.

Liquidity

Secondary Markets

As "Robber Barons" emerges into the market and revenues are generated, all sales orders are reported in real time by the Business Manager to the Trust Administrator, who is accountable to report sales to REVPAC holders via a dedicated reporting platform on the Internet.

IPO investors and secondary market speculators can monitor the performance of the venture in the consumer market along with other factors that influence the value of the investment holding.

REVPAC holders can make accurate projections of returns based on consumer response to the venture, and easily track the current value of holdings in near real time.

As REVPAC Bond Units trade on inter-bank open auction systems or on trading
exchanges, market fluctuations are reported by traders, independently of the venture reporting system.

Windfall Yield Impact

In our case study of Joe's Cyber Sleuth Games, we assume that Joe meets all his sales objectives. The software game "Robber Barons" is a phenomenal consumer market success, with $100 million in sales over a five-year period.

The Zero-Risk REVPACs yield $20.00 for each $5.00 invested! — and we haven't even taken into account the Windfall Yield Premium!

How Windfall Entitlement Yields Work:

At full term of the REVPAC, the IP and Capital Assets of the Venture revert back to the Innovator/Venture Manager, or whomever is in possession of the Buy Back Option.

The Equity Interest of the Commercial Venture is held by the REVPAC Investment Trust (as chattel) and is sold at the Buy Back "valuation" computed

as follows:

1.   *Venture Equity Market Value*
– established as the Average Adjusted Annual Yield to REVPAC Holders for the full term of REVPAC Bond.

2.   *Venture Performance Buy-Out Schedule*
– established as a Sliding Scale Payment Schedule, wherein the purchase price is based on the accumulated Returns-of-Investment, realized by REVPAC Bond Holders.

REVPAC Holders Accumulated Yields (1)	Capital Asset Purchase Price (2)
Less than 10% ROI	100%
10% to 25%	90%
26% to 50%	80%
51% to 75%	70%
76% to 100%	60%
101% to 150%	50%
151% to 200%	40%
201% to 300%	30%
301% to 400%	20%
401% to 500%	10%
Over 500%	0%

(1) Based on IPO price
(2) Based on replacement cost for capital assets owned by Investment Trust

To demonstrate the impact of the Windfall Yield, we calculate: (a) Venture Equity Market Value: $2.8 million (five year average of accumulated yields) and (b) Venture Performance Buy-Out Schedule: $350,000 (401% to 500% ROI Capital Asset Purchase Price).

This increase will result in Windfall Yield distributions to investors of an additional 15.7% percent ($4.50 per REVPAC Bond Unit). Total REVPAC Bond payout to investors is a whopping 490 percent ROI - $24.50 per Bond. Not bad for Bond holders who paid a $5 IPO price, 60 months ago!

Secondary Trading Market Pro-Forma

The Secondary Trading Market Pro-Forma predicts Joe's REVPAC Bonds to hit a high of: $7.50 in Year 1, $15 in Year 2, and over $22.50 in Year 3. These secondary market prices are based on the accumulated, undistributed yields, the anticipated continued success of "Robber Barons" for the duration of the revenue-sharing term, and the estimated market valuation of the Future Participation Warrant.

After the first yield distribution Year 3, secondary market trading prices adjust to reflect real-time revenue-sharing yields and the approaching maturity of the REVPAC while continuing to be influenced by the value of the Future Participation Warrant.

TRADING PERFORMANCE

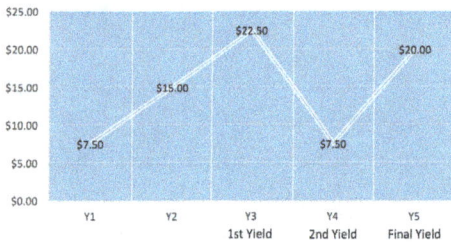

$25.00			$22.50	
$20.00				$20.00
$15.00		$15.00		
$10.00				
$7.50	$7.50		$7.50	
$5.00				
$0.00				
	Y1	Y2	Y3 / 1st Yield	Y4 / 2nd Yield	Y5 / Final Yield

The Future Participation Warrant may significantly impact trading prices of REVPAC Bonds in secondary markets. Joe waited until Year 5 to introduce his Warrant activation venture, "Patent Pirates." Inevitably, investors will speculate on the future revenue-generation potential of the new emerging product, creating a demand for REVPAC Bonds in the trading markets and further escalating trading prices. Note the upswing in the pro-forma trading market chart when Joe announced his Warrant activation venture.

Imagine that Joe had activated the Warrant in Year 3. Trading prices may well have hit the $35 mark. Isn't that a stunning trading performance – 7 times the IPO price – in less than 3 years!

REVPAC Life Cycle Chart

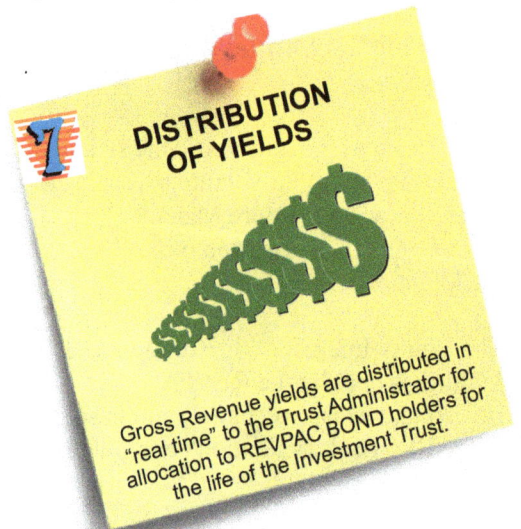

1 INNOVATOR

After developing a new idea, product, or service, the innovator bundles the IP and proprietary rights to capitalize and commercialize the innovation into a REVPAC BOND Wrap

4 BUSINESS MANAGER

The Business Manager is responsible for developing the venture project and reporting the progress of the market emergence of the venture to the Trust Administrator.

7 DISTRIBUTION OF YIELDS

Gross Revenue yields are distributed in "real time" to the Trust Administrator for allocation to REVPAC BOND holders for the life of the Investment Trust.

2 REVPAC BOND Wrap

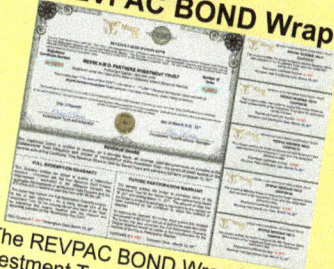

The REVPAC BOND Wrap forms an Investment Trust that represents the Innovator, Investors and business/fiduciary stewards responsible to commercialize the Innovation into a viable business venture

3 INVESTMENT TRUST

Investment Trust finances 100% of the venture from investors' funds and distributes future gross revenue entitlements, derived by the venture from the marketplace.

5 TRUST ADMINISTRATOR

Trust Administrator allocates investment capital to the Business Manager and oversees future revenue yields to REVPAC Investment Trust BOND holders.

6 EMERGE INTO MARKETPLACE

The venture project emerges into the marketplace, and revenues are remitted to the Trust Administrator for distribution.

8 FULL REDEMPTION GUARANTY

In the event REVPAC BOND Holders fail to recover 100% of their investment, upon full maturity of the REVPAC BOND, the GUARANTY reimburses the holder the difference between distributed yields and their investment.

9 FUTURE PARTICIPATION WARRANT

Entitles the Innovator to receive additional funding for subsequent ventures while assuring REVPAC BOND Holders the right to invest in and share revenue entitlements in future ventures of the Innovator.

REVPAC in Action

World financial markets have long awaited a financial instrument that is revenue-powered — not equity-diluting or debt-laden.

REVPAC is a leading-edge financial instrument designed to fuel cutting-edge endeavors and optimize revenue opportunities for the rapidly expanding global consumer market.

REVPAC financing supercharges business, sports, and artistic ventures — launching them rapidly into the competitive arena with industry giants.

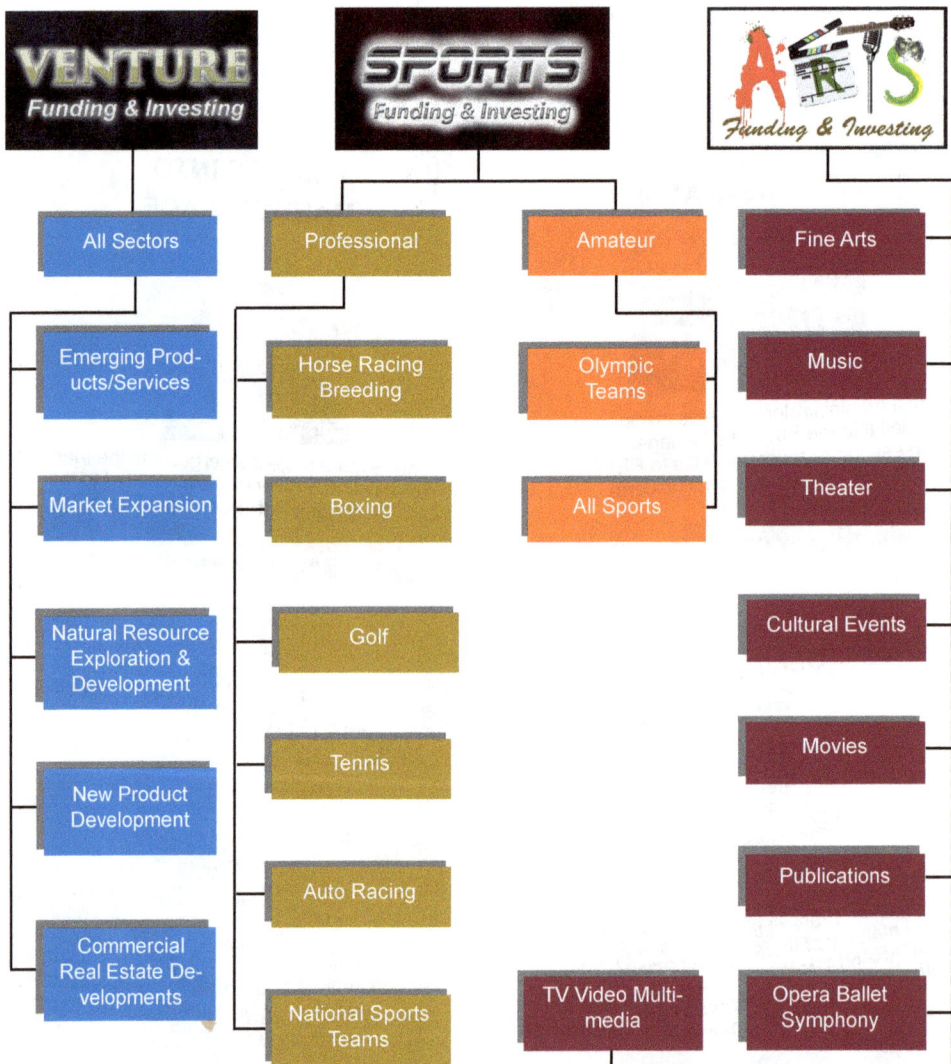

Business Ventures

Approximately 500,000 new business ventures are launched worldwide each year. Of these, 70 percent are engaged with emerging proprietary products and services and 30 percent are focused on incubating new ideas at the research and development stage.

It is estimated that over 90,000 publicly traded companies exist in the world today, with over one-half actively seeking additional financing to complete development of new ideas or to market fully developed ideas that are ready to emerge into the marketplace.

Worthy business concepts, offering genuine opportunities for extraordinary revenues, are being turned away daily by underwriters because of lack of investor confidence. It is not that investors have stopped believing in innovation. Rather, traditional investment mechanisms have offered consistently disappointing returns.

> REVPAC satisfies all the concerns holding wary investors at bay from promising ventures — assurance of yields if the venture is successful, Full Redemption Guaranty of zero risk, liquidity in a rich secondary trading market, and absolute accountability.

A real-world example of the global impact and power of REVPAC to generate start-up capital, while producing meaningful returns to investors, is already in action.

An Example of a Business REVPAC in Action

The principals of a leading Health Maintenance Organization (H.M.O.) with its own Hospitals, laboratories, radiology and pharmacies in the Republic of Mexico – 5 minutes across the U.S. border in Tijuana – developed a business plan to expand its health care business into the international marketplace – targeting the large population of Hispanic expatriates residing in California. The plan - known as "MexRx" - entailed the marketing of a proprietary *Herbal Care Immune System Activator* product line and deep-discounted pharmaceuticals as well as affordable surgical services.

The proprietary Immune System Activator product line contained universal remedial applications, including: *Rheumatoid Arthritis, Carpal tunnel Syndrome, Herpes zoster, Psoriasis, Diabetes, Acne and various skin disorders, as well as various Cancers.*

Additionally, the product line was in the final stages of Federal Testing to qualify as a pharmaceutical within Mexico. The MexRx program also included over 1,250 prescription/non-prescription medical products – with average discounted pricing of 50% as compared with U.S. price levels – and over 100 surgical procedures with similar discounted pricing. Marketing of the Mex-Rx program was to be primarily implemented via the Internet.

The principals of the H.M.O. sought a solution to financing the MexRx plan.

The solution was REVPAC.

The principals appointed a Trust Administrator and formed a REVPAC Investment Trust to raise $4.5 million to fund market emergence of MexRx.

The H.M.O. opted to do an underwriting to their members. An independent underwriter, working cooperatively, marketed 900,000 REVPAC Bond Units at $5.00 each, completing a successful IPO in less than 45 days.

The capital is being used to manufacture and market the unique Herbal Care Immune System Activator product line in addition to marketing non-proprietary pharmaceuticals and surgical services.

All capital assets, along with Intellectual Property rights, are assigned to the Investment Trust for the term of the REVPAC to secure the investors' stake in the returns.

The Business Manager, forecasts $907 million gross revenues over the seven-year term of the Investment Trust - with 20 percent of the gross revenues derived from the worldwide sales of the Immune System Activator product line and 7.5 percent of the gross revenues derived from all non-proprietary pharmaceutical /surgical sales – to be allocated to REVPAC investors. If those projections are achieved, bearers of Zero-Risk REVPAC will reap 18.64 times ROI.

The success of this inaugural REVPAC offering is a prime illustration of the REVPAC potential to deliver capital to worthy endeavors, as well as substantial return-on-investment potential for investors.

The prospectus, investment brochure and organic documents employed in the MexRx Investment Trust offering is included in this book under Table of Authorities.

This is only one application of REVPAC to a business venture. REVPAC will traverse virtually every business sector to revitalize the venture-capital industry and renew investor confidence in emerging enterprise.

*   *   *

Another Example of a Business REVPAC in Action

COSTA RICA

Legendary Bluewater Action in Central America

Seafood Export Venture

Recently, the Republic of Costa Rica extended its national territorial fishing rights to the 10 mile limit and enacted proactive legislative enforcement of environmental protection regulations. The impact on the country's fishing industry, swift, severe and largely unanticipated. The territorial extension drove foreign fishing vessels from the newly defined Costa Rican waters and eliminated the harvest of those vessels from Costa Rican processing plants. The well-intentioned environmental initiatives shut down many processing plants unable to meet the financial requirements of compliance.

As an unintended result, the country's fishing exports had suffered a 62 percent decrease – a devastating blow to the regional economy, those steeped in the tradition of the fishing trade, and the families, dependent upon the income it produced.

The consultant who recommended the initial reforms – a steering committee member of the nation's largest fishing cooperative – was called back to the table to find a solution to the industry crises.

Once again! That solution was REVPAC.

The fishing cooperative, comprising 3,000 industry tradesmen, fleet owners, and processing facility managers, formed a REVPAC Investment Trust to raise $2 million to revitalize the fishing industry in Costa Rica.

Two independent underwriters, working cooperatively, marketed 400,000 REVPAC Bonds at $5 each, completing a successful IPO in less than one week.

The capital was allocated to complete the purchase of two state-of-the-art processing plants, three additional fishing vessels, and to cover operational expenses during the ramp-up stage.

All capital assets, along with the cooperative's exclusive national fishing rights, are assigned to the Investment Trust for the term of the REVPAC to secure the investors' stake in the returns.

The Business Manager for the cooperative, forecasts $1.14 billion gross revenues over the seven-year term of the Investment Trust, with 4 percent to be allocated to REVPAC investors. If those projections are achieved, bearers of REVPAC Bonds will reap 10.75 times ROI.

The success of this REVPAC offering is another prime illustration of the potential of REVPAC to deliver capital to worthy endeavors, as well as substantial returns for investors.

In fact, the legal, accounting, and investment communities of Costa Rica were so impressed with the accomplishments achieved by REVPAC for the fishing industry, they compelled the government to consider the incorporation of the REVPAC model into its regulations governing public trusts and other public offerings.

Competitive Sports

The business of competitive sports is among the Top 10 revenue-producing industries in the world. However, the investing public has never had the opportunity to tap the rich economy driven by the careers of talented athletes and the related businesses spawned by their success.

The economics of team sports such as football, baseball and basketball is distinctively different from that of individual competitive sports such as professional golf, tennis, boxing, motor sport racing, and horse racing. However all sports offer affinity investment opportunities that — when tapped with REVPAC — provide capital resources to struggling team franchises and much-needed financial support for individual competitive sports.

REVPAC offers an advantage to team franchises for the financing of stadiums and may be used to overcome salary-cap issues when incorporated into athletes' contracts. REVPAC also provides a new access to capital for emerging athletes in individual competitive sports, while providing potentially phenomenal returns for investors. This is especially true when endorsement royalties are incorporated into the revenue-sharing rights.

Imagine a REVPAC Sports offering wrapped around 100 emerging tennis, golf, or boxing professionals. If that wrap includes only one athlete with the talent of Tiger Woods or Oscar de la Hoya — the ROI could soar to the hundreds-multiple range.

An Example of a Sports REVPAC in Action

Thoroughbred Horse Racing & Breeding Venture

Let us take a look at a hypothetical case using the sport of kings, Thoroughbred horse racing, to demonstrate the potential of sports REVPAC.

A historically successful, licensed trainer forms an Investment Trust to purchase and maintain in racing condition 35 Thoroughbred racehorses, with the goal of participating in approximately 1,500 races during a five-year period.

The Investment Trust comprises 600,000 REVPAC Bond Units at $5 each, for an aggregate $3 million. REVPAC investors will receive 50 percent of the gross revenues derived from purse earnings and 40 percent of the net sales revenues derived from the sale of the horses during the five-year term of the REVPAC.

As with all REVPAC -underwritten ventures, the capital assets and intellectual property of the stable — purchased with the proceeds of the IPO — are indentured to the Investment Trust through the Collateralized Yield Obligation to secure the revenue-sharing rights of investors.

The seasoned trainer is appointed Busness Manager and is responsible for all acquisitions, development, management and sale of the racehorses within the stable. The Business Manager intends to maintain 40 percent of the horses at the "maiden" and "claiming" race levels and 60 percent at the "allowance" and "stakes" race levels. A majority of the races for the stable are scheduled for California racetracks with select allowance and stakes races at other major U.S. tracks, to be strategically scheduled as the thoroughbreds mature.

The Business Manager, tasked to optimize revenues, only selects races that afford maximum opportunities for both purse winnings and claiming race sales values. Reasonably accurate revenue projections can be made based on the average annual performance of all racehorses trained by the Business Manager — win, place, show and fourth place finishes — during the preceding five-year period.

The Business Manager, over the preceding five-year period, has a record wherein the Thoroughbred racehorses under his control have placed in the win, place, show and fourth place finishes in over 65 percent of all races entered.

The Business Manager intends to utilize 45 percent of offering proceeds, earmarked to purchase the initial stable of racehorses from other owners, that have successfully competed in claiming races, starting at $15,000 up to $45,000; 25 percent will be applied to purchase promising maidens or racehorses that either, because of their age, have never run a race or have competed without winning. The balance of the proceeds are to be used to acquire allowance-class horses with the potential to become stakes winners.

The trainer-Business Manager forecasts that approximately 10 percent of the capital asset base — *monies spent to purchase Thoroughbreds* — will be lost through horses unable to compete successfully or that become injured.

In this scenario — based on the Business Manager's past training record — we forecast that REVPAC investors will receive an average 35 percent Return on Investment per year via Revenue Yield distributions and a 220 percent increase in the overall value of the Thoroughbred racing stable at the end of the five-year term.

Value of a Champion

The extraordinary revenue potential and sales value of a champion Thoroughbred is legendary — which provides an enticing lure for speculators to buy and sell horse-racing REVPAC in secondary trading markets. Wouldn't you like to own a piece of the action in a racing stable with such promising champions as the recent stakes winner, American Pharoah? If American Pharoah had been included in a REVPAC stable as a foal, his value would have increased to $22.5 million (i.e. Race Purse Earnings and Sale of Breeding Rights) in only three years!
An unbelievable return of 10,000 percent in only 11 races!
American Pharoah, alone (not taking into account, the other revenues from the Racing Stable) would increase the value of the REVPAC Bonds from $5 to over $150!

Now, with REVPAC, owners can access the financing they need to purchase promising horses and train them throughout their careers.
Investors will be able to cash in — at any time — while speculators clamor to buy REVPAC in developing champions.

Breeding programs for Thoroughbreds can likewise be financed with REVPAC through stables that own promising sires and dams. Breeding REVPAC will realize revenues from stud fees, sales of yearlings, and/or lifetime revenue-sharing rights in foals. Approximately 4,000 sires "stand" currently in the United States. One hundred percent of those sires are financed through breeding syndicates or partnerships, both of which are illiquid securities. REVPAC provides investors with an opportunity to buy and sell future revenue-sharing rights in maturing breeding programs and gives breeding farms access to funding for the development of racing champions — while providing investors extraordinary potential returns at zero-risk.

A breeding stable may offer, through an affinity program, breeding rights to REVPAC holders owning 5 percent of outstanding REVPAC Bonds. This affords investors in the industry an additional incentive — the option to breed their dams to proven sires — to the inherent benefit of the REVPAC investment.

If you couple the Full Redemption Guaranty with the affinity program, a breeder, owning 5 percent or more of a REVPAC Investment Trust, would be able to not only breed promising dams to proven sires — but also to, be guaranteed 100 percent ROI capital at full term — in effect receiving breeding

rights and potential revenue yields at zero risk.

Breeding REVPAC becomes a "futures commodity" tradable on world securities exchanges, just as futures are traded in precious metals and grains on today's commodity markets.

Thoroughbred racing is the most complicated of the Sports REVPAC models. Even within this complex scenario, it is easy to see the impact REVPAC can have throughout virtually every professional sport.

Yet Another Example of Sports REVPAC in Action

Professional Boxing Venture

At the time of this book's publication, a group of sports trainers and media specialists were planning a REVPAC denominated Investment Trust to fund an ongoing development team of top amateur and professional athletes excelling in the sport of boxing.

The team has strategic alliance partners in China and throughout the Far East with the technical capabilities to launch reality shows and weekly "HBO" style Saturday-night Boxing telecasts, Closed-Circuit, Pay-Per-View Major event transmissions and Digital Streaming to portable devices – that will feature Professional Boxing.

The team has been in negotiations with Professional Boxing Champion, Manny Pacquiao, to head the Boxing Management Production Team (similar to the style of Oscar de La Hoya with Golden Boy Productions).

Manny Pacquiao is a Boxing Icon and the single best-known symbol of Boxing throughout the Far East.

The underlying strategy is that CHINA IS THE NEXT GREAT FRONTIER FOR PROFESSIONAL BOXING! Boxing was banned in China in 1966, as part of the "Cultural Revolution". The sport reemerged on the amateur level during the 1990's - and in 2004, China won its first Olympic medal. In 2012, Professional Boxing emerged, in earnest, and Xiong Zhao Zhong won a major pro world boxing title. Boxing is now, one of the fastest growing sports in China. There currently are no regular televised boxing matches and Pay-per-View fight matches are unknown within the People's Republic – however, the technology is currently in-place to stream to an estimated marketplace of 300 Million mobile devices.

Whereas, the North American television market for Boxing is saturated - wherein Pay-Per-View events are charging $60 to $70 per Buy and attracting an audience of between 350,000 to 2,200,000 Buys – the Pacquiao Team has deemed the Far East Market and specifically, the Chinese Market, is the future of Professional Boxing. *It's a numbers game:* If the Pacquiao Management team can offer 300 Million Chinese Boxing Fans a major Championship Event for $5 per Pay-Per-View Buy – the audience Buy will generate 10 times more revenue than the greatest Pay-Per-View success in North American history.

The REVPAC Investment Trust will own a Twenty Percent (20%) gross revenue entitlement in all revenues derived from media promotions of the weekly boxing telecasts, Prize Fight Purses, Pay per View (PPV) Buys, Live Gate and Endorsements by Professional Boxing Athletes that are under management of the Business Manager – and Manny Pacquiao.

Arts and Entertainment

REVPAC finds its roots in the funding of the arts and, in fact, was primarily developed for the world of arts and entertainment to reinvent the archaic and exclusionary financing practices of the industry. REVPAC was originally designed as a fine arts investment tool to satisfy the dearth of capital available to budding masters and to provide for meaningful participation for art lovers in the careers of successful artists.

REVPAC is the perfect investment instrument for both the fine and performing arts and the entertainment industry. REVPAC provides a vastly more lucid and equitable underwriting method than the traditional process of funding creative ventures through the capital stock of corporations or interests of limited partnerships.

Arts and entertainment corporations, by their nature, are not intended to and in fact do not effectively function as capital venturists within business markets that demand new products with each new season. All too often a corporation develops a single art or entertainment venture as its underpinning, and the future of the corporation and its shareholders relies on that one venture to succeed. An arts and entertainment development corporation is under constant pressure from the consumer marketplace to develop new products. A film production company with a single film will sink or swim with that production. Likewise, a stage production company, fine art development company, or music production company with a single product or artist faces a similar dilemma.

One of the most creative financing methods in recent history for long-term arts and entertainment development was the funding of the now legendary Touchstone Pictures. The management behind Touchstone Pictures set out to develop a series of film productions — *rather than rely on a single production's becoming a blockbuster* — and prudently floated $1 billion worth of limited partnership interests in four limited partnerships known as Silver Screen Partners. Though many of the films succeeded, the Silver Screen Partnerships have not rewarded their investors commensurably or provided a durable liquid market where the investors might liquidate their holdings. Consequently, the door

on this type of long-term financing is temporarily closed for film production companies trying to emulate Touchstone Pictures.

Touchstone Pictures

In the absence of REVPAC, there exists no financial instrument that can serve an arts and entertainment corporation's long-term funding requirements while satisfying venture-capital investors' needs for meaningful reward and liquidity.

REVPAC affords arts and entertainment development companies the opportunity to structure a series of ventures, independent of one another, without encumbering the financial resources that the company has available as working capital. Furthermore, the companies do not suffer financial duress from a single failure — or even several failures — as would be the case if the companies used their economic base and revenue streams in the role of venture capitalists.

With the advent of REVPAC, arts and entertainment development companies are able to reconceptualize their purpose, i.e., *"Let's get out of financing and owning 100 percent of the products and into revenue partnership with REVPAC holders."* These companies are now able to get back to what they do best — business management and managing artistic franchises.

Arts and entertainment development companies are finally afforded the luxury of experimenting with new forms of art without risking their hard-earned revenues and diluting equity ownership.

With REVPAC, investors have an avenue to participate in enormous revenue-generating arts and entertainment ventures and the careers of emerging artists, at zero risk.

Or — similar to the REVPAC Sports wraps — imagine an entertainment wrap including dozens of promising movie producers or up-and-coming musical groups. How many artists, with all the talent of a Steven Spielberg or a Garth Brooks, simply lack the requisite funding to launch them into megastardom?

There exists an untapped wealth of opportunity for the individual investor to reap huge benefits — with REVPAC *for the Arts* investing — while nurturing emerging artistic talent with no risk.

Further, now investors can buy and sell revenue "futures" of artistic careers as they mature in the consumer marketplace.

REVPAC introduces requisite accountability, real-time reporting, and affinity investing to the arts and entertainment community, that — for the first time — includes the individual investor in the revenue participation of a single successful project or a wrap of promising emerging talents!

The investment community traditionally shies away from arts and entertainment ventures because of the high risk associated with such investments and a perception of the industry as rife with erratic accounting and management practices.

A few public companies, such as Warner Bros. and Viacom, allow investors to speculate on the success or failure of the company over time or the future trading performance of the stock. But never before have investors been invited to the table to reap a percentage of *gross revenues* of a potential blockbuster motion picture or a record label's upcoming releases.

Future Warhols and Dalis, Spielbergs and Stones, Clancys and Grishams, Brookses and Madonnas, and Andrew Lloyd Webbers are now able to be franchised by arts and entertainment developers and financed by REVPAC as investors worldwide network their venture-capital investments into arts and entertainment ventures.

*   *   *

REVPAC in Action

An Example of an Art REVPAC in Action

Fine Art Limited Editions

Our hypothetical case involves fine arts and a famous Fine Art Master who desires to finance his unsold limited editions and the development of five promising sculptors and painters in his school of art.

The Fine Art Master has 169 Fine Art sculptures and 500 oil canvas masterpieces among his lifetime achievements and 500 paintings. Molds for the sculptures are in place and have been previously employed in the production of limited-edition bronze fine art. There remain 9,000 limited-edition pieces that are "open" and yet to be cast. Likewise, there remain 15,000 "unsold" limited edition prints.

The Master forms an Investment Trust to finance the casting of limited-edition bronze sculptures — from the "open" inventory — to be displayed for sale at Fine Art galleries and to cast limited editions of 25 future works of sculpture art and 250 painted works from five promising sculptors in his school.

The Investment Trust comprises 600,000 REVPAC Bond Units at $5 each, for an aggregate $3 million. REVPAC investors will receive 30 percent of the gross revenues derived from the sale of 9,000 bronze sculptures and 25,000 limited edition prints of the Master's works and 50,000 bronze sculptures and 25,000 limited edition prints from the future works of the Master's students for an aggregate 12,000 limited edition sculpture pieces and 75,000 prints during a five-year period. In addition, one pure silver casting will be cast of each of the 25 future works of art and sold at auction prior to the REVPAC Bond Units' reaching full term. The REVPAC holders will receive 50 percent of the gross revenues derived from the auction sales.

The proceeds of the REVPAC offering are to be used to develop an inventory of 1,100 limited edition Fine Art sculpture pieces (15,000 prints) and to implement the marketing programs for the inventory. The bronze sculpture inventory will be maintained at the 1,100 sculpture (15,000 print) piece level throughout the REVPAC term and represents the capital assets of the Investment Trust. The capital assets have an inventory value — *which is defined as 25 percent of retail value* — of $3.18 million. The capital assets are to be maintained at a minimum inventory value of $3.18 million throughout the term of the REVPAC — unless the inventory is depleted through sales.

As with all REVPAC-underwritten ventures, the capital assets and copyrights of all works of art are indentured to the Investment Trust through the Collateralized Yield Obligation to secure the revenue-sharing rights of investors.

The Master appoints a well-known Fine Art marketing company as the Business Manager. The Business Manager's obligations are to optimize sales revenues and to select highly saleable works of art that will be cast to maintain the inventory at the required minimal level as gallery sales are realized.

In the event that all limited-edition pieces

are sold during the term of the REVPAC, there will be total gross sales revenues of $73.5 million. The Investment Trust's 30 percent revenue share is $22.05 million — $36 per REVPAC Unit — for a Return on Investment of over 700 percent in only five years. *This does not include the 50 percent revenue-sharing yields from the auction sales of the 25 silver sculptures and 250 original oil masterpieces.*

As an added incentive for the Fine Arts Investment Trust, the Master has included an affinity program wherein any investor that owns a minimum 7,500 REVPAC Bond Units at the end of each year receives a limited edition bronze sculpture or Fine Art print from a future masterpiece to be created by the Master.

In the event that a REVPAC holder elects the Full Redemption Guaranty option and purchases the minimum 7,500 REVPAC Bond Units, the holder will be entitled to receive five bronze sculptures or Fine Art prints in addition to the revenue yields plus be assured of 100 percent return of investment at full term.

The Future Participation Warrant is of significant value — entitling REVPAC holders the opportunity to own Revenue Shares in the Investment Trust's Master Artist as well as the five developing Masters throughout their long and productive careers. It is feasible that the emerging artists from the Master's school

with a $5,000-per-limited-edition-piece valuation can mature into a $50,000-per-piece-valuation commodity during a successful 10-year art-development program.

Now, with REVPAC, fine art development programs can access the financing they need. Investors will have the potential of realizing multiple returns-on-investment with a zero risk option — and future revenue shares in the careers of developing fine art masters will trade in securities markets just as breakthrough corporations trade on stock exchanges.

The Fine Arts scenario can be applied throughout the arts and entertainment industry. Motion pictures, theater, television production, book publishing as well as fine arts can now finance their A&E products through REVPAC. Investors can speculate on the short-term success of works of art and entertainment products while being afforded long-term revenue-participation rights in the careers of artistic talent.

Global consciousness is awakening to the stirrings of a new renaissance. World peace and global communications foster an opportunity for a new generation to vault cultural barriers and expand artistic expression as never before.

A voice from Tibet can instantaneously be heard across the globe — *through art.* That voice can manifest new semiotic imagery in differing cultures through distinct symbols of understanding — generating art movements unimaginable from even the artists's perspective.

This dramatic landscape is the canvas upon which the new renaissance will be painted — *fueled by* REVPAC *financing.*

Impact of Art REVPAC

Stabilizing Economics of Global Art Development

REVPAC represents a significant step in a new era of global marketing of art and entertainment. Yes, REVPAC accesses capital resources for development companies. Equally significant is the potential that REVPAC represents a common unit of exchange — *a new pseudo currency* — to unite art and entertainment developers and distributors around the world behind a common goal, a single art venture.

Expanding Art and Entertainment into Foreign Markets

There are many art and entertainment ventures that succeed on a national basis but rarely realize their full potential in foreign markets. This is because they lack the capital required to aggressively market the art and entertainment venture abroad.

Advertising, marketing, and promotion are the key elements in selling art and entertainment ventures. Whether the venture is a motion picture in Japan, a music album in Germany, or fine art in Australia, promotional dollars are the difference between a moderate return and a raving success. *Art delights, marketing sells!*

REVPAC provides two important advantages for art and entertainment developers seeking to expand into foreign markets:

- *They finance foreign marketing campaigns*

  It stands to reason, if the art/entertainment venture has promotional dollars behind it, the foreign distributor will give priority status to the venture — ahead of other art and entertainment products without promotional budgets. The art and entertainment developer is thereby provided with a stronger negotiating position to demand favorable revenue sharing, and can even require the distributor to guarantee minimum sales revenues.

- *They afford incentive to foreign distributors*

  Art and entertainment developers can issue **REVPAC** to foreign distributors, achieving revenue milestones within their markets. Incentive **REVPAC** affords the distributor the opportunity to earn a global stake in the art and entertainment venture while providing the developer with a means of stimulating territorial revenue performance.

  Through REVPAC, an art and entertainment developer can create its own distribution network around the world.

  The developer appoints distributors as Business

Managers of Investment Trusts in their respective territories. REVPACs are underwritten to finance sales-support promotional campaigns for a series of art/entertainment ventures in each territory.

Access Capital to Commercially Package Art and Entertainment for Foreign Markets

Art is not merely a product or a package of information. Art is an expression of culture. In effect, art belongs to a people enjoying a common language and points of reference. The world's population today enjoys neither a common language nor a common culture. The arts are much more nationalistic than global in consumer response. Although futurologists forecast that cultural homogeneity will eventually subsume nationalism, it is hardly the vision of contemporary businessmen and certainly not a prediction on which investors rely.

The exportation of works of art exemplifies the nationalistic resistance facing art-and-entertainment-development companies today. There exists the same resistance on the part of many foreign consumers to buying American works of art that exists on the part of Americans to purchase foreign works of art. When was the last time you purchased a foreign book or magazine? Have you seen a foreign-language motion picture recently?

REVPAC provides a common unit of exchange for art-development companies around the world to unite behind a single art venture — and to package works of art for their respective domestic markets.

Imagine a motion picture, funded via REVPAC to finance all preproduction costs (special effects, sets, sound, costumes, etc.), that is marketed to film production companies as a turnkey, ready-for-production package. The REVPAC holders participate in a revenue share of the box office receipts from each country. The film production company from each country modifies the script to meet national consumer criteria, casts its own artists and directs their own production. *A German production company will shoot the set on Monday, a French production company on Tuesday and a Spanish production company on Wednesday — all using the same special effects, sound, and costumes.*

Since sets and special effects account for a major portion of today's film-making budgets, the national film companies realize significant production savings, while being afforded the opportunity to create a marquee megadollar production that would otherwise be cost-prohibitive. The consumer market in each country will enjoy its national artists, surrounded by expensive sets and costumes and enhanced by cutting-edge special-effects technology. *For the first time, a true world premiere can take place — with markets around the world opening on the same date.*

This method of globalizing motion pictures will export behind-the-scenes artistic genius from scriptwriters to special effects in a new and refreshing way, permitting decentralized groups — *outside of the film-making capitals* — to impact world markets.

The globalization of works of art can be translated into every field of art — *book publishing, theatrical productions, music, as well as fine arts* — and into every language.

The only reason that the arts lag behind today's business world in reaching all corners of the global marketplace is the lack of a common unit of exchange to unite art developers.

REVPAC fuels new alliances between artists, art developers, and investors worldwide. New art forms and movements will develop on a global scale during the next 25 years, making the way the art community does business today appear as archaic as black-and-white television.

Access Capital from Foreign Investors

The REVPAC standard overcomes traditional cognitive dissonance to invest in foreign art ventures. Gross Revenue Sharing coupled with Trust Administrator accountability afford art developers the opportunity to access funding from a global audience. Whether the investors are domiciled in the U.S., Japan or Germany, they share the same appreciation of art and the same mind sync: *Does the work of art contain salability?* Investors worldwide can now network their capital into an art venture with the confidence of financial reward — whether the revenues are generated in the U.S., Japan or Germany.

*   *   *

Role of REVPAC in Paving the Way Toward Tomorrow's Hybrid Consumerism for the Arts

Consumers Become Productivity's Capital Base

Consumer activists have long crusaded to put the participatory relationship between producers and consumers into action. REVPAC paves the way for a new dimension in this relationship with the arts.

Traditionally, consumers and producers meet only at the point of purchase. REVPAC financing provides a potentially revolutionary hybrid consumerism process, wherein consumers/end users can cast their economic support in a new and meaningful way via the underwriting of tomorrow's artistic/media expression.

Shifting Art Development from Centralized Institutions to Decentralized Special-Interest Groups

Investment Bankers have already taken to the Internet which ushers in a potential new democratization process for consumerism where consumers not only set the tone, but actually *create* the pace for productivity.

During the last three decades, the splintering of mass-audience media and large umbrella organizations serving art and entertainment consumers has provided the bases of influence that today's REVPAC Art Investment Trust issuers can target for financing. Many art and entertainment associations are fragmenting into regional and specialty factions. Consumer profiles and special interests are documented, compartmentalized and easily available via information process services that are readily accessible by art and entertainment developers to target analogous consumer tastes, interests, and needs. This information is valuable for both investment bankers and art/entertainment developers to utilize in planning future REVPAC Art and Entertainment Investment Trusts — not only as a basis for funding, but also as an indicator of potential consumer appeal.

Imagine how readily a cultural profile group can be identified to fund an art/entertainment venture for a select work of art, a series of works, or even an entire art movement.

REVPAC affords art/entertainment developers a unique opportunity to easily identify a potential end-user/consumer base and to synthesize end-user consumption into venture-capital financing.

This synthesis affords the existing consumer base not only the ability to foster its own desired works of art for self-consumption, but also the opportunity to be rewarded financially by enlarging the consumer base for the artistic genius behind the works of art — thereby perpetuating future artistic expression. This is

especially critical in the development of tomorrow's artistic and cultural movements.

The most intriguing factor for consumerism is the liberation of art forms and media content from centralized corporate dominion. REVPAC allows cultural groups to render their votes of confidence in an artist or artistic expression via the purchasing of the art ventures' REVPAC Bond Units. Artists, authors, directors, and producers will be able to float new concepts and visions to targeted audiences for financing — without interference from corporate management interests.

REVPAC provides a financial liberation for art forms that will find means and ways to foster independent development of cultural expression — unimaginable from today's perspective.

Consumer Interaction in Art Development

Consumers, by becoming REVPAC holders, can follow the process of art development, voice an active role in that process and be able to interact with Art venture developers. One cannot dismiss or underestimate the underlying intellect and genius of the consumer marketplace — especially when that intellect can manifest its voice via the Internet. Thousands of consumers and investors, with a stake in emerging art ventures, constitute a mass synergistic think tank, possessing a powerful potential to contribute a myriad of design, function, production and marketing ideas for the art developer.

Why REVPAC Will Be the Financial Instrument of Choice by 2025

Today's economy is global in principle. Trade barriers have all but eroded, consumers are more affluent and educated than ever, and media and Internet services accelerate access to information at unprecedented speed.
Yet the multi-national venture-capital investment community still awaits its emergence into this new era of progress and prosperity. REVPAC represents a quantum leap in 21st-century global financing. Its currency-in-trade is *gross revenue percentages,* and gross revenue is *universal.* Extraordinary ROIs are available only through venture-capital investments. Basing those yields on gross revenues provides a simple equation with which savvy international investors can evaluate investment opportunities — both at the IPO stage and when speculating on emerging ventures in the secondary securities markets of the world.

REVPAC establishes a new standard for investment benefits sought by sophisticated global investors.

- The financial success of a new business venture is translated into straightforward yields that pass directly from consumer sales to investors without management interference or arbitrary deductions.

- Returns are based on gross revenues — *not net earnings* — simplifying the evaluation, tracking, and accountability of investment, while providing a hedge against inflation.

- The Full Redemption Guaranty option removes all risk from investing in venture-capital opportunities.

- The built-in Risk-Insurance Wrap stimulates foreign investing and enhances liquidity in a rich international secondary trading market.

- The Future Participation Warrant affords investors with long-term revenue participation in successful ventures, or future developments from proven innovators and management teams. In effect, innovative genius and management talent become investment franchises.

- The Intellectual Property rights underlying the venture project are afforded an additional layer of litigious recourse to protect the proprietary rights of the Investment Trust and REVPAC Investment Trust Unit holders.

REVPAC is the gateway to new-venture financing sought by corporations with global vision.

- New businesses can access capital not previously available through traditional forms of financing.

- No longer must companies incur debt or endure equity dilution to launch innovations into the competitive consumer marketplace.

REVPAC establishes a World Standard unit of exchange that can be used as a virtual currency in the acquisition of assets, intellectual property rights, and services for emerging business ventures. Businesses can now leverage future-revenues — *without debt* — to incubate innovation even prior to the IPO stage.

speculators. Securities analysts, brokers, and traders will be attracted to REVPAC in the secondary trading markets, in which they can forecast and effect transactions based on anticipated consumer response to innovative tangibles.

The business of underwriting emerging ventures will one day be dominated by REVPAC, as the global investment community recognizes that the more modern and unified system is vastly more lucid and equitable at all strata of the financial community than the current process of underwriting the capital stock of corporations.

- Because the patents, copyrights, and other intellectual property claims protecting the proprietary rights of the business are held as chattel by the Investment Trust, those rights become integral to the investment instrument itself. For the first time, intellectual property is bundled into a financial instrument, bringing a new and effective method to defend against intellectual property infringement. Compelling litigious pressure can now be brought to bear against offenders of IP rights in the courts of foreign countries *by citing securities laws violations.* This results in significantly greater opportunity for enforcement than ever before. This additional layer of litigious recourse will enable swift judicial action — enhancing the protection of REVPAC proprietary and revenue rights.

An essential, and largely neglected element of the world venture mercantile marketplace will be filled and maintained by REVPAC — in much the same way as the world's natural resources are serviced by today's commodity futures, and through which a rich liquid trading market will be provided to investors and

What will result will be not only an Investment Banking system of new venture development but the ultimate barometer for comprehensively indexing consumer market response to those new ventures. *Imagine the impact of trading markets for venture projects wherein the investors' yields flow directly from the end-user marketplace to the investor.*

The venture synergism created by the REVPAC Financial Model promises to create a surge of interest and confidence from the investment community in taking an idea and cashing in, *which the public can follow through a system of real-time reporting* and which, in the historical perspective, can pave the way into a new era for the relationship between venture capital and innovative resources, launching a creative renaissance for the next generation.

CAPITAL MARKETS
SEEKING REVPAC SOLUTIONS

Institutional and Corporate Sector

While potential institutional funding market application of *REVPAC Bond Funding* is extensive - select *Stand-Out* market sectors have exigent needs and goals...that will be especially attracted to the potential benefits and solutions offered by REVPAC BONDS. Here is a "short-list" of ready-to-market Institutional Funding Sectors that clearly illustrate the *Power of REVPAC Bond Funding Standard...* and the creative solutions available through *REVPAC Funding*. These Sectors represent largely - un-tapped and viable - *Niche Markets* for all REVPAC Bond Investment Products and Programs.

BANKING INSTITUTIONS

• *Small Banking and Brokerage*

Small to Mid-Size Financial Institutions do not usually possess fulfillment capability or network infrastructure to offer "private label" Capital and Investment Programs to their Clients. Directors seek opportunity to operate "in-house" capital/investment centers to participate in the potential lucrative profits afforded by these Programs.

Small Banks & Brokerage are extremely sensitive of sharing the identity and contact information with outside service providers, regarding their Accounts.

REVPAC Solution:

The REVPAC Bond Wrap allows smaller banking institutions that are "associated" through membership organizations (i.e. alliances, associations, unions, etc.) to "Build customized REVPAC Funding Programs" that allow the Small Institution, total autonomy while, networking the collective membership's resources into expanding Small Business Development and Venture Capital Services.

The theme: "Build Customized REVPAC Funding Programs" consists of Turn-key, Off-the-Shelf and Private Label Programs - that: operate under the name of the Financial Institution - derived from the "collective membership" products and services that deploy the REVPAC Bond Wrap.

The Program operates in a similar manner as "Credit and Financing Packages" that are fulfilled under "private-label" to small banking Institutions that do not possess the infrastructure to fulfill and network their own Programs. All "fulfillment" services are performed by the Membership Collective Service Provider and the final product is delivered to the banking institution to be conveyed to the end-client in the name of the banking institution.

The Private Label Programs may include:

Small Business Development Program
* Vetting, trust, funding and B2B networking services managed through collective membership platform
Small Business Capital Funding Program
* Underwriting and Syndication Service through Open-Auction Membership Primary Market
* Matching Funds Program through a membership ANNUITY entity
Social Entrepreneur Program
* Fund-Raising planning for NGOs through a customized Private Label Annuity – utilizing Membership infrastructure

• Public Pension Funds

Many Public Pension Funds (especially within the U.S.) are mandated to allocate a fixed percentage of their assets toward minority Interest investments. Minority interest is defined by a designated minority group of persons that may be categorized by ethnicity, gender, physical/mental limitations, etc. At present, many Public Pension Funds are unable to meet the mandates due to the lack of an adequate financial instrument providing a surety-guaranty that the investment capital is not at risk.

REVPAC Solution:
REVPAC BOND denominated Investment Products provide the surety and the potential for extraordinary yield (not to mention the "transparency") that Public Pension Funds have long sought to be able to fund minority interest Venture Capital opportunities.

It is estimated that over $30 Trillion U.S. Dollars resides in Pension Funds throughout the world – with *Twenty-Five Percent of the world's retirement assets, deposited in U.S. Pension Funds.* Depending upon the available percentage of pension-fund assets that are mandated yet unallocated, the amount of fresh venture capital available - through REVPAC BOND INVESTMENT PRODUCTS - is significant.

• Islamic Banks - And other select Fundamentalist driven Financial Institutions:

Islamic Fundamentalist Financial Institutions are proscribed by "Shariah" or Islamic Law from the application of "debt-interest" in money management. Many Banks and Financial Institutions throughout the Middle East, Malaysia and Indonesia deploy a non-interest bearing financial instrument-named **SuKuk** - that is used to denominate select investments.

The Sukuk is not widely used - outside of Islamic circles - and has failed to generate an international following from non-Islamic capital markets - though interest is slowly expanding.

The limitations of "fundamentalist money management" - *especially in a "debt-driven world-marketplace"* - severely shrinks the field of available choices in developing capital and investment programs for Financial Institutions that adhere to the rigid code of Islam.

-Please Note- The "Sukuk" is the Arabic name for Islamic Bonds. Islamic financing differs; from conventional financing in its strict adherence to *Shariah* or Islamic Law - which calls for ethical and equitable financing, and bans speculation.

REVPAC Solution:

REVPAC BONDS are unique and flexible financial instruments that are "purely" revenue driven. The generally accepted form of REVPAC BONDs has been designed for "yield pass-thru" in the form of a subordinated debenture -with 'so-called' nominal 'interest'- to satisfy the accounting and tax requirements of those nations that base many of their favorable accounting and tax regulations on "debt". This however, should not limit the fundamentalist financial institution participation in the universal form of REVPAC BONDs - ideally: designed for the non-Islamic capital markets...because the "interest" feature of the REVPAC BOND is "non-recourse-debt"...and All Yields of the REVPAC BOND are tied to Revenue Participation - **not recourse-debt-interest**. Additionally, the REVPAC BOND designed to be flexible - can be modified (if required) to be able to account and administer the flow of Revenue Participation from Venture Capital Opportunities to be in full compliance with Islamic Law.

REVPAC BONDs provide the ultimate financial instrument for Islamic Fundamentalist Financial Institutions. They offer extraordinary Returns-on-Investment, 100% Surety Guaranty (zeroing out Risk) and is in full compliance with closely held tenets of Shariah. What's more...it is "Universal" for all capital markets... which is significant - because NOW Venture Capital Funding within Islamic Capital Markets can be linked with all other Capital Markets throughout the world... significantly enhancing the flow of innovation and investment capital.

The Market Segment

of Fundamentalist-driven Financial Institutions includes other-than-Islamic institutions with growing demands to seek 'non-debt-interest' bearing solutions to capital management... *i.e. fundamentalist*

Christian based financial institutions are an example within the western hemisphere. REVPAC BOND Funding is a universal financial instrument in full conformity and compliance with the World's fundamentalist-driven Financial Institutions mandate - proscribing "debt-interest" in money management

CORPORATE LEGAL & ACCOUNTING (ADVISORY & PLANNING)

Corporate Legal/Accountant Advisory & Planning teams are continually called upon by Management for solutions to business challenges and opportunities. These teams are engaged in intense competition to influence corporate decision makers and are in an ongoing-search for cutting-edge tactics to advance the fiscal welfare of their corporate clients.

These Legal/Accountant Advisory teams are a key target sector to address the merits and real-time solutions of the REVPAC BOND Funding Standard. The following is a 'short-list' of exigent Issues facing Today's Corporate Decision Makers and the creative solutions and advantages offered by the REVPAC BOND Funding Standard.

• Acquisitions - Licenses - Franchises & Strategic Partner Relationships

Corporate Relationships, pursuant to the terms/conditions of Acquisitions, Licensing, Franchising and other similar business accords, can NOW be effectively wrapped into "Revenue Sharing Investment Products" denominated in REVPAC BONDS.

The REVPAC BOND wrap is an all-inclusiveTurn-Key package - warrantied and insured to deliver "bonded" Oversight, Monitoring and Reporting TRUST GUARANTY services - assuring all parties of absolute transparency and enforcement of rights and entitlements.

• Patent & Copyright Protection

The REVPAC BOND wrap self-encompasses a modern and effective litigious tool against Intellectual Property infringement.

The "wrapping"of Intellectual Property into "Revenue-Sharing-Investment-Products" which are denominated in REVPAC BONDS - is a powerful weapon in the hands of IP holders and their licensed developers for swift and strident enforcement of Intellectual Property rights under any and every nation's securities and banking laws.

- The Patents, Copyrights and other IP claims, *protecting the Business Venture*, are held as "chattel" within the framework of the Collateralized Yield Obligation. Since the IP is part of (and integral to) the registered investment instrument - both the IP and the REVPAC Bond qualify for protection under securities, banking statutes and commercial laws of all nations.

NOW - *for the first time* - Intellectual Property is bundled into a universal financial instrument...bringing a new and effective method to defend against IP infringement. Compelling litigious pressure can now be brought to bear against offenders of IP rights in the courts of all countries throughout the world by citing securities laws violations. This results in significantly greater opportunity for property protection and swift enforcement of infringement.

Some of the Advantages and Benefits of the "wrap":

- obviates the need to dilute equity ownership of corporate entities;
- securitizes license performance covenants;
- collateralizes revenue sharing pledges;
- affords extra layers of litigious recourse against intellectual property infringement;
- qualifies access to Open-Auction Banking System / Secondary Funding Markets for funding and divestiture;
-Trust Monitoring and Full Transparency Reporting ensures absolute accountability of revenues.

NON-GOVERNMENT SOCIAL ORGS

•   *Funding of Mission Programs*

Funding of NGO Mission Programs has presented a perennial economic challenge for NGO Members. Traditional methods of capitalizing a campaign usually consists of: public fund-raising efforts, private and government endowments and altruistic patronage.

There are major obstacles to adequately funding a Mission Program. The costs associated with soliciting funding are often equal to or greater than the proceeds that ultimately reach the project.

REVPAC Solution:

REVPAC BOND Donor Programs afford members with the opportunity to purchase REVPAC BOND Investment Products and to donate all or a portion of the investment to the NGO. REVPAC BONDS can be donated to fund single Mission Program or a series of Programs, with investors and the NGO never risking a penny of their investment principal.

The REVPAC BOND Funding Standard for Social Entrepreneur Donor Fund Raising Programs provides that all "yields" (above and beyond the original investment) be contributed to fund the Altruistic Cause, leaving the Investment Principal intact and available to be reinvested into future similar causes. Thereby affording a perpetual source of funding… on roll-over of Investment Principal… while extending to the DONOR, the potential for extraordinary Tax write offs.

The NGO may opt to participate as a Small Business Developer in the Social Entrepreneur Program… and develop small business ventures (i.e. Franchise retail businesses) funded from the proceeds of the donated REVPAC BONDS. This program affords the NGO with the extraordinary leverage of not only receiving the contributed portion of the REVPAC BOND donation… but also the NET INCOME from the business venture… PLUS – at full term of the REVPAC BOND – the NGO may continue to operate the small business venture in order to generate an uninterrupted stream of proceeds for the Mission patronage… or the NGO may opt to divest itself of the equity ownership… and apply the proceeds to the Mission Program.

How the Social Entrepreneur Program can Work for the NGO:

Imagine the NGO operating a chain of fast food franchise outlets - funded by the Donors thru REVPAC BONDS. In addition to receiving the REVPAC BOND Yields from the Franchise operations - the NGO also participates in the Net Revenues of the Franchises. At full term of the REVPAC BOND - the NGO receives Equity Ownership of the Franchises.

REVPAC BOND Funding Standard coupled with the Social Entrepreneur Program provides the following benefits:

* Facilitates and accesses unique Alternative Fund Raising Opportunities that offers significantly greater capital resources (flow of money into NGO) than is feasible thru conventional Fund raising methods.

* Provides Long-Term Capital stability for Mission Programs because the stability of the economics assures long-term funding support. ALSO: Stimulates a perspicuous focal point for private and public interest & activist groups toward a system of checks and balances for Economic Development.

* Substantially decreases the cost of Fund Raising - increasing the overall efficacy of the Mission.

REVPAC BONDs provide the ideal financial instrument and Funding Standard for sponsorship wherein the fragmented financing methods and vehicles currently in use by NGOs often fall short of requisite funding goals.

NGO Fund Raising System

... in Action

Non Government Organization (N.G.O.)
Revenue Participation FUND RAISING SYSTEM
In association with
REVPAC BOND Funding of the Mission Program

1. NGO Donors purchase REVPAC BONDS.
2. Donors' REVPAC BOND Investment purchases a Business Entity that is 100% owned and operated by NGO. *Cash Flow Forecast for the annual sales of the Business Entity must be minimum Four Times the Purchase Price of the Business per year (7 Year Average)* .
3. Donors receive Ten Cents of every Dollar on ALL Sales! *This 10% Revenue Participation Program is called a "DADDY" – Dime-a-Dollar-Dividend -Yield. DADDY payments are streamed directly to Donors' Smart Cards – in REAL-TIME!*
4. NGO (owner/operator of the Business Entity) receives the Net Operational Revenues of the Business Entity (Net Revenues are equivalent to a *Daddy – 10% Gross Revenue Participation*).
5. NGO FUNDS Mission Program from Net Revenues!

SOCIAL ENTREPRENEURISM & REVPAC

Social Consciousness in a Rapidly Changing Global Village

Since 2013, the number of registrations of Non-Profit Foundations outnumber For-Profit Stock Corporations within the United States. This phenomenon, coupled with the powerful deluge of the "alternative media voice" calling for social activism on over two thousand causes and issues - is accelerating the Global Call for a Change in the direction of the Future of the Global Village...that cannot be ignored!

The alternative choice voice is "growing in numbers and volume" with the message that the complexity of the socio-econ infrastructure has outgrown itself. The indictment charges that special interest groups - totally FOR-PROFIT driven and impervious to accountability, responsibility and reverence for life - is at the helm of an ill-fated mission. The alarm, being sounded, is that the high-cost of this continued and unchecked course, will culminate in the bankruptcy of our societies - morally and economically. While the message appears time-worn and reminiscent of the 60's and 70's...it is gaining momentum and is reigniting a multi-generational awareness that appears to have deeply seeded roots. The call for "activism" is being made on a "personal" and "community" basis with the underlying theme that value systems and personal ethics for the "common good of all people" have been overcome by materialistic goals and short-term objectives and instant-gratification fixes.

No one can deny that a massive and global movement for social reform is in progress - much like a sub-surface swell of an impending tsunami...

While the clamor for "change" grows in urgency and sound bites...the fiscal and sobering reality is that "change" requires financial resources. Capital is integral, from which to fund the support mechanisms for effective, "activism" campaigns and movements that can promulgate such change. However, outside of the traditional and perennial "altruistic donor-based fund-raising" campaigns, there exists a severe dearth of fresh capital sources for Social Activist Organizations.

The major impediment to adequately capitalize Today's Social NGO Movements is the lack of a Universal Funding Solution and STANDARD to attract meaningful resources.

The wait is over! REVPAC BOND FUNDING is the emerging Potent and Viable Alternative Funding Conduit that Social Activists desperately require to access meaningful capital resources, with which to effectively succeed in their missions.

Social Activists and Venture Entrepreneurs Unite Under a Unique Social Entrepreneurial Program

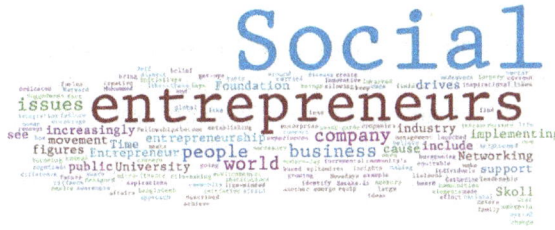

At first glance, it may appear incongruous...an Alliance of Small Business Entities, Insurance Underwriters and Financial-Banking Service Providers, brought together to develop emerging business ventures ...working in tandem with SOCIAL ACTIVISTS who share common goals and objectives. However, given the global conditions and the intrinsic values of the separate parts, there could never be a more "timely" and suitable opportunity for such an Alliance.

Venture Capital Entrepreneurs and Social Activists - in many ways - are birds of a common feather. They are "kindred spirits" - in every sense of the term... Albeit, that the aim of one is based on "Capital" and the other on "Social Reform". Actually, a working partnership, between the two holds a symbiotic potential of bringing about significant advantages for each one - separate and extraordinary rewards for both - as a team.

SOCIAL ENTREPRENEURSHIP 101
EVERYTHING IMPORTANT YOU'LL EVER NEED TO KNOW ABOUT SOCIAL ENTREPRENEURSHIP

definition: a social entrepreneur recognizes a social problem and uses entrepreneurial principles to organize, create and manage a venture that drives social change.

Entrepreneurial VS. *Social Entrepreneurial*

✓ serving markets with new products/ services for financial gain
✓ idea for product/service, startup, prototype, venture (investment), growth, exit plan, return on investment

✓ drive social change brought about by social challenges
✓ using business solutions to solve them
✓ aim is to further social and environmental goals
✓ a big win = sustainability and social impact

KEY TRAITS
INNOVATIVE
LEADER
HAS WILL POWER
RISK TAKER
COURAGEOUS
CULTIVATED

The **SOCIAL enterprise**
an enterprise that provides business solutions to social problems... *"good at doing good!"* Has a clear social purpose. Reinvests Profits back into the business / community.

{ A COMPANY THAT EMPHASIZES **CORPORATE SOCIAL RESPONSIBILITY** IS NOT A SOCIAL ENTERPRISE. MUCH LIKE AN ENTREPRENEUR WHO DONATES MONEY TO HIS FAVORITE CHARITY IS NOT A **SOCIAL ENTREPRENEUR** }

Starbucks + Fair Trade Coffee
SOCIAL RESPONSIBILITY

A social venture is NOT a charity... it is a business with social objectives

Social Activists and Venture Entrepreneurs share "kindred" and parallel paths in that, both are:

* Open to Change and Innovation;
* Think outside of the Box;
* Have no Borders or Barriers inhibiting the Networking of their causes;
* Dedicate significant amounts of time and donate sincere efforts toward the goal of "achievement"...without any guarantee of recompense;
* Linked throughout history...as the identical innovators and pioneers responsible for both venture capital breakthroughs as well as social improvements and;
* In Need of FUNDING...

Entrepreneur & Social Entrepreneur

Entrepreneur	Social Entrepreneur
• Exceptional ability to see new opportunities	• Targeting under-served / disadvantaged / broken markets
• Determination to take those opportunities	• Large scale and transformative change
• Unflinching willingness to take inherent risk	• Ethical process to reach that change (beyond compliance)
• Sees that a **suboptimal equilibrium** = OPPORTUNITY	• Sees a stable but unjust equilibrium (not just suboptimal)
• Outcome focused – **creative destruction**	• Is able to take the opportunity to reach new equilibrium

It is due to similar philosophies and "shared pathways" of these persons, who choose to become Entrepreneurs and Activists that "collectively" they share, as a group - the identical spirit that pioneers New Frontiers and inspires progress...

Today, the common pooling of Altruistic purpose with Entrepreneurial Resources - bound by the unique and equitable STANDARD of REVPAC BOND FUNDING - is implementing new funding methods that are fostering ATERNATIVE CHOICES toward a BETTER WORLD.

HOW the Social Entrepreneur Program Works - *A Capsule View*
The following is a "capsule-digest" of the REVPAC Bond Funding Program for Social
Activist Organizations.

Mission:

To fund and foster development of proprietary Venture breakthroughs that are compatible
with the Social Activist's Organizations' goals and mission.

Objectives:

(1) To secure funding of innovative ideas emerging into the marketplace, developed through
(and in association with) the Social Activist's Organization, Venture Entrepreneurs and
REVPAC BOND Underwriters.
(2) To network all phases of market emergence - utilizing the infrastructure of both the
Social Activist Organization's Member Network and that of the Venture Entrepreneurs.

Underlying Philosophy:

Teach Social Activist Organizations how to network
Venture Capital Opportunities with Entrepreneurs into
the Marketplace - and to provide a means for securing
the long-term financial stability of the Organization and
success of its Mission.
***Teaching Social Activist Organizations How to Deploy
REVPAC BOND FUNDING.***

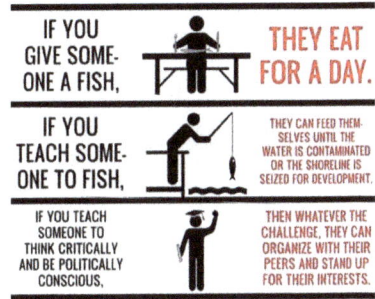

IF YOU GIVE SOME- ONE A FISH, **THEY EAT FOR A DAY.**

IF YOU TEACH SOME- ONE TO FISH, THEY CAN FEED THEM- SELVES UNTIL THE WATER IS CONTAMINATED OR THE SHORELINE IS SEIZED FOR DEVELOPMENT.

IF YOU TEACH SOMEONE TO THINK CRITICALLY AND BE POLITICALLY CONSCIOUS, THEN WHATEVER THE CHALLENGE, THEY CAN ORGANIZE WITH THEIR PEERS AND STAND UP FOR THEIR INTERESTS.

How It Works:

The Social Entrepreneur Program has three primary responsibilities:

(1) *Activist Organization-operating as N.G.O. Lending Authority- mobilizes their Member/*
Sponsor Network to identify worthwhile emerging business ventures
that are compatible and congruent to the Organization's Mission.

mobilize

* Qualify and select Funding candidates;
* Prepare Document Package and Application for Funding;
* Analyze Funding Requirements and Feasibility for success and;
* Maintain on-going relationship with Small Business Entity - to
  counsel and guide the management throughout the
  Funding Process.

(2) *Integrate Organization Members and Mission into the Business Plan of the Small Business Entity to support the emergence of the Business Venture.* To wit: coordinate and assist Small Business candidate through Organization Member Network to "package", and launch emerging products / services through B2B networking of services (management, marketing and strategic alliance relationships) from resources and Member network of Activist Organization and Small Business Entrepreneur- to procure meaningful sales from the Marketplace.

(3) Integrate Organization's DONOR FUND RAISING CAMPAIGNS with REVPAC BOND Financing of emerging business ventures on the Primary Open Auction Market. In other words: Donors purchase REVPAC BONDS and donate the REVPAC BOND to the Social Activist Organization as their altruistic contribution to the fund raising campaign and toward the Humanitarian cause.

Key Elements of Funding:

REVPAC BOND Funding opens new avenues of Fund Raising opportunities for Social Activist Organizations and their "Social Entrepreneur" Associate Members.

The Social Activist Organization is trained and appointed as an "authorized" clearing house for Emerging Business Ventures seeking REVPAC Bond Funding. Subsequent to qualifying and "packaging" a Business Venture for the Open Auction Market, the Social Activist Organization integrates the REVPAC Bond Underwriting into its "Donor's Portfolio" for the Fund Raising Campaign.

(1) *Three Donor Program Options*

The Organization's Donors (purchasers) of the REVPAC Bonds - who wish to make a contribution of the Bonds to the Social Activist Organization are afforded Three (3) Donor programs to choose from:

(a) **Donor Donates Bond**- allowing the Organization to receive all Revenue Sharing Yields - which, under favorable market conditions, has the potential of increasing the "donation" substantially - by 3, 4 or more times the Face Value of the Bonds,.. This Donor Program allows the Bond that is covered by Full Redemption Guaranty - to be "rolled-over" again and again...For many years, in perpetuity.
Provides for multiple Returns-of-Investment Yields to Organization and the potential of a never-ending revenue stream for the Organization.

(b) **Donor Retains Bond and donates a portion of the Yield Coupons** – Allowing the Donor to both participate in potential ROI of the Investment... without risk to the Principal-Investment...while sharing Potential future Revenue Sharing Yields with the Organization. *Organization and Donor are "Partners" sharing in the success of the Emerging Business Venture.*

(c) **Donor Retains Bond** – and donates all Yield Revenue Coupons to the Organization with the proviso that all Yields "above and beyond" the Face Value of the Bond is to be a charitable donation to the Organization. This guarantees the Donor that the Donor will recapture 100% return of investment capital while donating all profits from the investment.

Donor can use the Return-of-Investment to purchase a New REVPAC Bond and repeat the donation process...or discontinue the donation.

NGO Organization receives all Yields in excess of the Face Value of the Bond. Donor's Principal Investment is never at risk and is covered by Full Redemption Guaranty to be reimbursed, in full, to Donor.

(2) *Margin (Lending) Financing* - The Organization may "borrow" against the Face Value of the REVPAC Bonds or any other REVPAC Investment Product.

   * Donor donates REVPAC Investment Products and authorized Margin Financing:

   * Organization "margins" investment product to access funding - up to 50% of Face Value. This affords the Organization immediate access to donated funds;

   * If and when Yields occur... the Margin is "settled"... If NO YIELDS occur... the Full Redemption Guaranty retires (settles) the Margin.

(3) *New Dynamics for Fund Raising* - Among the many advantages offered Social Activist Organizations thru REVPAC Bond Funding over traditional Fund Raising Campaigns- there are two significant benefits that stand out:

* Cost Savings:
Traditionally, Non-profit Fund Raising Costs range between 50% to 70% of the gross contributions. Only half or less of the contributed capital reaches the "cause". REVPAC Bond Funding significantly reduces - and in-many-cases eliminates - the high-cost of Fund Raising. The Organization receives 100% of the Face Value of the investment...there are no-loaded costs above the Face Value of the investment.

* Increased Contributions:
The Donor is "assured" that the full FACE VALUE will be recovered - whether by the Donor or by the Organization - depending upon which of the Four Donor Programs is elected.

The Full Redemtion Guaranty /plus/ the potential of Revenue Yield Coupons returning extraordinary ROI's - contributes to the possibility that DONORS may receive extraordinary "write-offs" (tax-relief). Additionally, the donor has full Surety that - under any and all circumstances and market conditions - the full Return of the Investment Principal is guaranteed.

These unique features are in-and-by themselves- extraordinary for Fund Raising Programs. REVPAC Bond Funding provides a new dynamic for the world of Charity Donations for Worthy Causes...that may result in substantially increased capital contributions for Charitable Organizations than heretofore experienced.

Fiscal Benefits to Organizations:

The primary advantages and benefits for Charitable Organizations Participating in REVPAC Bond Funding are:

(1) Lucrative Revenue Sharing Program as Lending Authority;

(2) Organization and its Members will be at the forefront of emerging breakthroughs that have been Vetted, Qualified and Financed through the REVPAC Bond Funding Process... affording significant B2B networking and arbitrage opportunities;

(3) New and modern Fund Raising mechanism (REVPAC Bond Funding) that has the potential of:

> • Significantly increasing the amount of donations available to the Organization;

> • Substantial decrease of the cost of traditional Fund Raising expenditures - which increases the overall efficacy of the Organization's pursuit of it Mission and;

> • Provides a self-perpetuating source of future funding with which to plan long-term budgets, strategies and objectives.

REVPAC BOND STANDARD - *Universal Solution to Social Issues*

The unique features of REVPAC Bond Funding include: Gross Revenue Sharing - Transparency of Financial Reporting - Guaranty of Investment Principal and Surety of Fiscal Fiduciary Accountability. The Surety and Integrity of the underlying covenants of REVPAC Bonds provide a viable and dependable "Check and Balance System" that - if responsibly deployed - may develop into the Universal Standard and Solution to ensure Social Reform Programs - long-sought-after by Social Activists. Here are a few of the many Social Issues that can be effectively brought into "check-and-balance" through REVPAC Bond Funding.

* Labor Rights
Labor is not participating in fair share of market revenues generated from their production. Example: Latin American/Asian Labor receives less than 5% of wholesale value of their production.

REVPAC Solution
Portion of REVPAC Bonds (or special Bond Issue for Labor) is issued to Labor Organization/Union/ Cooperative that is representing Labor Force.

Bond Yields (from Gross Revenues) provide fair, meaningful and equitable method of rewarding work force and funding requisite benefits.
/ALSO/ Bond Issue provides transparence and accountability that can be readily monitored by Labor Representatives and easy-to-follow (in Real-Time) by work force.

* Indigenous Land/Resource Rights

Protected Native People with land/ resource rights have little or no litigious recourse to monitor the accountability of concessionaires – commercially exploiting the property/resource.
Example: In U.S. Bureau of Land Mgmt. grants concessions on Native American land with less than fair value /or/ no Value distributed to Indigenous right holders. Identical violations occur in S.E Asia and Latin America.

REVPAC Solution
Concessions to develop Indigenous properties/ resources are wrapped into REVPAC Bonds, The Bonds are issued to Indigenous rights holders therein indenturing all future gross revenues derived from property/resource exploitation.

Bondholders rights, entitlements and benefits are safeguarded by Fiscal Fiduciary Monitoring, with stringent Remedial Enforcement in the event of default.

* Government, Privatization and Monopoly Concessions

Governments - Regional/National - granting Monopoly rights to foreign developers - either through Privatization Programs or Resource/ Utility / Commodity Concessions (i.e. as above Indigenous example)... is being conveyed, in many cases, in the absence of competitive bids and for ulterior purposes that often lie outside the national interest of the people.

Example: Bolivia granted utility monopoly rights for Water and Electricity to a private French Company that increased utility prices and caused civil unrest and the departure of the former President. This is occurring throughout the world - especially for energy/mineral rights and concessions.

REVPAC Solution

Same as Indigenous Issue. Additionally, Concession Agreements – wrapped into REVPAC Bond – include Social Programs - i.e. integration of local micro-economic programs into End-User Marketplace of Concessionaire; contribution of funding and/or market-orders for local business ventures. REVPAC Bonds - protecting the entitlements of the People in the "indentured" future gross revenues of the Concession - is transferred in trust to an accredited and bonded Trust Institution, outside the government or private business sector.

Example: REVPAC Bond Yields Coupons provide for "gross revenue sharing" entitlement of any/all resource, commodity or other product (included in Concession) derived from END USER Sales in Marketplace. Thereby providing for maximum value of resources in "exported" end-user market. These Yields from Bonds may be reinvested by the Trust Institution in Social Programs - with Trust Administrator monitoring and enforcing all covenants of the Concession Agreements and the REVPAC Bonds.

* Minority Interest Business (US) Non-Equality Issues

Venture Capital Investment into Minority Interest Small Business developers of emerging innovation accounts for less than 2% of all VC capitalization in last decade.

Govt. SBA Program is inadequate / Venture Capital/ Investment Bankers respond to Venture Capital Investment Opportunities with inequality and there is a dearth of available capital for minority entrepreneurs.

Example: There are a handful of "black" owned securities brokerage firms in the United States. Minorities, in the U.S. have few places to seek investment capital. Of all the Initial Public Offerings filed with the SEC during the last decade...less than 3.5% (three and one-half of one percent) of all the capitalization from Public Offerings was earmarked for Minority Interest Management.

REVPAC Solution

REVPAC Bonds eliminate the Risk of erosion or loss of Investment Principal. Public Pension Funds and many Financial Institutions have been delinquent in complying with an existing Government mandate to invest a fixed (minimal) percentage of their assets in Minority Interest controlled or related Investments. The non-compliance is largely due to the stringent investment parameters that these funds and institutions are required to apply to investment decisions. These parameters - all but disqualify Venture Capital Opportunities - not to mention the misunderstood and undocumented "minority marketplace".

Now, with REVPAC Bond Funding, Minority Investment Opportunities take on a Non-Risk dimension that can persuade Investment Bankers to consider the merits of ROI potential... and to rethink the addition of Minority Investments for their portfolios. What is especially persuasive and promising... is that with Full Redemption Guaranty Coverage - REVPAC Bonds provide Social Activist Organizations with the "fodder" they need to demand that Public Pension Funds and Financial Institutions comply with Government Mandates...and commit the "public sector investment capital" into promising Minority Interest Small Business Entities with Venture Capital Opportunities.

Also, the Insurance Package that is part of REVPAC Bond Funding promises to qualify Minority Interest Management Teams with the requisite Financial Services and "Image Surety" to forge Strategic Alliance relationships.

* *Cultural & Fine Arts Funding / Heritage Preservation Patronage* is unable to finance next season's costs - without Govt. Endowments (and these are being steadily decreased or eliminated).
The costs associated with soliciting patronage-funding are often equal to or greater than the proceeds that ultimately reach the project.

REVPAC Solution

REVPAC Bonds can be applied to fund an individual production, a season, or a series of seasons of the cultural arts of a community, with investors never risking a penny of their investment. The REVPAC Bond Funding Standard for Social Entrepreneur Donor Fund Raising Programs provides that all Yields (above and be-yond the Face Value of the Bonds) be contributed to fund the Cultural & Fine Arts/Heritage Preservation Cause...leaving the Investment Principal (intact) and available to be re-invested into future similar Causes. Thereby affording a perpetual source of Funding...On roll-over of Investment Principal.

REVPAC Bond Funding Standard provides the following benefits:

* Substantial decrease of the cost of traditional Fund Raising expenditures - increasing the overall efficacy of the Cultural/ Art Mission;

* Providing Long-Term Capital Resources: Stabilizes the economics of Cultural/Art Programs / affords artistic talent to commit its future development to the Cultural/Art World (rather than the commercial) /and/ stimulate a perspicuous focal point for private and public interest / activist groups toward a system of checks and balances for Cultural economic development.

REVPAC FUNDING... *Uniting the Possible with the Responsible*

REVPAC Bond Funding promises to create a surge of interest and trust from the investment community in taking an idea and cashing in - which can be followed through a transparent system of real-time reporting. The integration of Social Consciousness - as a vital component - in the REVPAC Bond Funding Process... through the Social Entrepreneur Program...can pave the way into a new era for the relationship between **venture capital possibilities and social responsibilities,** launching both a creative and humanitarian renaissance for future generations.

The following is a summation of the highlights and benefits the REVPAC Bond Funding offers the Social Entrepreneur Program:

* Provides a method and process to distribute meaningful yields from the success of emerging business ventures;

* Provides a transparent fiduciary system of ensuring integrity of accounting and administrating the Business Venture and Revenue Yields;

* Provides a system of monitoring the distribution of the "value and yields" of a Business Venture – thereby assuring "visibility" of revenue sharing and who gets how much. This affords an easy-to-understand barometer from which to gauge fulfillment of responsibility and fairness in distributing "just rewards" to the principal elements of Venture Development: Creative Genius, Property (Intellectual and Real), Capital, Labor and Management.

* Establishes a "universal standard" that can be used as "virtual currency" and "meaningful barter" in the acquisition of assets, property and services for emerging Business Ventures. Small Businesses can now leverage "indentured future revenues" to incubate innovation - especially in situations and environments where capital is not readily available.

* Establishes a system of checks and balances, providing a dependable method of monitoring and distributing the "wealth" of Ventures. This is especially applicable to national, regional, community, social or cultural "concessions' - i.e. indigenous property rights, government monopoly rights, natural resource concessions, etc. Now, these concession licenses can be "assigned under chattel" and the chattel can be wrapped into REVPAC BONDS, providing the certainty that:

1) The "wealth" and Yields will be distributed fairly and without interference or deductions of any kind. Yields flow directly from the marketplace to BOND holders.

2) The Yields represent the "real-time market value" of the underlying products/ services of the Venture. This prevents developers (concessionaires) from manipulating the price and value of the product/service and thereby allocating an unfair portion of the "wealth" to the "rightful sources" (Creative Genius, Property Titleholders, Capital, Labor and Management) - i.e. NOW, in lieu of Concessionaires being able to pay a pittance for natural resource commodities /or/ a fraction of a penny on the Retail- Dollar for labor's contribution for produced goods...a fair portion of "Revenue Sharing" - based on the "end market valuation" ...is Yielded.

3) Since Yields are based on Gross Revenues - derived from the end-user market - the Yields are "inflation proof". The end-user market prices - and therefore, the Yield Revenues - rise in tandem with inflation, as a cork.

Socially Conscious Institutions and Governments can deploy the REVPAC BOND with confidence that the "wealth and value" of a proprietary resource, assigned to a Concessionaire will be distributed to those responsible for bringing the resource to market.

The TRUE WEALTH of a Nation or People is the Real-Time Market Value of its "Resources". REVPAC BONDS protect the Rightful Recipients to share in the Wealth and serves to monitor the Oversight of Custodians and Developers of National Resources, including those of Creative Genius and Labor.

84

REVPAC *Social Entrepreneur Plan*
... In action

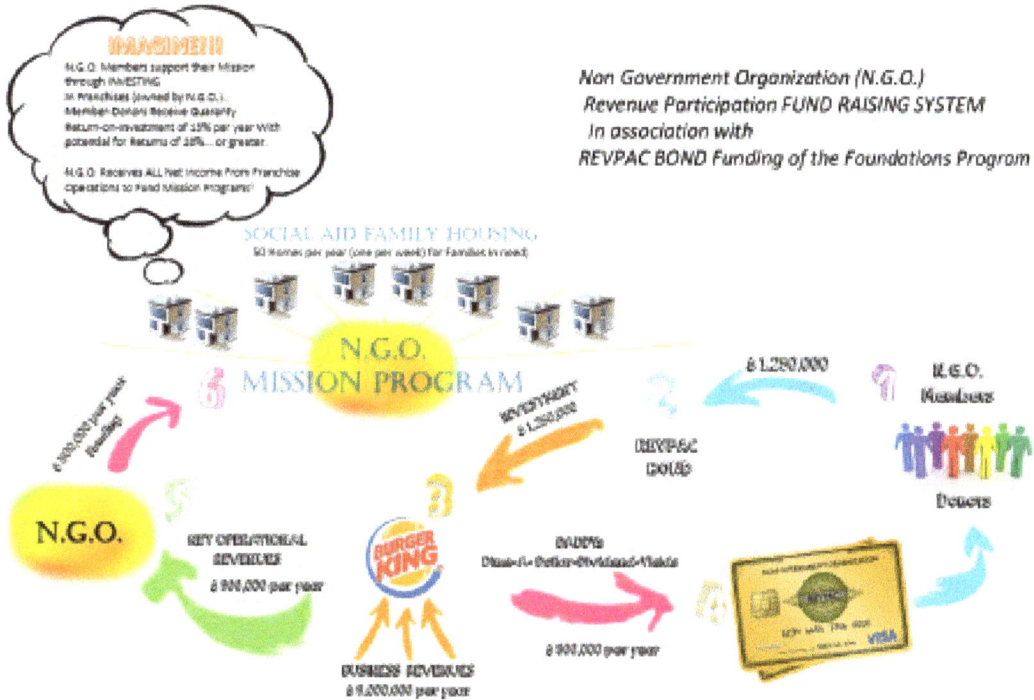

Non Government Organization (N.G.O.)
Revenue Participation FUND RAISING SYSTEM
In association with
REVPAC BOND Funding of the Foundations Program

1. NGO Donors purchase $1,250,000 of REVPAC BONDS for the NGO to own and operate a BURGER KING Franchise.

2. Cash Flow Forecast for the nnual sales of the BURGER KING must be minimum $5 MILLION per year.

3. Donors receive Ten Cents of every Dollar on ALL BURGER KING Sales! This 10% Revenue Participation Program is called **"DADDYs"** - *Dime-a-Dollar-Dividend-Yields*

4. DADDY payments are streamed directly to Donor's Smart Cards - in REAL-TIME!

5. NGO (owner / operator of the BURGER KING) receives one-half of the Net revenues (equivalent to a DADDY - 10% Gross Revenue Participation).

6. NGO FUNDS 50 Single Family homes each YEAR...almost one per week!

REVPAC Variations

Incubating Ventures

REVPAC Bonds are designed to finance the emergence of post-development ventures into the marketplace. However, there is substantial cost associated with incubating any venture to the market-emergence stage. The REVPAC Structure offers an alternative method of funding — or partially funding — the innovator or creative genius through that incubation stage: " The Incubating REVPAC."

The Incubating REVPAC is a "founders' stake" issued in the formative stage of a venture — to initial-stage investors, contractors and service providers — to fund start-up costs even before the REVPAC Bond IPO stage. Incubating REVPAC Trusts can be variably structured, but generally afford holders with long-term revenue-sharing rights in the gross revenues of a finite number — or all — of the ventures spawned during the career of an innovator, and a percentage of gross REVPAC Bond IPO proceeds when the ventures are underwritten successfully.

Similar to the standard REVPAC Bond, Incubating REVPACs are structured around an Investment Trust established by the innovator or venture developer when seed-capital investors and service providers are identified. All costs of development of the IPO stage, and the costs of the public offering, are covered by the Investment Trust for one or more REVPAC Bond offerings bred in the incubator of the Incubating REVPAC.

For example, a sculptor may garner $500,000 in pre-production capital, products, and services required to bring to fruition 10 master works of art for sale — and from which limited editions will be promoted and sold, often with proceeds from REVPAC Bond IPOs.

The original investors and other Incubating REVPAC holders may receive a 5 percent share of gross IPO proceeds upon the successful completion of each REVPAC Bond offering, as well as 5 percent of gross revenues derived from the sales of each of the 10 works of art.

If only 5 of the 10 works of art are completed, and the resultant aggregate IPO proceeds are $40 million, the Incubating REVPAC holders will receive $2 million in yields — four times their original investment — *plus* their venture-revenue participation rights.

Unlike standard REVPAC Bonds, Incubating REVPACs cannot be traded in secondary markets. Because Incubating REVPACs are by nature higher-risk securities, zero-risk assurance is not always available via the Full Redemtion Guarantee option. In some cases, though, Full Redemption Guarantee coverage is available, depending on specific criteria of the guarantor and the term of the Incubating REVPAC.

Incubating REVPAC may be defined as convertible to IPO REVPAC at the time the Incubating REVPAC Investment Trust is chartered.

Incubating REVPACs may include the Future Participation Warrant for future ventures beyond the initial IPOs, offering further incentives for investors to participate in the embryonic stages of a promising career or venture development.

Incubating REVPACs act as an incentive to entrepreneurial service providers to perform development-stage services in return for future revenue participation. This can significantly reduce the start-up and development costs necessary to bring a venture, or series of ventures, to the REVPAC Bond IPO stage.

With Incubating REVPACs, innovators have an alternative to debt financing and partnership equity allocations prior to market emergence. Promising enterprises can enter the consumer marketplace with *zero debt!*

Using Incubating REVPACs to finance a start-up prior to a REVPAC Bond IPO can have significant public relations benefits — both during the IPO stage and in the consumer market. The confidence demonstrated by service providers (presumed industry insiders) betting on the success of a venture will foster an image of credibility and bolster investor confidence.

Incubating REVPAC provide the business venture developer with requisite funding to structure, register and sell venture REVPAC offerings to the investment community. Investment proceeds from the offerings are employed to develop, produce and market the venture's products or services to the consumer marketplace.

Cultural Ventures

Funding of the cultural arts — opera, ballet, concerts, theater, and fine arts — has presented a perennial economic dilemma for communities, public-broadcast networks and production companies. Traditional methods of financing a production or a season of events is usually centered around public fund-raising efforts, private and government endowments, and altruistic patronage.

There are major obstacles to adequately funding the arts. The costs associated with soliciting funding are often equal to or greater than the proceeds that ultimately reach the project. Art productions are rarely self-sustaining; revenues seldom outdistance production costs.

Once again, REVPAC offers a solution in a modern and unified system of supporting the arts.

REVPAC Bonds can be used to fund an individual production, a season, or a series of seasons of the cultural arts of a community, with investors never losing a penny of their investment. With the Full Redemption Guaranty option, investors receive 100 percent return of their capital investment at full term — typically at the end of the seventh year.

Other advantages of Cultural REVPAC Ventures include:

Fiscal Accountability

All service providers engaged in the development of productions are backed by performance bonds. This ensures that the IPO cost disclosures — delineated in the offering prospectus — are honored and safeguard the capital investment dependent upon the successful performance of service providers. Performance bonding and requisite, real-time reporting provide REVPAC investors with assurance that the projects they fund will reach the cultural community on time and within budget.

Quick Read of Cultural Investing

The distribution of gross revenue yields to investors in Cultural REVPAC Bonds provides a simple method of measuring the success of cultural art productions. Because a cultural season comprises a full calendar of productions, the gross revenue yields provide a lucid view of the economics of cultural art and a means by which to identify those productions that have the capability of being self- sustaining. Sponsors of cultural arts may now have a definitive snapshot of their investment and an uncluttered vantage point from which to survey the potential and actual financial landscape of a season's cultural art development.

Structuring Entertainment Productions into a Cultural REVPAC

The Cultural REVPAC Venture can be structured to include entertainment productions with lucrative revenue potential to offset losses of less consumer-driven cultural productions. Investors can now participate, with zero risk and potentially generous returns, in both multiple cultural art productions and commercially successful entertainment productions within one REVPAC Bond Trust.

Potential Windfall Value of Future Participation Warrant

The Warrant guarantees investors the identical revenue-sharing rights in a subsequent cultural arts production or season as provided in the current Cultural REVPAC Venture. A cultural season of productions involves the development of a variety of artistic geniuses and their works. Any one, or even several artists, may be on the threshold of consumer discovery - as well as the works of art themselves. The Future Participation Warrant ensures the investor the altruistic opportunity of securing a sponsorship role in the development of cultural art and artistic genius *as well as* a potential long-term windfall return on investment.

Franchising Artistic Genius for Communities

By adopting the REVPAC model for cultural arts, communities can finance homegrown artists — in essence franchising the artistic talent of the local community. If a community's cultural consciousness is committed to the art renaissance for the next generation, it must incubate today's local talent into future commercial art ventures as well as the cultural arts. Cultural REVPAC Bonds secure a financial and management stake in local artistic talent, ensuring that the community benefits from the success of the talent it fosters.

Cultural REVPAC Bonds develop cultural programming for communities, public broadcast networks and fine art production companies on a long-term basis for single or multiple seasons. REVPAC provides the financial instrument standard for cultural sponsorship which the fragmented financing methods and vehicles currently in use have failed to do.

REIT Ventures

REVPAC Real Estate Investment Trusts (REITs) offer yet another sorely needed restructuring of an archaic financial model that takes advantage of the investors' dollar with little or no yield.

With traditional REITs, investor returns are based on Net Operating Income (NOI) — offering little opportunity for windfall yields and no guaranteed return on investment. Although generally viewed as stable long-term investments, just like any other publicly traded entity, REITs are structured to maximize the benefits for insiders — *not* toward maximizing revenues or investor returns.

With REVPAC REITs, the financial landscape is again changed in the arena of commercial real estate development and management.
For high-income-producing properties — such as hotels and resorts, amusement parks, shopping centers, franchise outlets, and the development of timeshares — REVPAC REITs represent yet another watershed, redesigned to breathe life into a stale financing mechanism.

REVPAC REITs are long-term — 10 or more years — Investment Trusts providing revenue yields derived from the *gross receipts of the businesses domiciled on the properties.* Since the REVPAC REIT holds the properties as chattel — through the Collateralized Yield Obligation — the Full Redemption Guaranty option is not attached to REVPAC Bond Units, but is replaced with a Capital Asset Redemption and Windfall Appreciation Yield Coupon.

A REVPAC REIT will divest its properties at full term with 100 percent of the capital asset investment and 50 to 70 percent of profits distributed to the REVPAC holders concurrently with the final Revenue Share Coupon. The balance of the profits is distributed to the Business Manager.

REVPAC REITs offer:

- Annual revenue-sharing yields based on the gross receipts of the businesses (commencing on the third anniversary of the completed offering);

- Return of invested capital based on the divestiture of the properties at full term;

- Windfall appreciation yield from the profit-sharing rights upon divestiture;

- A currency-calamity hedge with the built-in Insurance Wrap; and

- The guaranteed right to participate in subsequent real estate development projects of the REVPAC REIT through the Future Participation Warrant.

With REVPAC, the synergy of gross revenue participation derived from the sales of condominiums, time-shares or retail services and products coupled with the security of the Full Redemption Guaranty, Real Estate Investment Trusts become kinetic investment vehicles.

Short-Term Ventures

Certain ventures are ephemeral and don't require a minimum five-year term to mature. Concert tours, educational and promotional seminar circuits, live or Internet events, and infomercials can all produce substantial revenues in only a year or two.

Short-Term REVPACs offer an attractive mechanism for funding these short-lived endeavors into the consumer marketplace, while offering investors a chance to participate in a lucrative venture that might otherwise never emerge.

Short-Term REVPAC differ slightly from standard REVPACs as defined thus far and may be structured for one, two, or three years — depending upon the time required for the venture to achieve, and exhaust, its potential in the marketplace.

The Short-Term REVPAC is composed of the Revenue Share, one Revenue Yield Coupon for each year of the term, a Future Participation Warrant, and the built-in Insurance Wrap. Although the Full Redemption Guaranty is generally not available with Short-Term REVPAC, the rapid generation of yields makes this an attractive short-term investment.

The Full Redemption Guaranty option may be made available, providing the fulfillment date of the Guaranty is at least seven years from the completion of the IPO — regardless of the date the venture is completed.

An Example of a Short-Term REVPAC in Action

A television production and marketing company produces a television infomercial for an emerging line of hair- and skin-care products. The promotion is scheduled for a six-week saturation of the Southern California market, with 30 percent of sales, derived from the program, committed to fund an identical follow-on campaign in South Florida and Arizona. Each six-week campaign will similarly fund an ensuing campaign — eventually covering all regions of the United States — for a total of 16 six-week campaigns, or 96 weeks.

The company establishes an Investment Trust and sells 200,000 Short-Term REVPACs, at $5 each, to raise the $1 million needed to produce the infomercial and purchase the television time-slots in Southern California for the first six-week campaign. The REVPAC holders are allocated revenue-sharing rights of 20 percent of the gross sales revenues and 30% of gross revenues are allocated to fund follow-on campaigns in other regions during a two-year term. The television production and marketing company — the Business Manager in this scenario — is allocated the remaining 50 percent of the sales revenues to defray the cost of the products and from which to realize net income.

A Future Participation Warrant is attached to the Short-Term REVPAC and exercisable upon the second anniversary of the REVPAC term, or before if the Business Manager so declares. This guarantees REVPAC IPO investors the opportunity to reinvest, at the same price and with the identical revenue-sharing rights, in subsequent productions.

Affinity Ventures

Any number of affinity programs can be bundled with the REVPAC instrument. This is especially appealing for issues with highly targeted or limited demographic appeal — such as sports teams or municipal projects — and big-ticket issues with high prestige factors — such as fine art or luxury items.

Issuers can integrate an additional incentive to investors in the form of season tickets, annual recreational passes, limited-edition prints and casts, or any number of benefits to accompany the revenue share.

Investors can now watch as revenues and revenue-share yields accumulate — while enjoying the additional reward of exclusive benefit programs, services, and products.

Affinity Programs are especially appealing for motor sports racing (e.g., Indy, CART, Nascar), recorded music, book publishing, etc. wherein the end users become the investors in REVPAC issues sponsoring select race car drivers, recorded artists and authors.

An Example of Affinity Ventures in Action

An example of an Affinity Venture in action is the Fine Art REVPAC discussed in this book wherein a REVPAC holder of 7,500 REVPAC Bond Units is allocated an annual limited-edition bronze sculpture created by the Master Artist. In this example, an investor may elect Full Redemption Guaranty coverage and, while never having the investment at risk, be assured of five limited-edition bronze sculpture disbursements during a five-year REVPAC term.

In a like manner, a racehorse-breeding program, financed via REVPAC, may incorporate "Stallion Shares" for breeding rights to a select stallion. This means that breeders can purchase a designated block of REVPAC Bond Units, exercise their breeding rights and be assured that all of their capital investment will be returned to them.

Currently, there are over 4,000 stallions standing in the U.S. Most of the stallions have been syndicated to breeders purchasing Stallion Shares — *that are illiquid and difficult to re-sell in a private market*. Now, breeders are afforded a new instrument to syndicate promising stallions wherein the investors not only receive Stallion Shares, but can liquidate their investment in secondary trading markets *and* have the surety of receiving a full return of their investment at full term.

Not only will horse owners, desiring to breed their mares to a select stallion, purchase sizeable blocks of REVPAC Bond Units *to qualify for guaranteed breedings,* but also speculators from outside the horse industry will be stimulated to invest their capital in a promising breeding program. As the
breeding program matures — *and the price of breedings with the select stallion increases* — the trading value of the REVPAC Bond Units will be enhanced. *In effect, Breeding REVPACs will become a "futures commodity" that can be traded on secondary exchanges, just as futures are traded in precious metals and grains.*

Collateralized Revenue

Obligation Hedge Funds

A number of prospective issuers in the United States desiring to employ the REVPAC model have determined that the registration process for Initial Public Offerings (IPOs) — especially for new financial instruments — is encumbered with a qualification process that could delay an offering for up to nine months. This time-consuming process is unrealistic in terms that most prospective issuers can afford. The issuers, in their search for a solution, determined that a vehicle qualifying for an exemption from registration was desirable.

The U.S. Securities and Exchange Commission Rules and Regulations provide a number of registration exemptions for investment vehicles capitalized with investments from accredited investors. The prospective issuers selected the investment vehicle known as *Hedge Fund* as the optimal vehicle to be employed in the United States together with the REVPAC Financial Model under an alternative trade name: Collateralized Revenue Obligation.

Hedge Funds offer an exemption from registration, allowing up to 99 accredited investors to participate in an IPO. Additionally, Hedge Funds are commonly accepted as a vehicle of choice for large financial institutions and fund managers.

The Collateralized Revenue Obligations (CROs) will parallel a REVPAC and in some cases be provided the additional advantage of offering a guaranteed rate of return for the first three to four years of the Hedge Fund — to provide the CRO the complexion of an Industrial Revenue Bond.

CRO-denominated Hedge Funds will be 100 percent underwritten with Full Redemption Guaranty coverage in place. The Full Redemption Guarantor is to receive a percentage of the gross revenues, directly from the Business Manager — as do the CRO holders. These Revenue Share Yields are to be allocated by the Guarantor into a *sinking fund* until such time that the sinking fund achieves a fixed benchmark amount to accommodate the Guarantor's risk. During this period of time, the CRO holders receive a fixed and guaranteed rate of return — *for example 7 percent per annum.* Once the sinking fund has achieved the benchmark, the CRO holders will receive the full amount of the Revenue Share Yield — *for example 50 percent of the IPO price.*

The CRO-denominated Hedge Funds are of particular interest to U.S. pension funds. The pension funds are mandated by the federal government to allocate a fixed percentage of their assets toward *minority interest* investments. Minority interest is defined as a business founded and dominated by a designated minority ethnic group (black, Hispanic, etc.). At present, many pension funds are unable to meet the federal mandates because of lack of an adequate financial instrument that provides the surety guaranty that 100 percent of the investment capital is not at risk. Once again, the REVPAC Financial Model plays an important role.

Now, CRO Hedge Funds can be utilized by underwriters to fund minority interest businesses. It is estimated that over $500 billion resides in U.S. pension funds. Depending upon the available percentage of pension-fund assets that are mandated yet unallocated, the amount of fresh venture capital available can be significant.

LONG-TERM

Long-Term Venture

A digital communications systems contractor is currently employing the REVPAC Financial Model to fund fiber-optic installation for a city of approximately 50,000 inhabitants. The city awarded a 30-year monopoly to the contractor in return for 5 percent of subscriber revenues. The cost of the installation is $16 million.

The Contractor opted for REVPAC financing. The REVPAC Investment Trust Unit has a 30-year term and yields 60 percent of subscriber revenues to REVPAC holders.

Revenue Yield pro-forma is based on the assumption that 50 percent of the households and 80 percent of the businesses will have gone online by the third year following completion of the IPO.

In the event that the Revenue Yield pro-forma is realized, the REVPAC holders receive a 32-to-1 ROI for full-risk REVPAC participation and Full Redemption Guaranty REVPAC receive 16-to-1 — *an average annual yield of 53 percent ROI.* Additionally, the Full

Redemption Guarantor guarantees full recovery of investment by Year 7. Not bad for a *utility investment.*

The Business Manager intends to notice the REVPAC Unit's Future Participaition Warrant during Year 5 for the purpose of funding another city's digital communications system.

Securities analysts forecast that the Full-Risk REVPAC Investment Trust Units will trade upwards of five times the IPO price and that the Full Redemption Guaranty REVPAC Bond Units will realize secondary trading market valuations of 2.5 times IPO price during the first three years following completion of the offering.

The Business Manager's portion of subscriber revenues is 35 percent of gross revenues with a maintenance cost factor of approximately 2.5 percent of subscriber revenues.

This is one example of several Long-Term REVPAC Ventures that are currently in process — *wherein Business Managers are accessing funding for a venture project, retaining a generous portion of the resultant gross revenue stream and employing the Future Participation Warrant to access additional funding for a subsequent venture project.*

* * *

Bearer REVPACs

Similar to bearer bonds (bonds issued and payable to the holder, but not in the name of any entity) utilized by several international issuers and traded in secondary markets around the world. Bearer REVPAC may be issued within certain jurisdictions. These REVPAC are designed to provide high revenue-sharing yields, while protecting the yields from currency maladjustments, and providing — in many cases — guaranteed return of the investment capital at full term. Due to the extraordinary return-on-investment potential of REVPAC, the bearer form of certificate may stimulate and ease global trading — while creating a pseudo currency instrument for those financial institutions conducting international transactions that require discreet handling or investment banking anonymity.

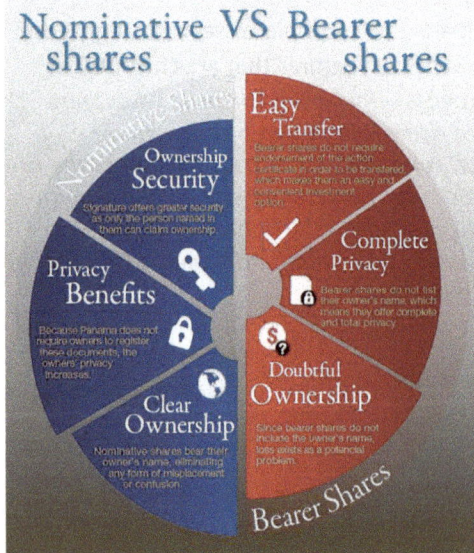

Subordinated Debenture-Wrapped REVPAC for select Markets

Why Consider a Debt Variation to the REVPAC Model? The REVPAC Financial Model is designed as an alternative to equity and debt financing and crafted as the ultimate financial tool for venture capital. However, the emergence of a new concept – such as REVPAC - will find a cognitive dissonance factor – *"outside the box"* – within capital markets that have been inured through decades of equity/debt practices and especially in those markets that have stringent taxation based on these practices. One of the primary benefits to the REVPAC Model is the undisturbed *pass-through* of a portion of the gross revenues, derived from a business venture to the holders, of the REVPAC Bond Units. There exist several capital markets with double or triple taxation levels for Financial Models passing through yields that are not structured on debt – *an example is the United States*. The Foundation has structured a variation to the REVPAC Model, specifically targeted at these capital markets.

Variation: Securitizing Subordinated Debentures into REVPAC Certificates. In this variation there does not exist an Investment Trust. The Issuer – *in place of* *the Investment Trust* - emits a Subordinated Debenture for a finite term, amount of the offering to take place and at a designated interest. *For Example: The Issuer issues a 7-Year Subordinated Debenture at 7% p/a for $10 Million.* Payment terms for the Subordinated Debenture are based on a designated percentage of future gross revenues derived from a business venture.

The Foundation, through a select banking institution, securitizes the debenture by issuing asset-backed securities – *"REVPAC Certificates".* The Certificates are guaranteed against loss of principal by a surety bond.

The REVPAC Certificates are offered by the bank for sale through Broker Dealers, participating in the Underwriting. Within capital markets, such as the United States, the bank registers the REVPAC Certificates with the Securities and Exchange Commission – through a shelf registration, which allows supplemental filings for each offering. *For Example: The bank may effect a "shelf registration" for $250 Million – of which the afore stated $10 Million offering is a part thereof.* Succeeding offerings, structured within a specific business sector and under the shelf registration, are affected without lengthy registration delays.

As revenues are derived from the business venture, that portion indentured within the Subordinated Debenture is distributed to the REVPAC Certificate holders – toward repayment of the principal and payment of interest. The principal is "paid down" over the 7-year term, dependent upon availability of revenue stream, as are the interest payments. In the event that the revenue stream results in an amount beyond the full-term principal and interest payments, the surplus is distributed as a "premium payment" (similar to "equity

kicker" for Real Estate investments) to the REVPAC Certificate holders. *"Equity kicker" is a term deployed in Real Estate transactions within the U.S., which provides for non-taxable pass-through of revenues – above and beyond principal and interest payments – and which provides a non-usury return-on-loan-beyond-interest.* In the event that there are inadequate revenues to effect principal payment, the surety bond is called upon at full term. The Issuer only indentures future gross revenues of the business venture – not assets or other revenue streams.

Summary.

The variation, in a sense, puts "inside the box" the "outside the box" REVPAC Model for select capital markets without sacrificing its creative genius. The holders of the securitized subordinated debentures enjoy identical revenue participation benefits, at no risk of principal, as do the holders of REVPAC denominated Investment Trust Units.

* * *

REVPAC in Review
Advantages of REVPAC to Issuer

REVPAC allows access to venture capital for the development of worthy innovations not readily available via equity, debt, or partnership financing.

The innovator/venture developer incurs no debt obligation, relinquishes no equity in his or her enterprise, nor incurs any long-term obligation of any kind.

REVPAC has a built-in Risk Insurance Package Wrap that empowers the acquisition of services for the development of ventures.

REVPAC provides meaningful enforcement of proprietary claims — protecting projects by collateralizing patents, copyrights, trademarks, and service-mark claims within the financial instrument. This significantly reduces the risk of intellectual property piracy in all countries wherein the REVPAC is registered and provides swift remedies in cases of infringement, through existing securities laws.

All proprietary rights revert to the Business Manager (or the Innovator/Developer when they are not the Business Manager) upon expiration of revenue-sharing rights of REVPAC holders.

Innovators can go directly to the business venture product/service end-user source to identify and target investors with substantial interest in the emerging venture and provide affinity financing. Affinity programs generate additional incentives to investors.

Management retains 100 percent control of the venture.

Advantages of REVPAC to Investor

Gross Revenue Yields
REVPAC is the *primary and universally accepted* instrument to provide an established percentage of Gross Revenues to the investor. This ties returns directly to consumer response and the business success of the venture — without management interference.

Optional Full Redemption Guaranty
This option transforms high-risk capital investment into a hybrid Gross Revenue Bond.

High Liquidity
Component elements provide potent secondary market potential. Each element is independently designed to produce a failsafe instrument — with both liquidity and long-term, high-yield potential.

Future Participation Rights
Investors are guaranteed an option to participate in subsequent ventures with the same innovator. Investors receive first pick of proven developers/enterprises, providing the opportunity to franchise innovative

genius through subsequent ventures.

Trust Administrator

The watchdog overseeing the Business Manager and overall development of the venture project. Investors are assured that the investment capital will be employed as designated in the Offering Prospectus and that revenues derived from the marketplace will be accountable.

Real-Time Reporting

Real-time, mandatory, lucid reporting eliminates the guesswork from predicting yields. Investors have constant access to financial and management reporting throughout the term of the revenue-sharing rights.

Built-in Risk Insurance Package Wrap
The package of Risk Insurance Coverage is integrated into both the REVENUE SHARE and the FULL REDEMPTION GUARANTY for the REVPAC BOND Investors - which guarantees: (1) the performance of the Business Manager to get the Commercial Venture to the marketplace plus fiduciary accountability for all revenues and; (2) Investors' 100% Return-of-Orignal-Investment as well as any other guaranteed yield covenants contained in the REVPAC Funding Program.

Advantages of REVPAC to Investment Bankers

Universal Banking

REVPAC affords Investment Bankers the opportunity to access capital for venture underwritings from investment sectors historically unresponsive to venture-capital opportunities.

The Full Redemption Guaranty feature of REVPAC takes the risk out of

venture-capital underwriting while providing the investor an easy-to-understand gross-revenue equation for gauging potential returns.

Now, Investment Bankers may approach fund managers of even the most conservative of pension funds with a financial instrument that is safe, yet that has the potential of multiple returns on investment capital.

The Collateralized Yield Obligation, Business Manager Agreement and Trust Administrator Agreement (see Table of Authorities) stabilize the economics of venture-capital underwriting wherein the Investment Banker can assure the investor of the integrity of the venture project development. There is absolutely no latitude for interference of investors' revenue-participation rights.

Investment Bankers can now approach equity issuers with a new financial instrument to revitalize public companies seeking additional capitalization to fund expansion programs without incurring further dilution of stockholder equity. Also, Investment Bankers may approach public companies seeking to decrease the number of shares outstanding by employing REVPAC Bond Units as a swap for stock.

One of the most significant considerations for Investment Bankers is the *exit strategy* for their IPO investors through secondary trading markets. REVPAC offers a potent secondary market potential for trading activity — *especially from foreign speculators.* Also, for the first time, fund managers will actively participate in secondary trading markets for venture-capital issues denominated in REVPAC Investment Trust Units. This means that the largest segment of the investment community can actively purchase Investment Bankers' issues, thereby affording deep liquid markets to fulfill *exit-strategy* targets.

Guide for the Innovator/Developer

Preparing Your Business Venture for REVPAC Financing

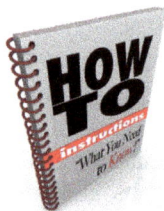

The first step in preparing your venture for REVPAC financing is the development of a comprehensive Business Plan. This plan should be prepared by qualified professionals, such as an accredited accounting firm. The plan should address, and confirm, that the venture meets the following criteria:

- Revenues are highly likely to be generated within one year of the projected completion of the IPO.

- High gross margins exist to provide for the allocation of the revenue-sharing rights to REVPAC holders, while leaving sufficient capital for the operation and profit of the Business Manager.

- The business venture is projected to enjoy a highly competitive edge in a largely untapped, but viable, market.

- Intellectual property and/or other proprietary rights protecting the business venture are secured and available to be pledged as chattel to the Investment Trust in return for financing the business venture.

If, upon evaluation of the Business Plan, it is determined that the venture is a bona fide target for REVPAC financing, then the following steps will need to be taken:

- Appoint a Business Manager to deliver the venture to the marketplace. The Business Manager must have sufficient credentials to be performance-bonded by an accredited bonding agency, to ensure that the success of the venture is not compromised by any failure on management's part.

- Appoint an accredited institution to act as Trust Administrator. This institution must have the demonstrated ability to sustain fiduciary accountability for the duration of the Business Venture, and have in place comprehensive errors and omissions (E&O) insurance to cover at least the amount of maximum anticipated revenue yields for any one Revenue Yield distribution period.

- Establish an Investment Trust employing the parameters of the organic documents appearing in the Table of Authorities.

- Execute the Business Manager and Trust Administrator Agreements and the Collateralized Yield Obligation.

Structuring Your REVPAC

How to Structure the Revenue Share

The rule of thumb for determining what percentage of gross revenues to allocate to the REVPAC holders is based on what is commonly referred to, within venture-capital financing, as the Hockey Stick Method.

The hockey stick represents the *expected* yield performance of a venture-capital investment in a new business venture from incubation through maturation.

Through the first three years the venture generates little to no revenue and, consequently, the investor realizes zero yield. However, upon emergence of the business venture into the marketplace, the venture experiences dramatic revenues. The hockey stick handle represents the investors' anticipated return on investment — *generally five to seven times the investment over a seven-year period.*

REVPAC provide the investor an opportunity to invest in an emerging venture *after the research and development "incubation" phase has been achieved.* Visualizing the hockey stick once again, the *ideal* IPO stage is represented at or near the elbow of the hockey stick — *just prior to the business venture's emerging into the marketplace.*

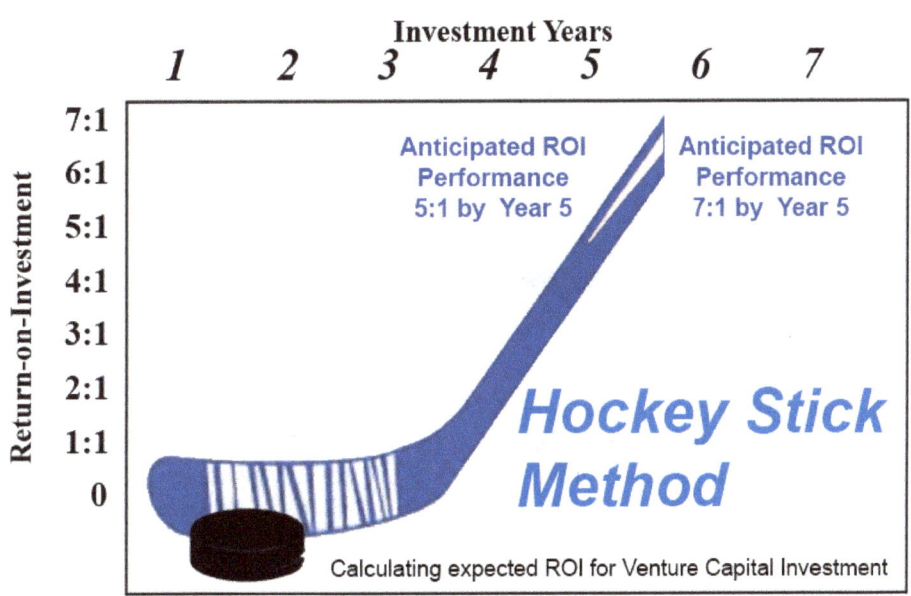

Investment Years

Anticipated ROI Performance 5:1 by Year 5

Anticipated ROI Performance 7:1 by Year 5

Hockey Stick Method

Calculating expected ROI for Venture Capital Investment

To determine the optimal revenue-sharing percentage for your future REVPAC investors, simply take the five-to-seven-year forecast of revenues in your Business Plan and apply the appropriate percentage to arrive at a 5x to 7x ROI for the gross proceeds that you intend to raise through your IPO. Also, when determining the revenue-sharing percentage for your REVPAC holders, take into consideration that you will be issuing underwriter's warrants — and perhaps other warrants — entitling the holders to purchase REVPACs in the investment trust at a discount. *The REVPACs available to warrant holders should not exceed 6 percent of all REVPACs comprising the Investment Trust.*

> *The higher the ROI potential for your investors, the easier it will be to raise the capital needed to develop the business venture.*

How to Structure a Warrant

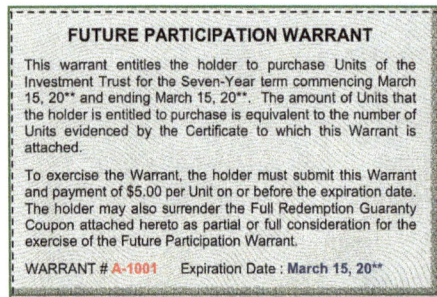

FUTURE PARTICIPATION WARRANT

This warrant entitles the holder to purchase Units of the Investment Trust for the Seven-Year term commencing March 15, 20** and ending March 15, 20**. The amount of Units that the holder is entitled to purchase is equivalent to the number of Units evidenced by the Certificate to which this Warrant is attached.

To exercise the Warrant, the holder must submit this Warrant and payment of $5.00 per Unit on or before the expiration date. The holder may also surrender the Full Redemption Guaranty Coupon attached hereto as partial or full consideration for the exercise of the Future Participation Warrant.

WARRANT # A-1001   Expiration Date : March 15, 20**

Warrants should be defined by the Business Manager during the venture's IPO, and may afford continued revenue participation in the initial venture for an additional term or the right to purchase a REVPAC in a subsequent venture by the same Business Manager.

The issuer may opt to define the Warrant — at the IPO stage — as continuing the identical revenue-sharing rights of the initial venture for an additional term, or in a to-be-determined future venture.

Warrants can be activated by the Business Manager at any time during the term of the REVPAC with at least 90 days' notice to REVPAC holders (but not less than 100 days prior to full-maturity).

The "Warrant Activation Notice" should include a detailed prospectus and must disclose all elements of the REVPAC to be issued pursuant to the Warrant. It should include all revenue projections, revenue-sharing rights, and a full description of the venture to be funded. REVPAC holders have 90 days from notice of Warrant Activation by the Business Manager to exercise their Warrants.

In the REVPAC models contained within this book, all Warrants dictate that at least 60 percent of REVPAC holders must exercise the Warrant in order to effect a second revenue-sharing term.

If 60 to 100 percent of holders exercise the Warrants, the Investment Trust will be renewed for the additional term and new REVPAC Bonds issued to those holders. The revenue-sharing rights for the subsequent term will be prorated to reflect the percentage of Warrants exercised.

> *Upon full maturity of the IPO REVPAC any REVPAC Warrants not exercised within the time frame allowed, in accordance with the conditions attached, will be retired, and all revenue-participation rights of these holders will expire.*

Should fewer than 60 percent of holders exercise the Future Participation Warrant, the Investment Trust will be dissolved upon maturity of the existing REVPAC Bonds.

As an alternative to dissolving the Investment Trust, the Business Manager may elect to make up for the shortfall in Warrants exercised by purchasing the necessary number of REVPAC in the secondary trading market, and exercising the Warrants attached within the required time frame.

To fund the purchase and exercise the Warrants necessary to continue the Investment Trust, the Business Manager may issue additional revenue-sharing rights with a second REVPAC offering, or use any form of financing available.

In cases of dissolution of a REVPAC Investment Trust, resulting from an insufficient percentage of Warrants exercised, the Innovator/Developer maintains first right of refusal to purchase the capital and intellectual property assets from the Investment Trust within a defined time frame.

In the event of failure of the Business Manager to produce a viable venture to satisfy the Warrant, the Trust Administrator holds the authority and responsibility to replace the Business Manager and effect a venture requisite to the Warrant. Disputes regarding the acceptability of any subsequent venture will be referred to the Arbitration Association.

In the event that the Business Manager fails during the initial term, the Trust Administrator is charged with

replacing the Business Manager, who is responsible to acquire whatever additional capital may be necessary to continue the venture. Any funding solution may be used. However, revenue-sharing rights of REVPAC holders may not be diluted, and all terms of the Warrants must be satisfied.

Structuring the Collateralized Yield Obligation

An important consideration when structuring the Collateralized Yield Obligation is the disposition of the capital assets once the Investment Trust reaches full term.

The Innovator/Developer may opt to purchase the capital assets for a nominal fee — provided the Investment Trust Unit holders have realized an established minimum-yield requirement. For example, if the REVPAC holders have achieved a 3-to-1 ROI, the Innovator/Developer may have the right to purchase the capital assets at a zero-cost base of the capital asset *replacement* value. A sliding scale may also be established whereby the purchase price may be set in accordance with the following schedule:

REVPAC Holders Accumulated Yields (1)	Capital Asset Purchase Price (2)
Less than 10% ROI	100%
10% to 25%	90%
26% to 50%	80%
51% to 75%	70%
75% to 100%	50%
101% to 150%	40%
151% to 200%	30%
201% to 250%	20%
251% to 300%	10%
Over 300%	0%

(1) Based on IPO price
(2) Based on replacement cost for capital assets owned by Investment Trust

REVPAC financing is designed to provide the Innovator/Developer and/or Business Manager the long-term benefit of enjoying the rewards of successful business ventures without equity partners, debt, or even long-term revenue participation encumbrance.

The structure of the Collateralized Yield Obligation must be fair and equitable to both the Business Manager (Innovator/ Developer) and the REVPAC holders. Once a business venture is successful, and the holders have achieved a generous Return-on-Investment, there is every reason to reward the Innovator/Developer with the opportunity to recapture the intellectual property rights and the capital assets — currently held as chattel by the Investment Trust - and to enjoy the fruits of the mature venture.

Preparing for Incubating REVPAC Financing

Incubating REVPACs are a long-term "founders" stake designed to fund the seed capital for the formative stage of a venture or to finance an innovator or creative genius through the incubation stage — long before the business venture is ready for its IPO.

Incubating REVPACs are the ideal financing tool for innovators, or even new venture-development companies seeking capital to finance the costs of incubation and its IPOs.

Once a business plan for the development of an innovation or a series of innovations has been designed, the following criteria must be met:

- Revenues are highly likely to be generated within three to five years of completion of the Incubating REVPAC funding.

- Projected gross margins should be sufficient to provide for the allocation of the revenue-sharing rights to to Incubating REVPAC holders, as well as future IPO REVPAC Bond holders, while leaving a sufficient portion of the revenues for the operation and profit of the Business Manager.

- The development of the innovation, or series of innovations, is projected to enjoy a highly competitive edge in a largely untapped but viable market.

- Intellectual property (IP) and/or other proprietary rights protecting the innovation, or series of innovations, are secured — or have a high likelihood of being secured — and are, or will be, available to be pledged as chattel to the Incubating REVPAC Investment Trust in return for financing the development.

Note: *The IP is later pledged from the Incubating REVPAC Investment Trust to the IPO Investment Trust for financing the business venture resulting from the innovation's development.*

In most cases, the innovator serves as Business Manager of Incubating REVPAC Investment Trusts. In situations where this is not the case, a Business Manager utilizing the identical appointment criteria as IPO REVPAC Bonds must be selected.

Once a Business Manager has been selected, the following steps must be taken:

- Appoint an accredited institution to act as Trust Administrator, utilizing the identical criteria as IPO REVPACs.

- Establish an Investment Trust employing the parameters of the organic documents appearing in the Table of Authorities.

- Execute the Business Manager and Trust Administrator Agreements and the Collateralized Yield Obligation.

Structuring Your Incubating REVPAC

How to Structure the Revenue Share
Incubating REVPACs are designed to provide the investor an opportunity to invest during the incubation phase of an innovation or
series of innovations. According to the Hockey Stick Method, the incubation stage is represented at or near the tip of the horizontal blade — three to five years prior to the innovation's becoming a business

venture and emerging into the marketplace.

In determining the potential ROI for your Incubating REVPAC investors, keep in mind that they are required to wait through a potentially protracted incubation period and are accepting significant risks. These risks include the viability of the future innovation in the marketplace — not to mention ultimate economic conditions within the future marketplace — both for the IPO and business venture. Incubating REVPAC investors warrant a generous return-on-investment opportunity — *usually 20 times ROI or greater.*

Now determine the source of revenue yields for investors. Generally, Incubating REVPAC investors participate in the revenues of the business venture like the IPO REVPAC Bond holders. As an example, when incubating a series of innovations, you may want to allocate 20 percent of the revenues to future IPO REVPAC Bond holders and 5 percent to the Incubating REVPAC holders. Incubating REVPAC Investment Trusts are usually capitalized for substantially less than an emerging business venture Investment Trust — *providing Incubating REVPAC holders with a higher ROI rate.*

You may also structure your Incubating REVPAC to receive a percentage of the proceeds from future REVPAC IPOs. For instance, you may allocate 5 percent of the capital raised in the IPO REVPAC Investment Trusts to the Incubating REVPAC holders.

Or, consider this: Why not also allocate 5 percent of future IPO REVPAC Bond Units to the Incubating REVPAC holders? In this way, Incubating REVPAC holders can look forward to receiving tradable REVPAC Bonds that can increase in value and be liquidated through secondary trading markets.

Remember that Incubating REVPAC are higher-risk than IPO REVPAC Bonds. The time line for the generation of yields is much greater than that which IPO REVPAC holders are required to endure. Additionally, Incubating REVPACs do not trade. There is no liquid market through which holders can sell their units. Therefore, it is prudent to provide Incubating REVPAC investors with generous revenue-sharing rights.

Determining the Term of an Incubating REVPAC

Since the projected time line for the incubation phase generally exceeds entrepreneurial expectations, and there exists the possibility that new proprietary innovations may be forthcoming, the term for the Incubating REVPAC holders should be long-term.

Incubating REVPACs are designed to provide the investor with "franchise rights" in the creative genius and talent of the innovator. The investors are risking their capital to buy a long-term stake in a person — or team — who they believe will mature into a valuable asset.

*You may launch many future IPO REVPAC Investment Trusts to finance your business ventures — but you will typically only launch **one** Incubating REVPAC.*

The life span of Incubating REVPACs *for innovators* should be structured for a term of 15 to 20 or more years, to allow investors the opportunity to participate in the long and fruitful careers of the creative genius and talent they are sponsoring.

The term for the Incubating REVPACs *of select business venture developments* may be structured for shorter terms, depending upon the projected incubation time line.

Incubating REVPAC holders continue to enjoy the benefits of their investment long after Incubating REVPAC reach full term, through revenue-participation rights in IPO REVPAC Bonds and emerging business ventures fostered by Incubating REVPAC financing.

How to Structure a Warrant

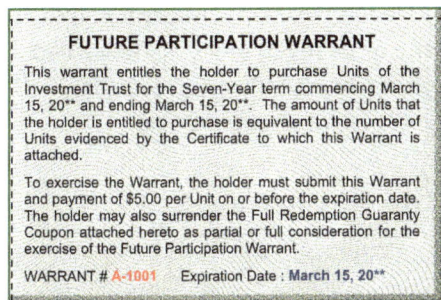

FUTURE PARTICIPATION WARRANT

This warrant entitles the holder to purchase Units of the Investment Trust for the Seven-Year term commencing March 15, 20** and ending March 15, 20**. The amount of Units that the holder is entitled to purchase is equivalent to the number of Units evidenced by the Certificate to which this Warrant is attached.

To exercise the Warrant, the holder must submit this Warrant and payment of $5.00 per Unit on or before the expiration date. The holder may also surrender the Full Redemption Guaranty Coupon attached hereto as partial or full consideration for the exercise of the Future Participation Warrant.

WARRANT # A-1001   Expiration Date : March 15, 20**

As with IPO REVPACs, Incubating REVPAC warrants should be defined by the Business Manager at the time the Incubating REVPAC is offered to investors. Since the Incubating REVPAC is generally long-term, the issuer may opt not to include warrants.

In the event that warrants are to be included, the issuer has two options:

- Afford continued revenue participation in the Incubating REVPAC for an additional term;

- Provide the right to purchase IPO REVPAC Bonds in one or several future ventures at a discount.

In all other instances, Incubating REVPAC warrants function in the same way as IPO REVPAC Bond warrants.

The primary function of the Warrant for issuers is to provide a ready source of financing for future capital requirements.

When structuring the Incubating REVPAC, an issuer should consider the possibility that additional capital may be needed — either to complete the incubation phase or to seize an opportunity. Perhaps a new innovation opportunity may arise from the incubation phase, having the potential for catapulting the issuer and Incubating REVPAC holders to unforeseen financial success. The issuer may structure the warrant to be called in such events — with as little as 90 days' notice.

Why Innovators should consider Incubating REVPAC Financing

Incubating REVPAC Financing enhances the long-term economic stability of the Innovator's career. The enfranchisement of Innovative genius — *wherein private investors share in the future revenues of the Innovator's works* — provides the following benefits to the Innovator:

- Incubating REVPAC finance future REVPAC Bond IPOs — which affords multiple opportunities for the Innovator's breakthroughs to achieve funding and development.

- The Future Participation Warrant feature of the Incubating REVPAC enhances the feasibility that the Innovator will achieve funding to develop future innovations.

- Assures the Innovator of account-ability from Business Managers in future Investment Trusts structured to develop the Innovator's works.

Guide for the Investor

What REVPAC Offers Investors

Investors seeking an advantage at the IPO stage of emerging business ventures can do no better than electing REVPAC denominated Investment Trusts. Only through the cumulative components of REVPAC Investment Trusts can investors receive:

- Gross Revenue Sharing.

- A simple-to-understand barometer for investment performance based on gross revenues. The value of a REVPACs is based on the direct market success of a venture — which simplifies investor evaluation, tracking, and accountability.

- An option to elect Full Redemption Guaranty — transforming high-risk venture-capital investments into secured Gross Revenue bonds.

- A Surety Risk Insurance Package that guarantees the performance of the Business Manager to get the Commercial Venture to the marketplace and ensures fiduciary accountability for all revenues. This stimulates investor participation in secondary trading markets for REVPACs — providing the potential of a large trading base into which investments may be liquidated.

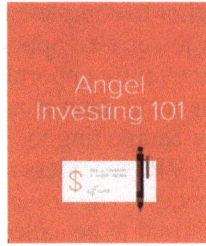

- A Future Participation Warrant, which affords investors long-term revenue-sharing potential in the careers of successful innovators and management teams.

The synergy of the REVPAC components offers investors a potent financial instrument whose value can outperform any other investment security in the market today.

What to Look for in a REVPAC

Opportunity

Investors should make sure that the following are wrapped into the REVPAC Investment Trust:

- **Return-on-Investment Potential**
Are the gross revenue-sharing rights structured to provide adequate ROI potential for the investors commensurate with the risk? Make sure that anticipated and feasible-revenue forecasts have been prepared by qualified professionals, such as an accredited accounting firm.

- **Intellectual Property Rights**
Are patent, copyright and trademark registrations or applications in good standing? Verify that proprietary rights are held as chattel by the Investment Trust, as provided for in the Collateralized Yield Obligation.

• **Commencement of Revenues**
Does the business plan provide for revenue potential within one year of IPO completion?

• **Business Manager Stability**
Does the Business Management team possess a successful history encompassing similar business ventures? Verify that requisite performance bonding is in place.

• **Trust Administrator Accountability**
Is the Trust Administrator accredited? Does it possess adequate errors and omissions insurance coverage to protect the forecasted revenue share yields?

• **Future Participation Warrant**
Is the warrant structured to provide unin-terrupted and identical revenue-sharing rights for the successive term at the same IPO price that investors enjoy in the current term?

Investment Considerations

REVPACs are revenue-driven. Investors should seek IPOs that have a high probability of generating optimal gross revenues.

Since any venture-capital investment is high-risk, REVPACs offer a Full Redemption Guaranty option.
IPO investors may, at point of purchase, elect the Guaranty to have 100 percent of their investment returned to them at full term. The premium for this election results in a reduction of their future yields by 35 percent.

Here is how this works. If the seven-year revenue forecast for a REVPAC business venture pegs the potential ROI at10 to 1:

• An investor electing Zero-Risk Guaranty and investing $10,000 will realize yields of $65,000, under optimal conditions. If the venture fails, and there are minimal or no revenues generated, the original investment of $10,000 is returned to the investor.

• An investor electing not to take the Full Redemption Guaranty and investing $10,000 will realize yields of $100,000, under optimal conditions. If the venture fails to produce any revenues, the investor loses the original investment of $10,000.

Investors purchasing IPO REVPAC Bonds should weigh the high-yield potential of a venture against the full return of investment security provided by Full Redemption Guaranty options. This is es-sential for investors adding REVPACs to long-term retirement portfolios. Investors who cannot afford to sustain a partial or full loss of their investment may consider a potential 650 percent sev-en-year investment return with zero risk more palatable than a potential 1,000 percent return with full risk.

Guide for the Investment Banker

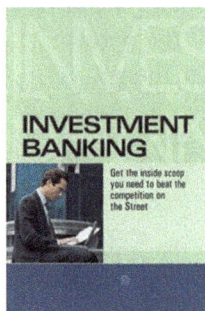

What REVPAC Offers Investment Bankers

REVPAC Investment Trusts are investment bankers' ideal underwriting products. They offer significant advantages rarely available through alternative investment instruments.

- The Full Redemption Guaranty option allows underwriters to:

  - Access otherwise high-risk venture capital IPO subscriptions from retirement account/pension fund sources.
  - Offer venture capital IPO subscribers margin services.

- Gross Revenue participation provides brokers with an easy-to-understand ROI formula for subscribers and secondary-trading market investors.

- REVPAC components offer potent secondary market potential — providing underwriter's IPO sub-scribers a highly active and liquid trading market.

- Investment bankers' issuers incur no debt obligation, relinquish no equity, nor incur any long-term obligation of any kind. Also, issuers retain 100 percent ownership rights to the venture project once the REVPAC reaches full term.

Due-Diligence Checklist to Qualify REVPAC Issuers

Investment bankers performing due-diligence and processing underwriting candidates should ascertain that the following criteria are met:

- Business Plan prepared or reviewed by qualified professionals — such as an accredited accounting firm — confirms that the issuer meets the standards for REVPAC securitization.

  See Guide for the Innovator/Developer: "Preparing your Business Venture for REVPAC Financing."

- Business Manager possesses adequate business history and credentials for performance bonding.

- Trust Administrator has a demonstrated ability to perform fiduciary accountability for the Investment Trust and possesses errors and omissions insurance to cover at least the amount of maximum an-ticipated revenue yields for any one Revenue Yield distribution period.

- Investment Trust is organized em-ploying the parameters of the organic documents appearing in the Table of Authorities.

- Investment Trust's Revenue Share provides a return-on-investment potential commensurate with the business venture risk.

- Full Redemption Guaranty is in place with an accredited risk-insurance institution.

- Future Participation Warrant is structured to provide rollover under identical or similar terms as the proposed current REVPAC.

- Risk Insurance Wrap, if elected, is in place with an accredited financial institution possessing demonstrated fiduciary history as a provider.

How to Structure Underwriter Warrants

REVPAC underwriter warrants should be structured not to exceed, *once exercised,* 3 percent of the Investment Trust's issued and outstanding REVPAC Bond Units. The exercise price is variable. However, 20 percent of the IPO price is recommended.

In the equity markets, underwriters are accustomed to receiving warrants for 10 percent of the securities underwritten. This is not advisable with REVPAC financing because the dilution dynamics for Revenue Sharing instruments is very different from those of equities and would prove a severe handicap for investors. The recommended REVPAC warrant exercise price (*approximately 15 percent of the traditional equity warrant exercise price level)* more than compensates the underwriter for this difference.

Secondary Trading Market Considerations

Underwriters are primarily interested in generous *short-term* trading market appreciation of securities valuations and reasonable assurance of an exit strategy for both their investors and the underlying securities of their warrants.

The REVPAC Investment Trust product is an underwriter's dream come true! The synergy of the unique components of the REVPAC Unit provide (for the first time) secondary market speculators with an opportunity to trade "revenue futures" in tomorrow's art/entertainment, sports, and corporate break-throughs.

The powerful influence of "revenue futures" that manifest themselves into meaningful yields for speculators have the potential of creating deep and active secondary trading markets.

Here is a capsule view of the potential trading performance of the REVPAC component parts.

- **Revenue Share**

  Since the revenue yields are based entirely on the gross revenues from the consumer to the business venture — *not on earnings* — ultimate REVPAC Unit values in the secondary trading market will rise or fall in direct correlation to that consumer response.

  Yields grounded in Gross Revenues provide an inherent inflationary hedge for unit holders, because the yields will adjust to inflation. The end-market prices of the business venture will rise in tandem with inflation, causing a commensurate increase in the value of the REVPAC Bond Units.

  Analysts forecast that REVPAC Unit trading market prices for the first three years — *prior to distribution of the first Revenue Share Yield Coupon* — will achieve a minimum trading level equivalent to 50 percent of optimal feasible yields during the term, or 200 percent of accrued yields, whichever is greater. *See MexRx Investment Trust Secondary Trading Market Pro-Forma in the Table of Authorities. Also, follow trading market performance in the real-time market.*

- **Full Redemption Guaranty**

  The Guaranty feature provides a trading floor for REVPAC Bond Units in the secondary trading marketplace. There will always be value — even if the business venture fails — since 100 percent of the face value or IPO price is redeemable at full term.

  The trading market value of REVPAC Investment Trust Units of failed business ventures will inevitably fall below the offering price — but never to zero. The market price will depend on the time remaining for the Full Redemption Guaranty to become effective and on real-time interest rates within world debt markets. Should a business venture fail, REVPAC Bond Units will witness a new class of speculator entering the marketplace as revenue-futures speculators exit. These new investors, sophisticated in interest arbitrage, will enter the market and provide a steadily increasing bid price until the day of redemption.

  Two classes of REVPAC Bond Units trade per Investment Trust: Full Risk and Zero Risk.

  Underwriters have the option of electing Full Redemption Guaranty coverage for the underlying units of their underwriter warrants.

  Full Redemption Guaranty REVPAC Bond Units are forecast to trade at one-half the secondary trading market price of full-risk REVPAC Bond Units during the first three years prior to the first Revenue Share yield distribution.

- **Future Participation Warrant**
The Warrant entitles the holder to purchase REVPAC Bond Units in the subsequent business venture of the issuer, or for the next term of the current business venture. Future Participation Warrants have the potential to entice speculators to purchase REVPAC Bond Units from the secondary trading marketplace — even though most yields of the current business venture have already been distributed and even if the current business venture has failed.

  The Warrant, in essence, is a windfall component — providing a "futures" trading market value enhancement based on speculators' prognosis of the future business venture or the next term of the current business venture. Since Warrants cannot be detached from REVPAC Bond Units, the trading value of REVPAC Bond Units will experience an increase in value commensurate with the speculators' confidence in the future potential revenues of the Investment Trust.

  Future Participation Warrants represent a new investment concept whereby innovators and management teams are "franchised" and investors can speculate on their future performance.

  The potential windfall value of Future Participation Warrants cannot be forecast. However, analysts believe that secondary trading market valuations will significantly increase upon the announcement of a new business venture, or as the REVPAC Unit approaches full term for successful ventures.

- **Risk Insurance Wrap**
The all encompassing package of Risk Insurance Coverage and the value of the currency in which REVPAC Bond Units are denominated, play a significant role in secondary trading markets — *especially for foreign investment participation.*

  If the currency in which the REVPAC is denominated — *usually the U.S. dollar* — decreases, the Currency Maladjustment Coverage sustains the interest of foreign speculators. This will maintain the trading market value of the REVPAC above levels that an unhedged financial instrument, denominated in a declining currency, might normally experience.

  Risk Insurance Wrap entails the forfeiture of interest payments on the accumulated, but undistributed, Revenue Share yields.

  The underwriter should determine the projected influence of hedging REVPAC Bond Units for potential foreign secondary trading market interest.

* * *

Role of Media in REVPAC

Real-Time Reporting

Every day in the real life of a business venture, something is happening. This *something* is the grist of real-time financial reporting. Since REVPAC yields are based on *gross revenue participation,* real-time reporting is especially critical for investors and brokers trading in REVPAC securities listed on secondary trading markets.

> *Never before have securities trading market valuations been so sensitive to consumer response as they will become with the REVPAC Financial Instrument.*
>
> *REVPAC Investment Trust trading markets will prove volatile — reacting in sync with theatrical box office returns, weekly literary/recorded music sales, performance of athletes, and reported gross-sales receipts of business ventures.*

> *Imagine the reaction of the trading market to reports of a REVPAC motion picture Investment Trust inking a major box office attraction or a REVPAC theatrical Investment Trust premiering in New York to critics' raves.*

Modernize Stylistic Journalism

As REVPAC business venture financing expands, business and financial journalism will experience a new demand from the investment community. An investment community appetite will emerge and expand, demanding a new brand of entrepreneurial stylistic journalism that gives sensitive insight and treatment to:

- the innovative genius behind breakthroughs;
- the tenacious spirit of business-venture developers;
- cutting-edge business and marketing techniques; and
- emerging consumer tastes and markets.

A plethora of human-interest stories — successes, failures, fortunes being made and lost, developers' dreams realized/dashed, aspiring geniuses' careers launched/trashed — will play out their dramas and comedies within a fishbowl environment, through the reporting of tomorrow's business-venture journalists.

Pioneer New Venture-Capital Information-Processing Methods

REVPAC will modernize the venture-capital world *that is currently lagging half a century behind contemporary investment banking and business practices.* So it will be for venture-captial journalism. The impetus of reporting *real-time* stories from the rapidly paced/highly competitive amphitheater of the emerging business-venture world will breathe color, flair, and ingenuity back into business journalism — similar to the way today's media treats art/entertainment and professional sports.

As business ventures of REVPAC Investment Trusts succeed in the consumer marketplace — under the spotlight that venture-capital success enjoys — and return-on-investment yields exceed those expectations available through alternative financial instruments, the clamor for new venture-capital business information will intensify. Media Reporting Services will create venture-capital departments, journalists will cultivate specialty niches, and emerging venture-capital business-information services will find themselves in real-time online demand.

> The synergy of emerging venture-capital business, information, and REVPAC yields will create an impetus to pioneer emerging business-venture information-processing methods. These will be used by investment analysts and investment banking sector specialists when they are called upon to make gutsy calls in a real-time marketplace — wherein judgment and forecast will achieve speedy verdicts.

Public Forum for Intellectual Property Protection

A clear perspective from the posture of a public forum on Patent, Trademark and Copyright development is achieved through active responsible disclosure and reporting by the media, thereby stimulating multisector — *not the least, academic and legislative* — focus on the processes and economics of innovative development and proprietary property rights and obligations.

Since the REVPAC Financial Instrument is wrapped with Intellectual Property, safeguarding the venture project, the media will play an important role as the voice behind the additional layer of litigious recourse in enforcing swift judicial action to protect REVPAC wrapped proprietary and revenue rights around the world.

Just as REVPAC will establish the index and standard for gauging commercial/industrial market exploitation of new ventures, the *venture capital* voice of the media will stimulate a perspicuous focal point for private and public interest/activist groups toward a system of checks and balances for commercial/industrial development and exploitation.

> New REVPAC venture-capital journalism will be as exciting and important to the world of business and finance as MTV is to the World of Music or ESPN is to the World of Sports.

Have A Question?
See if we have already
answered it

REVPAC FAQ
*Questions You May Be
Asking*

As an Innovator / Developer

How does the REVPAC Funding Program Work?

Once the Risk Insurance Package Wrap is completed and "in-place" - Your Venture is syndicated to the Lenders/Investors.
The Lenders/Investors purchase REVPAC "Angel" Bonds and the capital proceeds from the placement of the Bonds are distributed to you and Your Venture in the form of a SUBORDINATED DEBENTURE LOAN.

The "SUBDEB" Loan is not your normal business loan. It is paid back ONLY from a percentage of the future revenues of Your Venture - if and when Your Venture produces revenues.

If there are insufficient revenues from the Venture to pay back this loan - the Risk Insurers pay-back the Lenders/Investors what is owed.

The SUBDEB loan is a non-recourse loan. This means that you are not responsible to pay the loan back - in the event there are insufficient revenues from the Venture. Also, the "non-recourse" loan is an "off-balance sheet entry" on your financial statement. This means that the "debt" Subordinated Debenture loan does not count as a Liability and will not affect your Net worth - by General Accounting Practice Standards.

The Lenders/Investors and the Risk Insurance Underwriters share any future yields derived from the Revenue Participation Terms of the Subordinated Debenture Loan Agreement. They are YOUR REVENUE SHARING PARTNERS. Their expectations for a Return on their Investment (ROI) rely on YOU successfully managing the Venture into the marketplace. Their ROI expectations are structured on Your Pro forma Revenue Forecast for the Venture. The "guidelines" through which the REVPAC Funding is structured, assures the Lenders/Investors and Risk Insurance Underwriters a Return-on-Investment (ROI) of almost 500% - if you can achieve the CONSERVATIVE ESTIMATE of your Forecast. In the event, you achieve the higher rate of potential success - based on Your Pro-forma Revenue Forecast of FEASIBLE or OPTIMAL Scenarios - Your Revenue Partners realize significantly enhanced ROIs. The Lenders/Investors and Risk Insurance Underwriters are Your Revenue Partners for the long-term... they are available to financially support YOU and to provide a variety of integral financial services for your Venture during the foreseeable future. What is the Risk Insurance Package "Wrap"?

The Risk Insurance Package "Wrap" is comprised of a series of Surety Risk Insurance Policies comprised of 10 "major" insurance, bond, guaranty, surety and warranty "wraps" that guarantee Your Business Venture will reach the Marketplace and have the opportunity to succeed based solely on market conditions. The "Wrap consists - as a partial listing - of the following policies:

*Performance Completion Bond
*Credit/Receivable Insurance
*Business Liability Insurance
*Key Man Insurance
*Fraud Protection Insurance
*Business Interruption Insurance
*Political Instability Insurance
*Currency Calamity Insurance
*Professional Errors & Omissions Policy Surety
*Surety Risk Bond for Investor Guaranty

The Insurance wrap, does not guaranty the market response to the Business Venture or the eventual revenues that the Venture will enjoy - in essence, the wrap guarantees the investment group that is funding you that 100% of their investment will be returned to them via: (a) revenue yields from the Venture /or/ (b) Investment Redemption Guaranty Payments. Additionally, the Risk Insurance Package Wrap - which provides Your Venture with Full Risk Coverage - also affords a Surety to your directors, vendors, stockholders, associates and all other parties that have an interest in your enterprise and your Venture... that YOU AND YOUR VENTURE WILL REACH THE MARKETPLACE.

The afore-stated Risk Insurance coverage is wrapped into the FULL REDEMPTION GUARANTY for the Lender/Investors.

The FULL REDEMPTION GUARANTY guarantees the Lenders/Investors that the Revenue Participation Yields will equal certain minimum standards. These standards vary, depending upon the guaranteed yield provisions provided by the REVPAC Funding Certificate. In all cases, the standard includes 100% Return of Original Investment. This Guaranty provides that: in the event the Business Venture fails, for whatever reason, to yield revenue participation distributions to the Lenders/Investors - sufficient to fulfill the guaranteed yield provisions contained in the REVPAC Funding Certificate - the Surety Risk Insurance Coverage will effect payments equal to the difference between revenue participation yields received (if any) and guaranteed yield provisions. In effect: REVPAC Lenders/Investors are guaranteed never to be at risk of realizing any less than the Face Value of the REVPAC Funding Certificate.

REVPAC FAQ
Questions You May Be Asking

As an Innovator / Developer How does the REVPAC Funding Program Work?

Once the Risk Insurance Package Wrap is completed and "in-place" - Your Venture is syndicated to the Lenders/Investors. The Lenders/Investors purchase REVPAC "Angel" Bonds and the capital proceeds from the placement of the Bonds are distributed to you and Your Venture in the form of a SUBORDINATED DEBENTURE LOAN.

The "SUBDEB" Loan is not your normal business loan. It is paid back ONLY from a percentage of the future revenues of Your Venture - if and when Your Venture produces revenues.

If there are insufficient revenues from the Venture to pay back this loan - the Risk Insurers pay-back the Lenders/Investors what is owed.

The SUBDEB loan is a non-recourse loan. This means that you are not responsible to pay the loan back - in the event there are insufficient revenues from the Venture. Also, the "non-recourse" loan is an "off-balance sheet entry" on your financial statement. This means that the "debt" Subordinated Debenture loan does not count as a Liability and will not affect your Net worth - by General Accounting Practice Standards.

The Lenders/Investors and the Risk Insurance Underwriters share any future yields derived from the Revenue Participation Terms of the Subordinated Debenture Loan Agreement. They are YOUR REVENUE SHARING PARTNERS. Their expectations for a Return on their Investment (ROI) rely on YOU successfully managing the Venture into the marketplace. Their ROI expectations are structured on Your Pro forma Revenue Forecast for the Venture. The "guidelines" through which the REVPAC Funding is structured, assures the Lenders/Investors and Risk Insurance Underwriters a Return-on-Investment (ROI) of almost 500% - if you can achieve the CONSERVATIVE ESTIMATE of your Forecast. In the event, you achieve the higher rate of potential success - based on Your Pro-forma Revenue Forecast of FEASIBLE or OPTIMAL Scenarios - Your Revenue Partners realize significantly enhanced ROIs. The Lenders/Investors and Risk Insurance Underwriters are Your Revenue Partners for the long-term...they are available to financially support YOU and to provide a variety of integral financial services for your Venture during the foreseeable future. What is the Risk Insurance Package "Wrap"?

The Risk Insurance Package "Wrap" is comprised of a series of Surety Risk Insurance Policies comprised of 10 "major" insurance, bond, guaranty, surety and warranty "wraps" that guarantee Your Business Venture will reach the Marketplace and have the opportunity to succeed based solely on market conditions. The "Wrap consists - as a partial listing - of the following policies:

*Performance Completion Bond
*Credit/Receivable Insurance
*Business Liability Insurance
*Key Man Insurance
*Fraud Protection Insurance
*Business Interruption Insurance
*Political Instability Insurance
*Currency Calamity Insurance

*Professional Errors & Omissions Policy Surety
*Surety Risk Bond for Investor Guaranty

The Insurance wrap, does not guaranty the market response to the Business Venture or the eventual revenues that the Venture will enjoy - in essence, the wrap guarantees the investment group that is funding you that 100% of their investment will be returned to them via: (a) revenue yields from the Venture /or/ (b) Investment Redemption Guaranty Payments.

Additionally, the Risk Insurance Package Wrap - which provides Your Venture with Full Risk Coverage - also affords a Surety to your directors, vendors, stockholders, associates and all other parties that have an interest in your enterprise and your Venture... that YOU AND YOUR VENTURE WILL REACH THE MARKETPLACE.

The afore-stated Risk Insurance coverage is wrapped into the FULL REDEMPTION GUARANTY for the Lender/Investors.

The FULL REDEMPTION GUARANTY guarantees the Lenders/Investors that the Revenue Participation Yields will equal certain minimum standards. These standards vary, depending upon the guaranteed yield provisions provided by the REVPAC Funding Certificate. In all cases, the standard includes 100% Return of Original Investment. This Guaranty provides that: in the event the Business Venture fails, for whatever reason, to yield revenue participation distributions to the Lenders/Investors - sufficient to fulfill the guaranteed yield provisions contained in the REVPAC Funding Certificate - the Surety Risk Insurance Coverage will

effect payments equal to the difference between revenue participation yields received (if any) and guaranteed yield provisions.

In effect: REVPAC Lenders/Investors are guaranteed never to be at risk of realizing any less than the Face Value of the REVPAC Funding Certificate.

*   *   *

What are my Obligations for the Risk Insurance Wrap?

Once you qualify: the Risk Insurance Underwriters issue to you and your Business Venture the FULL RISK INSURANCE Coverage that provides the Surety for Your REVPAC Bond Funding.

The FULL RISK Coverage also serves to provide the assurance - for your Directors, Stockholders, Vendors, Associates and all other parties that have an interest in your enterprise - that YOU WILL EMERGE INTO THE MARKETPLACE - and Your Venture will have the Opportunity to generate Revenues and Succeed.

Furthermore: through the coverage of the Risk Insurance Wrap: Your potential to attract support for Your Venture is significantly enhanced. Strategic alliances can more readily be structured, because YOU have Insurance Underwriters bonding and warranting YOUR capability and future performance to reach the marketplace.

The All-Inclusive Risk Insurance Coverage is a coveted Security Assurance and Surety Guaranty that is an integral vital element in securing funding and strategic alliance support.

The coverage, traditionally requires significant "insurance premium payments" that are payable in advance of policy issuance. However, under the REVPAC Funding Program - the high-end advance costs are offset by the Insurers' participation together with Your Lenders/Investors - in the future Revenues of the Venture.

In order to ensure the Full Risk Insurance Underwriters that the fiduciary integrity of the enterprise and the Business Venture will be maintained throughout the REVPAC Funding term - a set of obligations for the Venture Developer (YOU) are put in-place. These obligations are the foundation for the long-term Insurance and Financial Service programs, implemented to safeguard and promulgate YOUR economic stability and the potential success of the Venture.

The following is a partial listing and summary of the Collateralized Yield Obligation covenants binding the Business Venture Developer and the Risk Insurance / Loan-Investment Group:

1. Revenue Sharing Pledge
This is YOUR promise to pay a percentage of your Venture's Gross Revenues in return for REVPAC Capital Funding. A percentage of any-and-all future gross revenues from the Business Venture are to be distributed to the Risk Insurance / Loan-Investment Group in return for funding the Business Venture. The gross revenue sharing is for the agreed-upon term (usually 7-Years).

2. Pledge Collateral Guarantee for Pledge
This is how YOU are "securing" Your Pledge to share Revenues in return for the Capital Funding:

All Intellectual Property claims, protecting the underlying Business Venture, is conveyed (under chattel) to collateralize the Revenue Sharing Pledge.

Capital Assets - especially those acquired through the REVPAC Capital Funding - are also conveyed under chattel. Capital Stock of the Venture Developer enterprise - in some cases is held under "chattel" to collateralize the Pledge.

Note: Chattel Collateral is returned to the Venture Developer (YOU) at Full term and as provided for by the Collateral Pledge Agreement.

3. Appointment of Administrator to oversee, arbitrate and enforce the Pledge
This is how the Capital Funding Group protects its interest and monitors the Fiscal Fiduciary Integrity of your management of the Business Venture.

An Administrator - representing the Risk Insurance / Loan-Investment Group - is appointed the "veto-power" Authority governing any-and-all Stockholder and Board-of-Directors resolutions that may impact the good standing of the Pledge. The Authority is appointed through the enactment of the following procedures:

* Stockholder Voting Trust: A voting trust between YOU and the Administrator, providing final consent and approval authority on any-and-all matters before the stockholders of your Enterprise (Venture Developer) that may affect or impact the compliance and good standing of the Pledge.

* Board of Directors Appointment: A new Director position is established on the BOD - "Insurance/ Financial Fiduciary Director". The Administrator is appointed - with stockholder approval - to the vacancy of the newly created Director position. The position is a "Term Appointment" - which means that the Administrator is to serve for the term of the Pledge. The BOD Director position of Insurance/Financial Fiduciary Director - is empowered with the deciding/ veto power vote on any matters and resolutions that are considered by the BOD that may affect or impact the compliance and good standing of the Pledge.

* Amendment to Articles and By-Laws: The Venture Developer (YOUR Enterprise) adopts requisite amendments in the Articles of Incorporation and By-Laws to provide for the following:

BOD Meeting Quorum: Notice and attendance of ALL BOD Members is required to hold any-and-all meetings. The Insurance/Financial Fiduciary Director - specifically- must be present at all meetings.

Plurality Vote Requirement to Approve Resolutions: Unanimous approval of ALL BOD Members -specifically including Insurance/ Financial Fiduciary Director - is required on any-and-all resolutions effecting the good standing and compliance of the Pledge.

4. Financial Reporting
How the Capital Funding Group tracks its Financial Interest in the Business Venture.

The Venture Enterprise is required to issue periodic Financial Reports concerning the Business Venture to Administrator reflecting Sales, Inventory, Capital Assets and other financial status reports required by the Administrator.

5. Renewal of Pledge
Under what terms and conditions can the Capital Funding Group Renew their Revenue Sharing Rights in the Business Venture

The Pledge is usually for a term of 7 Years. At the end of the Eighty-Fourth (84) month, the Pledge is terminated and the Revenue Sharing Rights of the Risk Insurance / Loan-Investment Group cease - unless renewed.

The Pledge may be renewed for an identical "renewal" term of 7-Years, at the sole option of the Risk Insurance / Loan-Investment Group, provided that Capital Funds for an additional Loan-Investment and equal amount as the primary Loan-Investment is remitted to the Venture Enterprise (YOU).

Upon remittance of the "Renewal" Loan-Investment, the Pledge is automatically renewed and will continue in effect, without interruption, however with the following adjustment:

If Revenue Sharing Yields - prior to renewal - equal less than 500% of Loan-Investment principal: all rights and privileges of Risk Insurance / Loan- Investment Group for the primary Business Venture will remain in effect for the entire Renewal Term (7-Years).

If Revenue Sharing Yields amount to 500% or more, the rights and privileges of Risk Insurance / Loan- Investment Group for the primary Business Venture will remain in effect for Four additional years.

6. New and Additional Business Venture for Renewal Term of Pledge

Can the Capital Funding Group buy into a Future Business Venture to be developed by you?

The Venture Enterprise (YOU) are required to notice the Administrator - prior to Term-End - if you intend to include a New Business Venture for the Renewal Term of the Pledge.

The Venture Enterprise - at its sole option - may include a new and additional Business Venture within the Pledge for the Renewal period. The Business Venture must contain identical rights and privileges for the Risk Insurance / Loan-Investment Group to share in the future potential revenues of the New Venture - as those that are in effect for the primary Business Venture.

The purpose of this option of introducing a New Business Venture to the Pledge for the Renewal Period - is to afford the Venture Enterprise (YOU) an opportunity to access additional venture capital investment to fund a New Business Venture - even in the event that the primary Business Venture failed to mature and yield anticipated and forecasted revenues.

7. Transfer of Controlling Interest of Stock Ownership of Venture Enterprise is Restrictive.

What happens if a Buy-Out or Merger-Acquisition Opportunity for YOU becomes available?

In the event, a third-party interest should seek acquisition of controlling interest of Venture Enterprise or out-right purchase of Business Venture - the Venture Enterprise is required to seek approval of the Risk Insurance / Loan-Investment Group. In most cases, the "Buy-Out" portion of the proceeds being paid to the Capital Funding Group will be required to equal minimum 500% of Loan-Investment principal -when added to the "earned" Revenue Sharing Yields credited to the Capital Funding Group at the time of the acquisition.

In the event, the approval is granted by the Trust Administrator, the conditions of Buy-Out Agreement will supersede Terms and Conditions of Pledge.

Under certain conditions, third party interest (acquiring controlling interest) may desire to retain Pledge active and "effective". The Purchasing Entity may desire to assume the obligations of the Pledge. In that event - provided there is no interruption or amendment to the Pledge (lessening the rights, privileges and benefits of the Risk Insurance / Loan-Investment Group) - and the Purchasing Entity is deemed "credit worthy" - the Trust Administrator will not unfairly withhold approval of the transfer or acquisition.

The Trust Administrator has final authority regarding said transfer. Approval is dependent, mainly, upon the qualification of the Buy-Out Purchasing Entity and the ultimate benefit of the trans action for the Capital Funding Group.

What happens if the Issuer has a buy-out offer for an Issuer-owned division, subsidiary or product/service property that is incremental to the Revenue Participation relationship with the Issuer?

In the event, the Issuer receives a buy-out offer, within this category, the Investment Trust receives the proportionate percentage of buy-out proceeds – in a like manner as the of buy-out proceeds – in a like manner as the Revenue Sharing percentage. However, in the event the REVPAC holders' aggregate Revenue Share allocations have not equaled minimum 5 times ROI, at the time of the buy-out offer, and said percentage will not, when computed with aggregate revenues-share allocations, equal a 5 to 1 ROI, said percentage must be adjusted upwards to provide the *minimum* 5:1 ROI.

Trust Administrate must provide written approval of such a buy-out. Such approval will not be unreasonably withheld and will be based on appraisal of fair market value.

What happens if the Issuer has a buy-out offer for controlling equity ownership of Issuer's entity?

In the event a buy-out offer occurs, the purchasing entity must honor the in-place Subordinated Debenture and REVPAC Investment Trust agreements – in which case, the Investment Trust will not participate in the purchase proceeds.

In the event the purchasing entity desires to terminate the in-place agreements, the Investment Trust will participate in the proceeds – in a like manner and participation percentage, as provided for in the agreements. However, in the event the REVPAC holders have not received minimum 5 times ROI and the participation percentage will not yield a 5 to 1 ROI, the percentage must be increased to provide a *minimum* 5 to 1 ROI.

The Trust Administrator must provide written approval of a buy-out. Such approval will not be unreasonably withheld and will be based on:

(a) *Buy-out with purchasing entity honoring in-place agreements -* the due-diligence validation of the purchasing entity and establishment of requisite documentation and banking instructions;

(b) *Buy-out with purchasing entity terminating in-place agreements* - appraisal of fair market value.

*   *   *

As an Investor

Can I buy REVPAC for my retirement plan portfolio?

Yes! REVPAC Bond Units — when protected by the Full Redemption Guarantee coverage and bilt-in Risk Insurance Coverage Wrap — are highly desirable financial instruments that provide security of investment capital, hedges against down-turn economic trends, and significant yield potential. REVPAC qualify for most pension plans and retirement programs.

How do I keep track of my investment?

The Administrator for the Investment Trust issues quarterly and annual reports to all REVPAC holders. Additionally, investors can access real-time Revenue Yields, Buy/Sell Trading Quotes, status of the Business Venture in the consumer marketplace (including revenue performance, scheduled marketing campaigns plus other pertinent data and information updated daily) via the Internet by accessing the Business Managers' Reporting Platform.

Can I borrow against my REVPAC? Investment Trust Units?

Yes! REVPAC Bond Units qualify as highly desirable collateral security instruments for lending institutions. REVPAC that are secured by Full

Redemption Guarantee coverage or those that have accumulated (undistributed) revenue yields are especially desirable. Select financial institutions may also provide margin services for REVPAC-denominated Investment Trusts.

When can I expect to receive Revenue Yields?

Revenue Yields are distributed 36 months following the completion of the public offering of the REVPAC Bond Units for the Investment Trust. To receive payment, the investor remits Coupon No. 1 from the REVPAC Unit to the Administrator for the Investment Trust. Additional revenue yield distributions occur each year thereafter, on the 48th month (Coupon No. 2), the 60th month (Coupon No. 3), the 72nd month (Coupon No. 4) and so on until the REVPAC reaches full term.

Who keeps track of my money?

The Investment Trust Administrator monitors, administers, and distributes all financial transactions conducted by the Investment Trust on behalf of the REVPAC Bond Unit holders. Full-disclosure reporting on all financial matters, including: business manager revenues, accumulated revenue share yields, and capital asset reports are sent to all investors quarterly and is also available via the real-time reporting platform of the business manager.

Would REVPAC make a good investment for my child's college trust?

Yes! REVPAC Investment Trust Units with Full Redemption Guaranty coverage provide excellent investment security for both short term - high yield and long term - growth investment programs. The REVPAC Bond

Unit with Full Redemption Guaranty coverage is a no-risk revenue share — with the potential of out-performing most secured financial instruments in today's marketplace. It is recommended that investors seeking long-term yields employ an investment advisor.

What happens to my investment when my REVPAC reaches full maturity?
The terms for REVPAC Bond Units vary between Investment Trusts. For example, on a seven-year REVPAC Bond Unit, the Bond is fully matured on the 84th month following completion of the public offering of the Investment Trust. Before the accumulated revenue yield for Year 7 (Coupon No.5) is paid, the investor may elect to exercise the Future Participation Warrant attached to the REVPAC Bond Unit. The investor may purchase the ensuing seven-year REVPAC Units by applying the accumulated (undistributed) Revenue Yields toward the exercise of the Warrant or by redeeming the Full Redemption Guaranty. The Investor may also elect to sell the REVPAC Unit via the securities trading markets (together with the accumulated Revenue Yields and Warrants) in order to realize potential windfall trading return.

How do I account for my Revenue Yields and are Investment Trust Yields taxable?
Please refer to the *Collateralized Yield Obligation* in the Table of Authorities, paragraph 4.03 - *Accounting Form for Allocations.*

The Trust Administrator accounting for all allocation disbursements of the Revenue

Share Yields are designated in the stated section.

REVPAC are structured to provide a tax-free *pass-through* from the gross revenues derived form the business venture to the Investment Trust to the REVPAC holder — *unlike dividend payments from stock ownership interests, which are required to deduct corporate taxes prior to disbursement in most jurisdictions.*

However, a REVPAC Bond holder's taxation liability will vary depending upon jurisdictional domicile of the REVPAC Investment Trust Unit holder. It is recommended that investors consult their tax accountants with regard to tax issues within the jurisdiction of domicile.

* * *

REVPAC BONDS PROTECT INTELLECTUAL PROPERTY
Putting Teeth into Litigious Recourse against IP Infringement.

The power of wrapping Intellectual Property into registered Banking-Financial-Securities Instruments... ... And The enforcement of Proprietary Entitlements - Deploying Banking-Financial-Securities Laws.

GETTING SERIOUS ABOUT PROTECTING PROPRIETARY PROPERTY RIGHTS:

1 *HOW IT'S DONE ...*

REVPAC BONDs Wrap Revenue and Property Claims within Bank and Financial Securities Registrations to protect License "Monopoly" Entitlements.

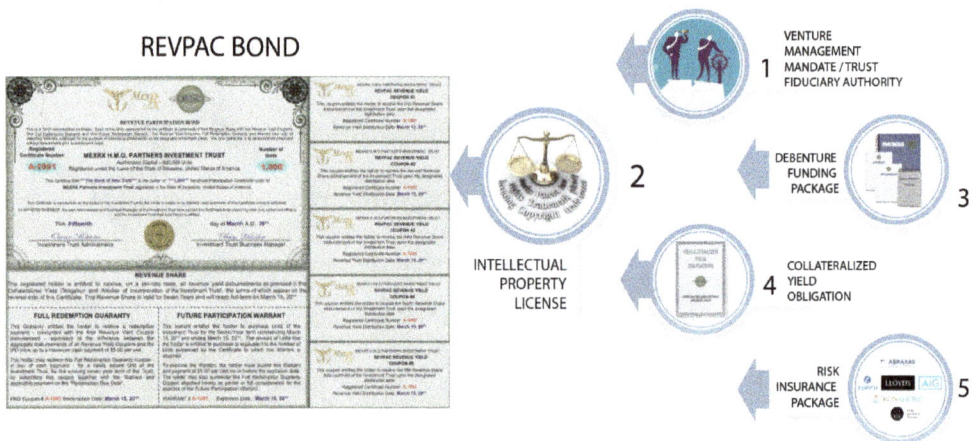

REVPAC BOND

1 — VENTURE MANAGEMENT MANDATE / TRUST FIDUCIARY AUTHORITY

2 — INTELLECTUAL PROPERTY LICENSE

3 — DEBENTURE FUNDING PACKAGE

4 — COLLATERALIZED YIELD OBLIGATION

5 — RISK INSURANCE PACKAGE

ONE: **The proprietary Business Venture is "enfranchised" as Territorial Master Franchise Licenses.**

• *The Territorial Master License – "enfranchises"* all property claims of the Business Venture. The Subordinated Debenture Package *"indentures"* all revenue claims of the Business Venture. Together and in tandem with the other component parts of the *REVPAC Wrap*, the right, title and interest of the Intellectual property of the Business Venture is "assimilated" into the *REVPAC BOND*.

TWO: The Master License is "wrapped" into the REVPAC BOND. The REVPAC BOND Wrap is registered as a "Bank Instrument under Banking Laws within the sovereign jurisdiction of the Territorial Master Franchise License.

- The *REVPAC BOND* – and its *property/revenue entitlement claims* to the Business Venture - is registered as a Banking-Securities-Financial and Commercial Trade INSTRUMENT with government and non-government agencies/organizations having jurisdictional and multi-jurisdictional regulatory standing and/authority. These agencies/organizations – with which the REVPAC BOND is registered include:

  - Financial Securities Regulatory Agencies/Orgs.
  - Bank Instrument Regulatory Agencies/Orgs.
  - Mercantile – Commercial Banking Agencies/Orgs.
  - Commerce & Trade Agencies/Orgs.
  - Intellectual Property Orgs.

THREE: REVPAC BOND Wrap secures OPTIMUM SAFEGUARDS for monopoly entitlements of the IP Entitlements.

- Effective Legal standing from which to deploy swift litigious recourse to protect and enforce the entitlements of REVPAC holders throughout all jurisdictions encompassed by the Business Venture Territorial Master License.

2 *HOW IT'S DEPLOYED …*

A Solution at last! Finally … Innovators and their Capital Partners have Meaningful Litigious recourse against Proprietary Property Infringement.

Litigious Recourse in NOW able to be brought to bear in *Intellectual Property Infringement Issues* through creative and effective litigation, citing:

- Banking Statutes
- Financial Securities Statutes
- Franchise, Trade and Commerce Statutes
- Insurance Statutes
- Mercantile – Trade Statutes
- Civil, Mercantile and Penal Laws protecting these Statutes.

Since the REVPAC Wrap integrates *right, title and interest* to Property and Revenues of a Business Venture *with Intellectual Property as the centerpiece for Investment Capital TRUST... Any infringement of the Property and Revenue Rights* (including Intellectual Property) represents a variety of potential violations of the Fundamental Laws protecting the economic stability and statutes of the jurisdiction in which the infringement is being alleged to occur.

NOW! Citing Banking, Financial, Securities, Trade, Commerce, Insurance VIOLATIONS (Civil, Mercantile and Penal) – *swift legal court action can be achieved to secure Temporary Restraining Orders (TROs).*

This multi-statutory / multi-law / multi-court and multi-jurisdictional legal action puts "teeth" into litigating the Infringements of Property Rights that has hitherto been lacking in the global trade and capital marketplace.

The practical – economic and IMMEDIATE impact of seeking TRO relief ... is that: *The TRO action expedites immediate relief and an effective measure to enforce the staunching of potential erosions to the Revenue Entitlements of Proprietary Properties (Business Venture) within Proprietary Venues (Enfranchised Master Licensed Territory).*

Especially poignant for the court, is the argument for Rapid Court Resolutions – to protect the small private investor in Revenue Participating Contract (REVPAC) Wraps - that may well fall within the scope of WIDOWS AND ORPHANS LAWS of the jurisdictions – in which the alleged infringement is brought before the court.

The *"wrapping"* of the Business Venture Property and Revenue Entitlements into the *Revenue Participation (REVPAC) BOND* is for the mutual benefit of both supply-side and capital side participants PLUS their Financial Service Providers to the Business Venture. It secures:

> • *REVPAC Bond holders* – Innovators as well as their capital investment partners within the jurisdictional territory of the Enfranchised Master License PLUS investors from outside the jurisdictional territory (foreign investment capital developing commercial business ventures within the jurisdiction);

> • Financial Institutions serving the REVPAC Bond holders and their underlying Business Venture (including risk-management/Insurance, Banking and Financial Underwriters PLUS all service-fulfillment institutions).

3 *PROTECTS INNOVATOR AND INVESTOR ENTITLEMENTS*

The REVPAC Wrap heralds a New Era for Investor Confidence in Emerging Business Venture Opportunities and foreign-export development of these Opportunities.

The benefits of Revenue Participation Entitlement (REVPAC BOND) Wraps – accompanied by registration as International Banking Instruments and the enforcement of Proprietary entitlements – *deploying jurisdictional banking-Financial-Securities Laws* – for the commercial development of Intellectual Property can be summed up as follows:

• Ensures Optimal Legal protection of Intellectual Property Rights in all jurisdictions in which the Business Venture is licensed and where the innovators (supply-side) and investment participants (capital-side) own Revenue Entitlements…

• Guarantees Future Participation Rights (reinvestment entitlements – *inherent in the Future Participation Warrant*) for the ongoing *expansion* of the Business Venture and future *new emerging* business venture development within the Master Licensed jurisdiction. This secures Long-Term enfranchisement of Innovative Genius and Entrepreneurial Management talent that is capable of developing successful Business Ventures within the Master Licensed jurisdictions…

• Secures Investment confidence within Capital Markets – to invest in Overseas Development of *"Emerging Proprietary Business Opportunities"* … which in-turn… enhance risk Management participation and renewable sources of capital investment for emerging business opportunities which have hitherto been lacking in the International Capital Investment Communities.

REVPAC ShareResourcing Plan

…The Ultimate Social Entrepreneur Program for Natural Resource Providers

…Reengineering the socio-economic benefits of Sharecropping for the Modern Era...

…stabilizing supply-provider-side economics of Natural Resource harvesting…

Custom Designed for
Agricultural – Sea Food – Natural Resource Providers
… To share in the Rich Revenue Entitlements of
OVERSEAS end-user Market Demand
for the resources that they harvest…

IT'S TIME HAS COME!!

The **REVPAC ShareResourcing Plan** is what the back-bone of the Natural Resource Cooperatives -*throughout the world's emerging nations*- have been waiting for!!!

Meaningful Sales Revenue Participation from OVERSEAS end-user markets.

The New-Revolutionary ShareResourcing Plan…

Annexes (apportions) a portion of ALL gross revenues (sales receipts) from the Points-of-Sale (P.O.S.) –into an electronic LockBox Depository – and digitally transfers the *Revenue Participation* proceeds to Natural Resource Providers *IN REAL TIME.*

The LockBox Depository disburses (digitally transfers) pro-rated portions of the "annexed" sales revenues to Cooperative Members that harvested the Natural Resources… The transfer is made directly to each Coop Member's REVPAC SmartCard…The entire transaction – from P.O.S. to Coop Member REVPAC SmartCard – occurs in milliseconds from the time-of-sale. Coop Members gain IMMEDIATE ACCESS to their Revenue Sharing yields – simultaneous to the OVERSEAS end-user customers' purchase of the Resource.

IMAGINE!!!
A Walmart Cashier in Los Angeles, California – rings up a sale for 5 Kilograms of frozen shrimp…The electronic terminal at the P.O.S. digitally transfers 10% of the sale to the depository Lock Box… which is immediately "streamed" to the REVPAC SmartCards of the fishermen in Costa Rica that harvested the shrimp – three weeks ago!

Here's How ShareResourcing Works…
Please refer to the ShareResource Flow Diagram. The following discussion – enumerated ONE THRU FIVE – relates to the corresponding number appearing in the Flow Charts.

ONE (1) – LOCAL COOP RESOURCE CORRAL *(COSTA RICA)*

All of the Local Cooperatives in Costa Rica Harvest Center agree to sell their future marine harvest to select processing plants that belong to the **REVPAC ShareResourcing Program.** The processing plants package and freeze the processed marine harvest in containers with barcode markers that identify the coop and members of the coop – *identified as harvesters.* The barcode is the "digital router" that identifies the members of the coop to receive Gross Revenue Participation Yields (royalties) for the OVERSEAS sales (of their harvest) as they occur … *and in Real-Time.*

All Coop Members receive ***REVPAV SMART CARDS.*** The Gross Revenue Participation Yields are digitally streamed to REVPAC SmartCards of the Coop Members – responsible for the harvesting of the resources sold.

TWO (2) – INTERNATIONAL EXPORT CENTER *(COSTA RICA)*

The frozen Processed Marine Harvest arrives at the International Distribution Center where the Harvest is containerized, placed in cold storage aboard shipment vessel and dispatched to final destination.

THREE (3) – NATIONAL DISTRIBUTION CENTER *(LONG BEACH, CALIFORNIA)*

Frozen Processed Marine Harvest Container is off-loaded at debarkation port and sent to National Distribution Center. Marine Harvest is "packaged" for end-consumer market. Consumer Packaging is marked with Digital Bar Code to identify COOP and COOP Members in COSTA RICA – responsible for harvesting the resources and placed in cold storage, awaiting shipment to Points-of-Sale destinations.

FOUR (4) – POINT-OF-SALE DESTINATION *(LOS ANGELES)*

End-Consumer market dispatcher (WALMART) receives Packaged Frozen Marine Harvest at warehouse and routes merchandise to store destinations. Merchandise is placed in display Point-of-Sale freezer for customer selection.

FIVE (5) – YIELDS DIGITALLY STREAMED TO COOP MEMBER *(COSTA RICA)*

As Store sales of Packaged Frozen Marine Harvest are transacted – ALL Sales Revenues flow through a common digital inventory control reporting system – which is linked to every sales transaction "Point-of-Sale" (P.O.S.) terminal throughout the Regional Market.

Concurrent with the sales being entered through the P.O.S. terminals, into the digital inventory –control reporting system – Coop Members receive their pro-rated Gross Revenue Participation Yields … *digitally streamed to them in Real-Time … and immediately accessible via their REVPAC SmartCard*

REVPAC White Papers

The REVPAC ShareResourcing Plan...In Action!

Today's economy is global in principle. Trade barriers have all but eroded, consumers are more affluent and educated than ever, and communication technologies accelerate access to information at unprecedented speed. Yet the economics of natural resource providers from emerging nations still awaits its emergence into this new era of progress and prosperity.

The **REVPAC ShareResourcing Plan** represents a quantum leap in 21st century global revenue participation. Its currency-in-trade is *gross revenue participation, and gross revenue is universal.*

Basing yields on gross revenues provides a simple equation with which ALL levels of the natural resource delivery system can evaluate opportunities – both at the "sharecropping" stage (farmers and fisherman) and at the investment speculation stage (investors to fund the infrastructure) for new and emerging ventures.

The venture synergism potential of the **REVPAC ShareResourcing Plan** promises to create a surge of interest and confidence from all strata of the natural resource delivery system... which everyone can follow through a system of real-time reporting and revenue sharing. In the historical perspective, The REVPAC Foundation ShareResourcing Plan, can pave the way into a new era for the relationship between natural resource providers, distributors and consumers...*launching a creative renaissance for the next generation.*

Here are a few examples of the immediate impact of this innovative ShareResourcing Plan:

(1) Remuneration to Harvesters – *Cooperative Members*

Cooperative Resource Harvesters (farmers, fishermen, etc.) can now receive Revenue Participation payments equivalent to Ten Percent (10%) of the end-market sales *gross revenues* ... for their Harvest. This is known as the *Dime-a-Dollar-Dividend Yield ("DADDY")*. The "DADDY" is effectuated in two installments:

• *Cash-on-Delivery (COD) Payment* – The "Harvester" receives a cash payment at the time that the Natural Resource is delivered to the "local" Coop resource-dispatch-and-Processing Center. Payment is accounted as a Cash-Payment-on-Delivery plus Advance-Payment-on-DADDY.

The amount of the COD Payment is equal to the "local market price" for the delivered Resource on the day of delivery. Additionally, the "Harvester" receives a "premium payment" (enhancement) above and beyond the "local market price" – which is accounted as the DADDY Advance Payment.

• **DADDY Revenue Participation Payment** – Ten Percent (10%) of the end-market gross revenue sales receipts are digitally disbursed to the Coop Member (Harvester) as the DADDY Revenue Participation Payment (less the "premium payment" – advanced with the COD Payment). DADDY is "digitally streamed" to the Coop Member's REVPAC SmartCard in Real-Time as the end-market sale is transacted.

DADDY Revenue Participation remuneration represents "greater" cash payments (between 50% to 75% greater) as compared to the level of payment that Coop Members ("Harvesters") – acting as independent Resource Providers – have been accustomed to receiving for their Resource Harvests, HITHERTO!

(2) End-Market Pricing Parameter for Harvested Resources

The establishment of Prices (for Resources) in the OVERSEAS end-market MUST meet the *REVPAC Program parameters* – of minimum 40% gross margin yield – in order to accommodate the "economics" of the REVPAC Standard and in order to allow ALL Revenue Participation Levels adequate remuneration for their contribution.

In the event that certain Resources are unable to be competitively "priced" – allowing for the Minimum *REVPAC Gross Margin parameter* – Innovative planning MUST develop alternative end-market products from the Resources that can accommodate the requisite 40% Gross Margin Yield...*i.e. Avocados become frozen guacamole/ seafood becomes processed specialty-Fine Food products/leather becomes shoes, luggage, accessories...etc.*

(3) Built-In Hedge against Inflation

Rides Inflation like a cork on water

The pricing of the Resources "fluctuates" to meet market-demand and economic conditions related to national currencies and their exchange markets. Since the Resource Coop Harvesters (supply-side) and the Infrastructure Investors (capital-side) are "remunerated" on a Gross-Revenue-Participation-Basis (DADDYs) … their yields adjust to inflationary conditions (automatically) since the end-market prices of the Resources adjust to meet the National Consumer Prices Indices of each market. Thusly, the supply-side (Coop Harvesters) and the capital-side (Investors) have a built-In Hedge against Inflation via the "economics" of REVPAC DADDYs.

(4) Overall Economic Significance for Natural Resource Providers

The **REVPAC ShareResourcing Plan** affords Natural Resource Providers the opportunity to eliminate the "middlemen" (export distributors) who have historically "exploited" Resource Providers of emerging nations … often leaving the independent Agriculture-Seafood and Natural Resource providers with an UNFAIR portion of the "true value" of their harvest.

NOW! ... The here-to-fore "exploited" Provider-base of the resource-Supply-Chain – *farmers, fishermen and resource harvesters of COSTA RICA – receive "end-market" Revenue Interest (Dime-A-Dollar-Dividend-Yields..."DADDYs").* **Thusly, instead of receiving pennies-on-the-pound "yields" from the harvest ... Coop Member Resource Providers can NOW realize far greater remuneration for their harvests.**

A Quick Glance at the Economics:
DADDY yields (10% of the Gross Sales Revenue) from an affluent *"Overseas-based market"* - represents far greater value than a 10% Revenue Interest from an Emerging Nation "National Currency-based market" ("Peso", Bolivar, Colon, etc.). The difference is EXTRAORDINARY! ...

It is the difference between 10% of $15 per Kg of Shrimp in the OVERSEAS Market and 10% of $3 for the same Kg of Shrimp in the local market of the Resource Provider. A DADDY is FIVE TIMES (500%) GREATER VALUE - for the Resource Harvester... deploying the **REVPAC ShareResourcing Plan.**

What's More! ... The *DADDY payments* – disbursed to the Resource Provider – are EQUIVALENT to the NET MARGIN that is disbursed to both the capital and merchant providers! AT LAST! ... The elimination of the "export distributor" and the deployment of a *fair and equitable Social-entrepreneur Program* allows Harvesters of emerging nations to SHARE in the financial rewards "fairly – equally – simultaneously" with the capital and merchant side-of-the-chain that operate and service Export Marketplaces for Natural Resources

ALSO ... The Resource Cooperative has the potential to develop *New Markets and Products for its Harvests... by forming "strategic-alliance relationships" with OVERSEAS RESOURCE PROCESSORS and "Private-Label" Merchandisers.*

ADDITIONALLY! The REVPAC PLAN Serves to provide a...
... *UNIVERSAL SOLUTION to ensure Indigenous Land/Resource Rights and Entitlements!*

Protected Native People with land/resource rights have, hitherto, little or no litigious recourse to monitor the accountability of concessionaires – commercially exploiting licensed property/resource belonging to the Indigenous Community.

NOW! Concessions to develop Indigenous properties/ resources can be wrapped into the REVPAC SHARERESOURCING PLAN, therein indenturing all future gross revenues derived from property/resource exploitation.

The Native People rights, entitlements and benefits are safeguarded by the REVPAC Fiscal Fiduciary Monitoring, with stringent Remedial Enforcement in the event of default.

The Surety and Integrity of the underlying covenants of the REVPAC PLAN provides a viable and dependable "Check and Balance System" that - if responsibly deployed - may develop into the Universal Standard and Solution to ensure Social Reform Programs - long-sought-after by Social Activists.

REVPAC SHARE RESOURCING
... IN ACTION

IMAGINE!!!
A Walmart Cashier-in Los Angeles CA rings
Up a sale for 5 kilograms of frozen Shrimp...
The electronic terminal at the Point-of-Sale (P.O.S.) digitally transfers 10% of
the sale to the "Bank Depository Lock Box"...
...Which is immediately "Streamed" to the
Smart Cards of the fishermen in Costa
Rica that harvested the shrimp.
Three weeks ago!

Local Coop Resource Corral
Costa Rica

1 Week One

A. Coop Members harvest one-Ton of shrimp... delivering the "Catch" to their Local Coop "Corral".

B. Local Corral processes and freezes shrimp... and Registers Shipment containers to identify Coop Member that harvested shrimp.

C. Coop Members receive REVPAC SMART CARD. Yields are streamed to SMART CARD when their Shrimp is sold.

COSTA RICA SEAFOOD COOPERATIVE
REVPAC
1234 6656 3756 0000
CARDHOLDER
Reunion Herd Distribution Date MARCH 15, 20●●
VISA

2 Week One
-Shrimp arrives at Intl. Distribution Center...
--Shrimp is "containerized" and shipped to destination market.

Intl. Export Center
Costa Rica

3 Week Two
-Shrimp is "packaged" for end user market...
-Consumer Packaging is marked with Digital Bar Code to Indentify... Coop Members that harvested Shrimp.

National Distribution Center
Long Beach CA

SHRIMP

4 Week Three
-Frozen Shrimp arrives at Walmart P.O.S. and is placed in Consumer Display Freezer for Sale.

Point-of-Sale Destination
Los Angeles CA

Walmart

5 Week Three
-Sale is made for 5 kgs of Frozen Shrimp
--10% of Sales Revenues is digitally streamed from Walmart to Coop Members SmartCard.

Yields Streamed to Coop Member

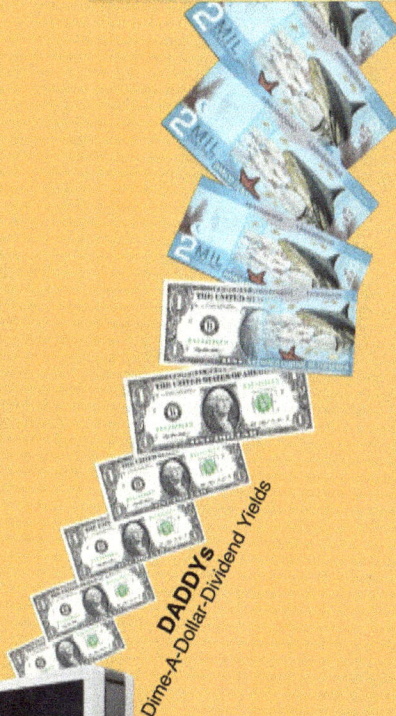

Thank you for
shopping with us!

DADDYs
Dime-A-Dollar-Dividend Yields

FINANCIAL PROFORMA STATEMENTS & FORWARD PROJECTION CALCULATORS

In Support of

THE REVPAC BOND CAPITAL THEORY

…The New Investment Banking Standard to Stabilize the Economics of SME Funding and Venture Capital Development…

This Actuarial Analysis is a companion publication to the Table of Authorities of the REVPAC-Guide and Handbook.

The Information contained herein is conveyed to Auditors and Actuaries for the purpose of evaluating and accrediting the REVPAC CAPITAL THEORY and its Financial-Banking Instrument - REVPAC BOND.

C O N T E N T S

HOW TO READ THE REVPAC BOND YIELD PERFORMANCE CALCULATOR

The Performance Calculator is based on the distribution of Ten Percent (10%) of the gross sales revenues, to REVPAC BOND Holders. This 10% yield is known as a "DADDY" – *Dime-A-Dollar Dividend Yield*".

The DADDY provides the REVPAC BOND Holder with an easy-to-follow formula with which to compute and project Returns-on-Investment (ROI).

For Instance: If a Retail Franchise Outlet (using the Burger King Brand example, costing $250,000 – employed in this Pro Forma) sells 25 meals per hour at $10 each – the Franchise Outlet will sell 250 meals, during the course of a 10-hour weekday operation – with total sales revenues of $2,500 per day. The REVPAC BOND holders receive $250 each day in DADDYs.

The Franchise Outlet ROI Performance is calculated, in Sales Revenue Variables, on the following basis:

MINIMAL
Daily Gross Sales Receipts equal to 1% of Franchise Cost:

DAY	MONTH	YEAR	AVERAGE SALES	BOND Holders ROI
$2,500 Weekday				
$3,000 Weekend	$ 80,000	$1,000,000	25 Meals per hour	16% per Annum

MEDIAN
Daily Gross Sales Receipts equal to 1.4% of Franchise Cost:

DAY	MONTH	YEAR	AVERAGE SALES	BOND Holders ROI
$3,500 Weekday				
$4,200 Weekend	$ 112,000	$1,350,000	35 Meals per hour	21.5% per Annum

OPTIMAL
Daily Gross Sales Receipts equal to 1.8% of Franchise Cost:

DAY	MONTH	YEAR	AVERAGE SALES	BOND Holders ROI
$4,500 Weekday				
$5,500 Weekend	$ 145,000	$1,700,000	45 Meals per hour	27% per Annum

The MINIMAL Variable represents GUARANTEED Sales Performance for the Franchise Outlet. The Full Redemption Guaranty, attached to the REVPAC BOND warrants that average daily sales will be equal to or greater than 1% of the Cost of the Franchise. If average daily sales receipts fall below this "floor" – the Integrated Risk Insurance Wrap pays the shortfall.

SECTION 1.0
SUMMARY OF INTENTS AND PURPOSE

The REVPAC BOND CAPITAL THEORY ... is a new Investment-Funding strategy aimed at the global Venture Capital marketplace.

The "nexus" of the REVPAC THEORY centers around the "annexing" (apportioning) of future gross revenue entitlements of select emerging business ventures for the benefit of Investment Capital and Risk Insurance Interests that underwrite the funding of those Business Ventures.

The "REVPAC" strategy is facilitated via a unique and proprietary series of Financial Products and Funding Programs - spearheaded by the new and revolutionary REVENUE PARTICIPATION CAPITAL (REVPAC) Financial Instrument.

The REVPAC enables Investors to financially participate within the lucrative high-stakes opportunities of Venture Capital without risk of Investment Principal. In effect: the proprietary REVPAC Financial Products (ANNUITIES AND FUNDS) - denominated in REVPAC BONDS - combine the best of what risk-insurance underwriting has to offer with the best of what Venture Capital Investment Banking should be all about - the minimizing of risk - the maximizing of potential reward - and the surety of fiscal fiduciary integrity and accountability for the Investment.

A number of "stand-alone" Investment benefits - above-and-beyond the gross revenue participation feature - accompany the REVPAC Investment Products ... such as - (a) "Real-Time Revenue Yields that are digitally streamed from the Point-of-Sale (P.O.S.) to the REVPAC Investors' Smart Cards;(b) Minimum Fixed Income Guaranty of 14% p.a. and; (c) re-investment programs for Revenue Yields that offer 200% R.O.I., in 5 Years (Rule of 52) and 300% R.O.I., in 7 Years (Rule of 73).

The global sponsor of the REVPAC Revenue Capital Theory is an alliance of Risk Insurance and Investment Banking Underwriters - associated under the organization name of REVPAC BOND RE-INSURANCE & FUNDING ALLIANCE. The Alliance, in search of the ideal and universal Investment Products through which to launch the global premiere of the REVPAC BOND CAPITAL THEORY and its REVPAVC BOND Financial Instrument - has determined that the solution rests in a series of Investment Products whose underlying business ventures (enterprises) have both: extraordinary yield potential and multicultural "universal" appeal.

The "universal enterprise" selected as the touchstone, upon which the Alliance intends to emerge the REVPAC BOND CAPITAL THEORY into the world's capital markets, is the Retail Franchise Point-of-Sale Enterprise.

REVPAC BOND denominated Investment Products, organized as Closed-End-Funds and Annuities will fund U.S. and Non-U.S. Franchise Brands that are both new /or/ well-known, within regional markets that have not yet expanded into the global marketplace.

Subsequent to securing a foothold for the REVPAC Investment Products in the International Capital markets - through the debut of the Franchise Brands – the Alliance intends to develop the REVPAC Investment Products for a variety of diversified business sectors that will serve to promulgate expansion and process the projected accelerated demand of emerging business ventures seeking funding through the REVPAC BOND CAPITAL THEORY.

This Economic Package is developed in furtherance of the mission of the Alliance and in support of the economic "soundness" of the REVPAC BOND CAPITAL THEORY.

SECTION 2.0

REVPAC YIELD PERFORMANCE CALCULATOR

ANNUAL FINANCIAL PRO FORMA STATEMENT

Business Venture - Single Franchise

This Calculator performs the all-important function of illustrating the "Micro- Economics of the REVPAC BOND CAPITAL THEORY" - through the example of how an emerging small-business venture (funded via the REVPAC BOND Financial Instrument) proposes to administer gross (sales) revenues.

The "selected" Business Enterprise for this Calculator is a Retail Franchise Point-of-Sale Outlet - *Imagine: a Burger King, Domino's Pizza, 7 Eleven, etc.* The "Franchise Enterprise" is an Ideal Business Model - through which attributes of the REVPAC BOND CAPITAL THEORY can be brought to light...for evaluation by serious examiners.

The Franchise Enterprise meets the requisite fundamental parameters for REVPAC BOND Funding. These parameters include: (a) Minimum Gross-Net-Margin Requirement of 35%; (b) Expectation of Sales Revenues within One Year of Funding; (c) Proprietary Product or Service that is protected by Intellectual Property claims and; (d) Niche Market - supported by accredited market study - projecting highly- favorable conditions for securing near-term and extraordinary market-share of target consumer patronage.

The Pro Forma Financial Statement contains Variable Sales Revenue Volume Scenarios - between $2,500 / Day and $5,000 / Day. This range is well within the present-day scope of most Retail Franchise Outlets.

The "selected" capital investment level - funding the Franchise Outlet is $250,000. This is the amount to be funded via the REVPAC BOND Investors. Note: the Variable Sales Revenue Volume Scenarios represent a range between One Percent (1%) of the total funding ($2,500 / Day divided by the $250,000 investment) and Two Percent (2%) of the total funding...This is an integral component (relation between gross sales revenues and Capital Investment) which will be revisited at the End of this Report in the section entitled "IPEG - Investment Performance Index of the REVPAC BOND CAPITAL Theory."

FINANCIAL PRO FORMA OPERATING STATEMENT - ANNUAL REVENUE BREAKDOWN FOR SINGLE FRANCHISE OPERATION

This Forward Projection Calculator is based on a single Franchise Point-of-Sale with an Original Cost of $250,000 - experiencing variable revenue volume scenarios. The objective of this Pro Forma is to serve as a Forward Projection of the feasibility of funding Franchise Ventures - via the REVPAC BOND STANDARD.

	MINIMAL PERFORMANCE (1)		MEDIAN PERFORMANCE		OPTIMAL PERFORMANCE	
	$2,500 / Day	$3,000 / Day	$3,500 / Day	$4,000 / Day	$4,500 / Day	$5,000 / Day
	$1,000,000 Year	$1,175,000 Year	$1,350,000 Year	$1,525,000 Year	$1,700,000 Year	$1,875,000 Year
INCOMING						
Annual Gross Revenues	$1,000,000	$1,175,000	$1,350,000	$1,525,000	$1,700,000	$1,875,000
OUTGOING						
Cost of Sale	400,000 (40%)	470,000	540,000	610,000	680,000	750,000
Cost of Operation (2)	250,000 (25%)	273,750 (23%)	297,500 (22%)	321,250 (21%)	345,000(20%)	368,750(19%)
Franchise & Capital Expenditures (4)	150,000 (15%)	176,250	202,500	228,750	255,000	281,250
REVPAC Yields	100,000 (10%)	117,500	135,000	152,500	170,000	187,500
Total Outgoing	$900,000	$1,037,500	$1,175,000	$1,312,500	$1,450,000	$1,587,500
Net Income (3)	$100,000 (10)%	$137,500 (12%)	$175,000 (13%)	$212,500 (14%)	$250,000 (15%)	$287,500 (16%)

Notes: (1) **Franchise Performance** appears as six variables. Each variable represents selected Revenue Volumes that are based on the Operation Performance of the Franchise. The nomenclature that categorizes the variables (MINIMAL PERFORMANCE – MEDIAN PERFORMANCE – OPTIMAL PERFORMANCE) represents the Forward Potential Revenues that are feasible for the Franchise Point-of-Sales under the following Market conditions: MINIMAL PERFORMANCE - Minimum Acceptable Sales to defray the costs of an on-going Operation (This variable represents the BREAKEVEN POINT for REVPAC Yields to offset Risk Insurance Coverage and Requisite Investor Yields to sustain Investor continued participation; MEDIUM PERFORMANCE - Average expected Sales for demographic location of Franchise Point-of-Sale under normal market conditions and; OPTIMAL PERFORMANCE - Best-Case-Scenario for Franchise Point-of-Sale under excellent market conditions. *Generally "OPTIMAL" represents above 65% sales performance of identical /or/ similar store Point-of-Sale comparables.*

The Revenue Volumes are computed as follows: **Daily Average** is "Weekday Sales Receipts" that are projected for 250 days. "Weekend and Holiday Sales Receipts" are generally 40% higher than Weekday Sales Receipts and projected for 115 days. The aggregate is often a "rounding-off" of the projected sales revenue volume. Example: $2,500 / Day - is computed for 250 days and added to $3,500 / Day (Weekends) for 115 days. The aggregate of $1,000,000 is a "rounding -off" of the TOTAL ANNUAL GROSS of $1,027,500.

(2) **Cost of Operation** is a "flat" budget-allocation of $250,000 per year and increases after $1,000,000 (sales) by $23,750 for each $175,0000 increase in annual gross revenues.

(3) **NET INCOME** is 10% for first $1,000,000 (Sales) and increases by $37,500 for each $175,000 (annual gross).
Please notice: (Notes 2 and 3) the combined aggregate always equal 35% of gross revenues.

(4) **Franchise & Capital Expenditures** are "Furniture, Fixtures and Extras" for maintaining Franchise in highly competitive/State-of=the-art condition. Expenditures also are allocated to expenditures, requisite to expanding the Franchise's Points-of-Sale throughout the Licensed Territory of the Franchise.

Actuarial Analysis

SECTION 3.0

REVPAC INVESTOR R.O.I. CALCULATOR
7-YEAR REVPAC BOND YIELD PRO FORMA STATEMENT

This Calculator is intended to introduce the fundamental "yielding" features of the REVPAC BOND CAPITAL THEORY as it applies to the REVPAC BOND INVESTOR.

The Calculator is based on the revenues of a Single Franchise Venture - *as presented in Section 2.0 of this Report.*

The Revenue Volume for each scenario is based on SIX Years of revenue- producing-operations. The first year of the SEVEN Year total Is computed with NO operational revenues - as the first year of the Venture is the "build-out"/ "ramp-up" period of a "start-up" business.

The two classifications of REVPAC Revenue Investment Products featured in the Calculator are the Investment Vehicles of the "ANNUITY" and the "FUND". These are the primary Investment products deployed in "bundling" Business Ventures (Franchise Models) that are funded via the REVPAC BOND CAPITAL THEORY.

The accompanying Notes - appearing in the Calculator - are integral to the understanding and application of the Investor R.O.I. Calculator.

REVPAC BOND INVESTOR - RETURN-OF-INVESTMENT CALCULATOR
7-YEAR REVENUE REVPAC YIELD PRO FORMA - SINGLE FRANCHISE VENTURE (VARIABLE REVENUE VOLUME)

This Forward Projection Calculator is based on a Single Franchise P.O.S. with an Original Cost of $250,000. The Pro-Forma/Calculator serves as a Forecast Feasibility Statement of potential Returns-of-Investment (ROI) for Investors in both Annuity and Fund Investment Products - funding Revenue REVPAC BOND Franchise Ventures.

	MINIMAL PERFORMANCE (1)				MEDIAN PERFORMANCE				OPTIMAL PERFORMANCE			
	$2,500 / Day		$3,000 / Day		$3,500 / Day		$4,000 / Day		$4,500 / Day		$5,000 / Day	
	$1,000,000 Year		$1,175,000 Year		$1,350,000 Year		$1,525,000 Year		$1,700,000 Year		$1,825,000 Year	
	Annuity	Fund	Annuity	Fund	Annuity	Fund	Annuity	Fund	Annuity	Fund	Annuity	Fund
REVPAC Revenue Yield (2)	$275,000	$390,000	$317,000	$458,250	$359,000	$526,500	$401,000	$594,750	$443,000	$663,000	$486,000	$731,250
REVPAC Windfall Yield (3)												
Equity Divestiture	80,000	130,000	94,000	152,750	108,000	175,000	122,000	198,250	136,000	221,000	150,000	243,750
Insurance Rebate	30,000		35,000		40,000		45,000		50,000		55,000	
Redemption	250,000	250,000	250,000	250,000	250,000	250,000	250,000	250,000	250,000	250,000	250,000	250,000
Total Windfall	360,000	380,000	379,000	402,750	398,000	425,500	417,000	448,250	436,000	471,000	455,000	493,000
Total Yield	$635,000	$770,000	$696,000	$861,000	$757,00	$952,000	$818,000	$1,043,000	$879,000	$1,134,000	$941,000	$1,225,000
R.O.I. (4)	254%	308%	278%	344%	303%	381%	327%	417%	352%	454%	376%	490%
Accumulated (5) Compounded Yield Re-Investment Plan	$750,000		$850,000		$1,000,000		$1,125,000		$1,250,000		$1,375,000	
Adjusted R.O.I.	300%		350%		400%		450%		500%		550%	

Notes: Appear on Addendum to this Statement

Notes to REVPAC BOND Investor — Return-of-Investment Calculator

(1) **Franchise Performance** appears as six variables. Each variable represents selected Revenue Volumes that are based on the Operation Performance of the Franchise. The nomenclature that categorizes the variables (MINIMAL PERFORMANCE – MEDIAN PERFORMANCE – OPTIMAL PERFORMANCE) represents the Forward Potential Revenues that are feasible for the Franchise Point-of-Sales under the following Market conditions: MINIMAL PERFORMANCE - Minimum Acceptable Sales to defray the costs of an on-going Operation (This variable represents the BREAKEVEN POINT for REVPAC Yields to offset Risk Insurance Coverage and Requisite Investor Yields to sustain Investor continued participation; MEDIUM PERFORMANCE - Average expected Sales for demographic location of Franchise Point-of-Sale under normal market conditions and; OPTIMAL PERFORMANCE - Best-Case-Scenario for Franchise Point-of-Sale under excellent market conditions. *Generally "OPTIMAL" represents above 65% sales performance of identical /or/ similar store Point-of-Sale comparables.*

The Revenue Volumes are computed as follows: **Daily Average** is "Weekday Sales Receipts" that are projected for 250 days. "Weekend and Holiday Sales Receipts" are generally 40% higher than Weekday Sales Receipts and projected for 115 days. The aggregate is often a "rounding-off" of the projected sales revenue volume. Example: $2,500 / Day - is computed for 250 days and added to $3,500 / Day (Weekends) for 115 days. The aggregate of $1,000,000 is a "rounding -off" of the TOTAL ANNUAL GROSS of $1,027,500.

(2) **REVPAC Revenue Yield** based on six (6) years of Average Annual Franchise Revenues - less apportioned Risk Insurance Premium payment. The Yields are computed with the following deductions that pays for the Risk Insurance Premiums: ANNUITY - 60% / FUND - 35% of the Average Annual REVPAC Full-Risk (no Risk Insurance) Yields. Example: REVPAC Full-Risk Investor Yield is 10% of Franchise Gross Revenues, REVPAC BOND Investor Yield is 6.5% of Franchise Gross Revenues (3.5% is allocated to Risk Insurance Coverage). REVPAC BOND ANNUITY Investor Yield is 4% of Franchise Gross Revenues (6% is allocated to Risk Insurance Coverage) and FUND Investor Yield is 6.5% of Franchise Gross Revenues (3.5% is allocated to Risk Insurance Coverage).

(3) **Windfall Yield** is cumulative sum of: (a) Equity Divestiture - sum of the Annual Revenue Yields for the two highest years; (b) Insurance Rebate - 10% of Original Investment (added-on as Bonus Enhancement Incentive Payment) computed on the basis of adding ALL Revenue Yields and re-investing annual yields(compounding the yields) and; (c) Redemption - 100% Return of Invested Capital.

(4) **R.0.I. (Return-of-Investment)** is computed on basis of comparing Original Investment ($250,000) to Total Yields. Sample: $2,500 / Day is computed as follows: Total Yields (ANNUITY - $635,000 / FUND - $770,000) ... which is 254% R.0.I. of the Original Investment of $250,000 for the ANNUITY (R.0.I. for the FUND is 308%).

(5) **Accumulated Compounded Yield Re-Investment Plan.** The Investor may elect to re-invest Revenue Yields (applicable *ONLY* to ANNUITY Investors) - in which event, the Revenue Yields are "re-invested" into successive new issues of: Franchise Revenue REVPAC BONDS. The re-investment frequency is performed on a monthly basis. The Accumulated Compounded Yield Re-Investment Plan represents the accumulated value of $250,000 - applied to varying Franchise Performance Yields that are re-invested and compounded monthly in successive Franchise Ventures that yield the MINIMAL PERFORMANCE of $2,500 / Day (16% p.a.). Example: $3,500 / Day yields $359,000 (ANNUITY) in annual Revenue Yields. These Revenue Yields - re-invested and compounded on a monthly basis (re-invested into Franchise Ventures that yield MINIMAL PERFORMANCE of $2,500 / Day (16% p.a.) - result in a 7-Year total of $1,000,000 ... This represents a 400% Return-of-Investment (R.0.I.) on $250,000 Invested Capital.

SECTION 4.0

REVPAC BOND FUNDED BUSINESS VENTURE OWNER-OPERATOR (NGO) CALCULATOR

7-YEAR REVENUE & EQUITY YIELD PRO FORMA STATEMENT

Business Venture - Single Franchise

The Forward Projection Calculator is intended for Owner-Operators (*i.e.* Non-Governmental Organizations N.G.O.) of Business Ventures - funded via the REVPAC BOND CAPITAL THEORY.

The Calculator deploys a Single Franchise Venture - based on the identical financial assumptions as the afore-presented Calculators of this Report.

The "ANNUITY" Investment Vehicle is the only Investment Product featured in the Owner-Operator Calculator - due to the stringent requisites of the Risk Insurance parameters for REVPAC BOND OWNER-OPERATOR (NGO) Risk Insurance Underwriting within the REVPAC BOND CAPITAL THEORY. All other Investment Products (including "FUND" Products) are excluded from Investment Risk Insurance Coverage, in conjunction with Owner-Operator Programs.

This Pro Forma Statement assumes that 100% of the funding proceeds for the Business Venture are derived via the Owner-Operator. This Calculator Is especially adaptable for Non-Governmental-Organizations (NGOs) deploying the REVPAC BOND CAPITAL THEORY for Fund Raising Campaigns and Social Entrepreneur programs.

7-YEAR OWNER-OPERATOR (NGO) PRO FORMA - SINGLE FRANCHISE (VARIABLE REVENUE VOLUME)
This Forward Projection Calculator is based on an Owner-Operator /and/ 100% Investor (REVPAC BOND Holders) of a Single Franchise with an Original Cost of $250,000.

	MINIMAL PERFORMANCE (1)		MEDIAN PERFORMANCE		OPTIMAL PERFORMANCE	
	$2,500 / Day	$3,000 / Day	$3,500 / Day	$4,000 / Day	$4,500 / Day	$5,000 / Day
	$1,000,000 YEAR	$1,175,000 YEAR	$1,350,000 YEAR	$1,525,000 YEAR	$1,700,000 YEAR	$1,875,000 Year
Revenues						
Revenue Yield REVPAC (1)	$275,000	$317,000	$359,000	$401,000	$443,000	$486,000
Windfall Yield REVPAC (2)	360,000	379,000	398,000	417,000	436,000	455,000
Operations (NET) (3)	600,000	825,000	1,050,000	1,275,000	1,500,000	1,725,000
Total Revenues	$1,235,000	$1,521,000	$1,807,000	$2,093,000	$2,379,000	$2,666,000
R.O.I.	495% ROI	608% ROI	723% ROI	837% ROI	952% ROI	1,067% ROI
EQUITY						
Market Value (4)	$1,000,000	$1,250,000	$1,550,000	$1,825,000	$2,100,000	$2,375,000
LIABILITY						
80% Buy-Out (5)	(187,500)	(187,500)	(175,000)	(162,500)	(150,000)	(137,000)
20% Purchase (6)	(200,000)	(255,000)	(310,000)	(365,000)	(420,000)	(475,000)
100% Liability	(387,500)	(412,400)	(485,000)	(497,500)	(570,000)	(612,500)
NET EQUITY	$612,500	$863,000	$1,065,000	$1,328,000	$1,530,000	$1,762,500
Total Revenues & EQUITY	$1,847,500	$2,384,000	$2,872,000	$3,421,500	$3,909,000	$4,428,500
R.O.I.(7)	740% ROI	953% ROI	1,149% ROI	1,368% ROI	1,564% ROI	1,771% ROI
Annual Avg. ROI	106% p.a.	136% p.a.	164% p.a.	195% p.a.	223% p.a.	252% p.a.

Notes to 7-YEAR OWNER-OPERATOR (NGO) PRO FORMA:

(1) **Revenue Yield (REVPAC)** is based en 6 Years of Average Revenues and 1 Year of MINIMAL GUARATY PAYMENT (This is First Year of Operation). Example: $2,500 / Day is computed with 6 Years of $40,000 p.a. (40% of $100,000 REVPAC Revenue) and 1 Year of $35,000 (Risk Insured - Minimal Guaranty Payment).

(2) **Windfall Yield (REVPAC)** is based on (a) Insurance Rebate - equal to 10% Enhancement of Invested Capital formula; (b) Redemption 100% Return of Invested Capital and (c) Equity Divestiture which is based on BUY-OUT Formula for 80% of the equity of the Franchise PLUS Outright Purchase of 20% of the equity of the Franchise. BUY-OUT and Outright Purchase formulas are described in REVPAC BOND Certificate.

(3) **Windfall Yield (REVPAC)** is based on (a) Insurance Rebate - equal to 10% Enhancement of Invested Capital formula; (b) Redemption 100% Return of Invested Capital and (c) Equity Divestiture which is based on BUY-OUT Formula for 80% of the equity of the Franchise PLUS Outright Purchase of 20% of the equity of the Franchise. BUY-OUT and Outright Purchase formulas are described in REVPAC BOND Certificate.

(4) **Operations (NET)** is based on ANNUAL REVENUE VOLUME for 6 Years. Year One is deemed as "Build-out and Ramp-up Period" which is credited with ZERO Revenues for purpose of this Pro Forma.

(4) **Equity (Market Value)** is based on Average Annual Operations (NET) PLUS REVPAC BOND REVENUE (Revenue Participation apportionment paid to REVPAC BOND Holders and their Risk Insurance Underwriter. The Average Annual Aggregate of Operations (NET) and REVPAC BOND REVENUE is multiplied by a factor of FIVE (5) to compute the "Equity Market Value" for the Franchise.

(5) **80% Buy-Out** is based on the Original Cost of the Franchise that is discounted, based on a BUY-OUT SCHEDULE that is described in the MASTER FRANCHISE LICENSE Document Package (included as part of the REVPAC BOND Registration). This BUY-OUT SCHEDULE permits the Owner-Operator to purchase 80% of the Equity of the Franchise at a Price "that is discounted in tandem with the ability and Performance of the Owner-Operator to generate Gross Revenues in connection with the Operation of the Franchise.

(6) **20% Purchase** is based on a Price that is computed as Twenty Percent (20%) of the Equity Market Value of the Franchise. Example: $2,500 / Day results in an Equity Market Value of $1,000,000 (the aggregate of Operations NET and REVPAC BOND YIELDS is $200,000 - multiplied by a Factor of Five)... the 20% Purchase Price is thusly computed as $200,000.

(7) **R.O.I. (Return-of-Investment)** is based on the Original Investment of $250,000, as compared to the Gross Yield(s). Example: $2,500 / Day is computed as follows: TOTAL REVENUES of $1,235,000 is 495% - *almost Five times the multiple of the Original Investment of $250,000.* TOTAL REVENUES & EQUITY of $1,847,500 is 740% - *almost Eight and one-half times the multiple of the Original Investment of $250,000.* ANNUAL AVERAGE R.O.I. OF 106% is the average Return-of-Investment each year over the Seven Year term - *is slightly greater than the Original Investment of $250,000.*

SECTION 5.0

INVESTMENT RISK INSURANCE PERFORMANCE CALCULATOR

FULL TERM (7-YEAR) FINANCIAL PRO FORMA STATEMENT

Business Venture - Single Franchise

This Calculator is intended for the use of Insurance Actuaries in the design and structure of Investment Risk Insurance Underwritings of REVPAC BOND funded Business Ventures.

The Calculator deploys a Single Franchise Model Venture - based on the identical financial assumptions as the afore-presented Calculators of this Report.

REVPAC BOND RISK INSURANCE UNDERWRITER

RISK INSURANCE PERFORMANCE CALCULATOR – UNDERWRITTEN RISK <u>vs</u> NET PREMIIUMS – *SINGLE FRANCHISE VENTURE* (VARIABLE REVENUE VOLUME)

This Forward Projection Calculator serves as a Forecast Feasibility Statement of potential Net Revenues for- the Risk Insurance Underwriter of REVPAC BOND funded Franchise Ventures. The Pro-Forma Calculator is based on a Single Franchise (P.O.S. Location) with an Original Cost of $250,000 - experiencing variable revenue volume scenarios (MINIMAL PERFORMANCE / MEDIAN PERFORMANCE / OPTIMAL PERFORMANCE). The objective of this Pro Forma is to serve as a Forward Projection of the feasibility of underwriting Franchise Ventures - via the REVPAC CAPITAL STANDARD (including its REVPAC BOND Financial Instrument - for Risk Insurance Underwriters for both Annuity and Fund Investment Products /with an emphasis on RISK to REWARD Ratios for the Underwriter.

	MINIMAL PERFORMANCE (1)				MEDIAN PERFORMANCE				OPTIMAL PERFORMANCE			
	$2,500 / Day		$3,000 / Day		$3,500 / Day		$4,000 / Day		$4,500 / Day		$5,000 / Day	
	$1,000,000 Year		$1,175,000 Year		$1,350,000 Year		$1,525,000 Year		$1,700,000 Year		$1,825,000 Year	
	Annuity	Fund	Annuity	Fund	Annuity	Fund	Annuity	Fund	Annuity	Fund	Annuity	Fund
INCOMING												
REVPAC Revenue Yield (1)	$325,000	$210,000	$388,000	$246,750	$451,000	$283,500	$514,000	$320,250	$577,000	$357,000	$640,000	$393,750
REVPAC Windfall Equity Buy-Out (2)	187,500	187,500	187,500	187,500	175,000	175,000	162,500	162,500	150,000	150,000	137,500	137,500
Equity Purchase	200,000	200,000	255,000	255,000	310,000	310,000	365,000	365,000	420,000	420,000	475,000	475,000
Total INCOMING (3)	712,500	597,500	835,500	689,250	936,000	768,500	1,041,500	847,750	1,147,000	927,000	1,252,500	1,006,250
OUTGOING												
Equity Divestiture (4)	80,000	130,000	94,000	152,750	108,000	175,500	122,000	198,250	136,000	221,000	150,000	243,750
Insurance Rebate (5)	30,000		35,000		40,000		45,000		50,000		55,000	
Redemption (6)	250,000	250,000	250,000	250,000	250,000	250,000	250,000	250,000	250,000	250,000	250,000	250,000
Total OUTGOING	360,000	380,000	379,000	402,750	398,000	425,000	417,000	448,000	436,000	471,000	455,000	493,750
Net Income	$352,500	$217,500	$451,500	$286,600	$538,000	$343,000	$624,500	$399,500	$711,000	$456,000	$797,500	$512,500

Notes to REVPAC BOND Risk Insurance **Underwriter - Risk Insurance Performance Calculator**

(1) **Revenue Yield** - The Revenue Yield from the franchise Gross Sales Receipts is Ten Percent (10%) of the Gross Revenues (as cited for computation purposes in this Calculator. The Risk Insurance Underwriter is apportioned (as a "Premium" payment) Sixty Percent (60%) of the Revenue Yield for ANNUITY Insurance Coverage and Thirty-Five Percent (35%) for FUND Insurance Coverage. In effect: the Risk Insurance Underwriter is allocated Six Percent (6%) of ALL Franchise Gross Sales Receipts and Three-and-0ne-Half Percent (3.5%) of ALL Franchise Gross Sales Receipts via ANNUTIY REVPAC BOND Ventures and FUND REVPAC BOND Ventures, respectively. These Premium Payments are denoted as "INCOMING" Revenue Yields for purposes of this Calculator. Revenue Yield Totals are from 6 years of Franchise operations.

(2) **Equity Buy-Out and Equity Purchase -** The Equity Buy-Out is the sale of 80% of the Equity of the Franchise Points-Sale location.
The BUY-OUT SCHEDULE OF PRICING is included in the MASTER FRANCHISE LICENSE Document Package (that is included in and made part of the REVPAC BOND Registration).. This BUY-OUT SCHEDULE permits the Owner-Operator to purchase 80% of the Equity of the Franchise at a Price that is discounted in tandem with the ability and Performance of the Owner-Operator to generate Gross Sales Revenues in connection with the Operation of the Franchise. The Equity Purchase is the sale of the (remaining) 20% of the Equity of the Franchise... The Purchase Price is based on 20% of the "Market Value" of the Franchise. "Market Value" is determined by the average of the two greatest Annual Revenue Yields to REVPAC BOND Holders and Insurance Underwriters (10% of gross sales revenues) added to the Net Revenues from the operation of the Franchise and Multiplied by a Factor of Five (5).

The proceeds from the Equity Buy-Out and Equity Purchase accrue to the benefit of the Risk Insurance Underwriters (as Premium Payment) The Risk Insurance Underwriter is the lien-holder of the Equity (as Collateral) in return for Redemption Guaranty and Equity Divestiture Guaranty.

(3) **TOTAL INCOMING** - Aggregate of all Incoming Revenues are accounted for as "Premium" payments and residuals - in return for Risk Insurance Coverage provided to REVPAC BOND Holders.

(4) **Equity Divestiture** - The full amount of the GUARANTY to the REVPAC BOND Holders for the Equity Buy-Out and Equity Purchase (designated as "Equity Divestiture") of 100% ownership right, title and interest in the Franchise Venture is the amount equivalent to the sum of the two-highest yielding years for REVPAC BOND Yields - received by the REVPAC BOND Holders during the 7-Year term.

(5) **Insurance Rebate** - (also known as 10% Enhancement Bonus) is applicable to ANNUITY Investors ONLY. The amount payable is equivalent to Ten Percent (10%) of the aggregate Revenue Yield distributions. In the event the ANNUITY Investor has elected the "Compounded Yield Re-Investment Plan" - the Insurance Rebate includes the REVPAC BOND Yields plus the "Compounded Yields that would have been realized via the Re-Investment Plan.

(6) **Redemption** - 100% Return of Invested Capital.

(7) **Insurance liability** is constant throughout ALL Franchise Performance (Variable) computations. The Risk Insurance GUARANTY covers - ANNUITY: Redemption of $250,000 PLUS Fixed Income (14% p.a.) of $245,000 - for an aggregate liability of $495,000 /AND/ FUND: Redemption of $250,000.

This page intentionally left blank.

SECTION 6.0

COMPOSITE INVESTMENT-RISK-UNDERWRITING ACTUARIAL CALCULATOR

FULL TERM (7 YEAR) RISK EVALUATION STATEMENT
$20 Million / Multiple-Franchise Funding Package

This Calculator is a companion to the INVESTMENT RISK INSURANCE PERFORMANCE CALCULATOR ... and represents MINIMAL-MEDIAN-OPTIMAL Expectations of Risk-Reward Ratios.

The Underwriting of Investment Risk - in connection with REVPAC BOND funding of Business Ventures (Franchise Models) is projected to be effectuated in "tranches" of (minimal) $20,000,000 each - consisting of multiple-ventures "bundled" into "risk packages". The Calculator is based on 80 franchises funded at an average of $250,000 each for an aggregate $20 Million.

The 7-Year Projection/Evaluation Statement is intended to present various Performance Pro Forma Statements from which Actuaries may evaluate and calculate risk insurance/annuity premiums, reserves and dividends in association with REVPAC BOND Financial Product Underwritings.

6.1 ANNUITY - MINIMAL EXPECTATION

7-YEAR REVENUE RIDR RISK-INSURANCE ACTUARIAL CALCULATOR (MINIMAL EXPECTATION) (1)

This Actuarial Calculator is a Forward Projection Pro Forma for the performance of 80 Franchises (each costing an average of $250,000) funded via an Underwriting of REVPAC BONDS that are wrapped into a $20 Million Funding Package, Each Franchise Is funded via an ANNUITY that provides a Full Redemption Guaranty (Risk Insurance coverage) for the Investment Principal ($250,000 each Franchise) and a Fixed Income Minimum Yield (14-% on the Investment Principal - $35,000 - per Franchise/per year) for an aggregate Risk Insurance Liability of $495,000 per Franchise. The following Performances of the Franchises within the $20 Million Funding Package are conservative Forward Estimates presented for purposes of Actuarial Evaluation of Risk.

Number of Franchises	% of Total Franchise Pkg.	Franchises Revenue Performance Category	Revenue Volume	Projected Risk Policy Value for Rev. Performance Category	Total Value of Risk Coverage
24	30%	TOTAL LOSS	-0-	($495,000) (2)	($11,880,000)
24	30%	MINIMAL (1)	$2,500/Day	$352,500	$ 8,460,000
16	20%	MINIMAL (2)	$3,000/Day	451,500	7,224,000
8	10%	MEDIAN (1)	$3,500/Day	538,000	4,304,000
4	5%	MEDIAN (2)	$4,000/Day	624,500	2,498,000
2	2.5%	OPTIMAL (1)	$4,500/Day	711,000	1,422,000
2	2.5%	OPTIMAL (2)	$5,000/Day	797,500	1,595,000
80 Franchises	100 %				$13,623,000

Notes: (1) The General Rule in Venture Capital Funding for Success-Failure Ratio Calculation is the 2-6-2 Rule. This generally accepted formula is applied in Forward Projections for Financial Feasibility Reports. The Rule's significance is that 2 of 10 Investments will lose money / 6 of 10 Investments will "Breakeven" /and earn "minimal returns" / 2 of 10 Investments will earn significant Returns-on-Investment.

The projection within this 7-Year Actuarial Calculator exercises greater caution in forecasting performance of the Franchise Investments. The formula deployed herein is 3-5-2.

(2) The assumed liability for the Risk Insurer for the $20 Million Investment Package is $39.6 Million. In the event all franchises incurred "Total Loss" - this is the amount that the Insurer is obligated to "pay-out". The assumed liability is based on Risk Insurance Coverage of the Principal Investment ($250,000) and Fixed Income Guaranty (14% of Principal Investment for 7 years/or/ $245,000)...an aggregate Liability of $495,000/Franchise.

6.2 ANNUITY - MEDIAN EXPECTATION

7-YEAR REVPAC BOND RISK-INSURANCE ACTUARIAL CALCULATOR (MEDIAN EXPECTATION) (1)

This Actuarial Calculator is a Forward projection Pro Forma for the performance of 80 Franchises (each costing an average of $250,000) funded via an Underwriting of REVPAC BONDS that are wrapped into a $20 Million Funding Package. Each franchise is funded via an ANNUITY that provides a Full Redemption Guaranty (Risk Insurance coverage) for the Investment Principal ($250,000 each Franchise) and a Fixed Income Minimum Yield (14% on the Investment Principal - $35,000 - per Franchise/per year) for an aggregate Risk Insurance Liability of $495,000 per Franchise. The following Performances of the Franchises within the $20 Million Funding Package are conservative Forward Estimates presented for purposes of Actuarial Evaluation of Risk.

Number of Franchises	% of Total Funding Pkg.	Franchise Revenue Performance Category	Revenue Volume	Projected Risk Policy Value for Rev. Performance Category	Total Value of Risk Category
16	20%	TOTAL LOSS	-0-	($495,000) (2)	($7,920,000)
24	30%	MINIMAL (1)	$2;500/Day	$352,500	$8,460,000
24	30%	MINIMAL (2)	$3,000/Day	451,500	10,824,000
8	10%	MEDIAN (1)	$3,500/Day	538,000	4,304,000
4	5%	MEDIAN (2)	$4,000/Day	624,500	2,498,000
2	2.5%	OPTIMAL (1)	$4,500/Day	711,000	1,422,000
2	2.5%	OPTIMAL (2)	$5,000/Day	797,500	1,595,000
80 Franchises	100 %				$21,183,000

Notes: (1) The General Rule in Venture Capital Funding for Success-Failure Ratio Calculation is the 2-6-2 Rule. This generally accepted formula is applied in Forward Projections for Financial Feasibility Reports. The Rule's significance is that 2 of 10 Investments will lose money / 6 of 10 Investments will "Breakeven" /and earn "minimal returns" / 2 of 10 Investments will earn significant Returns-on-Investment.

The projection within this 7-Year Actuarial Calculator (MEDIAN EXPECTATION) deploys the 2-6-2 Rule.

(2) The assumed liability for the Risk Insurer for the $20 Million Investment Package is $39.6 Million. In the event all franchises incurred "Total Loss" - this is the amount that the Insurer is obligated to "pay-out". The assumed liability is based on Risk Insurance Coverage of the Principal Investment ($250,000) and Fixed Income Guaranty (14%-of Principal Investment for 7 years /or/ $245,000) ... an aggregate Liability of $495,000/Franchise.

Actuarial Analysis

6.3 ANNUITY - OPTIMAL EXPECTATION

7-YEAR REVENUE RIDR RISK-INSURANCE ACTUARIAL CALCULATOR (OPTIMAL EXPECTATION) (1)

This Actuarial Calculator is a Forward projection Pro Forma for the performance of 80 Franchises (each costing an average of $250,000) funded via an Underwriting of REVPAC BONDS that are wrapped into a $20 Million Funding Package. Each franchise is funded via an ANNUITY that provides a Full Redemption Guaranty (Risk Insurance coverage) for the Investment Principal ($250,000 each Franchise) and a Fixed Income {Minimum -Yield (14% on the Investment Principal - $35,000 - per Franchise/per year) for an aggregate Risk Insurance Liability of $495,000 per Franchise. The following Performances of the Franchises within the $20 Million Funding Package are conservative Forward Estimates presented for purposes of Actuarial Evaluation of Risk.

Number of Franchises	% of Total Funding Pkg.	Franchise Revenue Performance Category	Revenue Volume	Projected Risk Policy Value for Rev. Performance Category	Total Value of Risk Category
16	20%	50% LOSS	-0-	($495,000) (2)	($4,000,000)
20	25%	MINIMAL (1)	$2;500/Day	$352,500	$7,050,000
20	25%	MINIMAL (2)	$3,000/Day	451,000	9,030,000
8	10%	MEDIAN (1)	$3,500/Day	538,000	4,304,000
8	10%	MEDIAN (2)	$4,000/Day	624,500	4,996,000
4	5%	OPTIMAL (1)	$4,500/Day	711,000	3,555,000
4	5%	OPTIMAL (2)	$5,000/Day	797,500	3,987,500
80 Franchises	100%				$28,922,500

Notes: (1) The projection within this 7-Year Actuarial Calculator deploys the formula **2-5-3**. The formula's Significance is that 2 of 10 Investments will lose money / 5 of 10 Investments will "Breakeven" /and earn "minimal returns" / 3 of 10 Investments will earn significant Returns-on-Investment. This formula is the "inverted" of the MINIMAL EXPECTATION (which is formula: 3-5-2).

ALSO The 2-5-3 formula is marginally "higher in expectation" than the General Rule in Venture Capital Funding for Success-Failure Ratio Calculation: the 2-6-2 Rule.

(2) The assumed liability for the Risk Insurer for the $20 Million Investment Package is $39.6 Million. In the event all franchises incurred "Total Loss" - this is the amount that the Insurer is obligated to "pay-out". For purposes of this OPTIMAL EXPECTATION Calculator - the assumption is that the average loss will be 50% of the total assumed liability of the Risk Insurer. This calculator has "rounded-out" the actual loss of $3.96 Million to $4 Million.

6.4 FUND - MINIMAL EXPECTATION

7-YEAR REVPAC BOND RISK-INSURANCE ACTUARIAL CALCULATOR (MINIMAL EXPECTATION) (1)

This Actuarial Calculator is a Forward Projection Pro Forma for the performance of 80 Franchises (each costing an average of $250,000) funded via an Underwriting of REVPAC BONDS that are wrapped into a $20 Million Funding Package. Each franchise is funded via a FUND (which owns investment portfolios denominated in REVPAC BONDS) that provides a Full Redemption Guaranty (Risk Insurance coverage) for the Investment Principal ($250,000 each Franchise). The aggregate Risk Insurance Liability for the Underwriters is $250,000 per Franchise. The following Performances of the Franchises within the $20 Million Funding Package are conservative Forward Estimates presented for purposes of Actuarial Evaluation of Risk.

Number of Franchises	% of Total Funding Pkg.	Franchise Revenue Performance Category	Revenue Volume	Projected Risk Policy Value for Rev. Performance Category	Total Value of Risk Category
24	30%	TOTAL LOSS	-0-	($250,000) (2)	($6,000,000)
24	30%	MINIMAL (1)	$2,500/Day	$217,500	$5,220,000
16	20%	MINIMAL (2)	$3,000/Day	286,500	4,584,000
8	10%	MEDIAN (1)	$3,500/Day	343,000	2,744,000
4	5%	MEDIAN (2)	$4,000/Day	399,500	1,598,000
2	2.5%	OPTIMAL (1)	$4,500/Day	456,000	912,000
2	2.5%	OPTIMAL (2)	$5,000/Day	512,500	1,024,000
80 Franchises	100 %				$10,082,000

Notes: (1) The General Rule in Venture Capital Funding for Success-Failure Ratio Calculation is the 2-6-2 Rule. This generally accepted formula is applied in Forward Projections for Financial Feasibility Reports. The Rule's significance is that 2 of 10 Investments will lose money / 6 of 10 Investments will "Breakeven" /and earn "minimal returns" / 2 of 10 Investments will earn significant Returns-on-Investment.

The projection within this 7-Year Actuarial Calculator exercises greater caution in forecasting performance of the Franchise Investments. The formula deployed herein is 3-5-2.

(2) The assumed liability for the Risk Insurer for the $20 Million Investment Package is $20 Million. In the event all franchises incurred "Total Loss" - this is the amount that the Insurer is obligated to "pay-out". The assumed liability is based on Risk Insurance Coverage of the Principal Investment ($250,000) per Franchise for an aggregate of 80 Franchises.

6.5 FUND - MEDIAN EXPECTATION

7-YEAR REVPAC BOND RISK-INSURANCE ACTUARIAL CALCULATOR (MEDIAN EXPECTATION) (1)

This Actuarial Calculator is a Forward projection Pro Forma for the performance of 80 Franchises (each costing an average of $250,000) funded via an Underwriting of REVPAC BONDS that are wrapped into a $20 Million Funding Package. Each franchise is funded via a . Each franchise is funded via a FUND (which owns investment portfolios denominated in REVPAC BONDS) that provides a Full Redemption Guaranty (Risk Insurance coverage) for the Investment Principal ($250,000 each Franchise). The aggregate Risk Insurance Liability for the Underwriters is $250,000 per Franchise. The following Performances of the Franchises within the $20 Million Funding Package are conservative Forward Estimates presented for purposes of Actuarial Evaluation of Risk.

Number of Franchises	% of Total Funding Pkg.	Franchise Revenue Performance Category	Revenue Volume	Projected Risk Policy Value for Rev. Performance Category	Total Value of Risk Category
16	20%	TOTAL LOSS	-0-	($250,000) (2)	($4,000,000)
24	30%	MINIMAL (1)	$2;500/Day	$217,500	$5,220,000
24	30%	MINIMAL (2)	$3,000/Day	286,500	6,876,000
8	10%	MEDIAN (1)	$3,500/Day	343,000	2,744,000
4	5%	MEDIAN (2)	$4,000/Day	399,500	1,598,000
2	2.5%	OPTIMAL (1)	$4,500/Day	456,000	912,000
2	2.5%	OPTIMAL (2)	$5,000/Day	512,500	1,025,000
80 Franchises	100 %				$14,375,000

Notes: (1) The General Rule In Venture Capital Funding for Success-Failure Ratio Calculation is the 2-6-2 Rule.

This generally accepted formula is applied in Forward Projections for Financial Feasibility Reports. The Rule's significance is that 2 of 10 Investments will lose money / 6 of 10 Investments will "Breakeven" / and earn "minimal returns" / 2 of 10~Investments will earn significant Returns-on Investment.

The projection within this 7-Year Actuarial Calculator (MEDIAM EXPECTATION) deploys the *2-6-2 Rule.*

(2) The assumed liability for the Risk Insurer for the $20 Million Investment Package is $20 *Million.* In the event all franchises incurred "Total Loss" - this is the amount that the Insurer is obligated to "pay-out". The Assumed liability is based on Risk Insurance Coverage of the principal Investment ($250,000) Per Franchise for an aggregate of 80 Franchises.

6.6 FUND - OPTIMAL EXPECTATION

7-IEAR REVENUE RIDR RISK-INSURANCE ACTUARIAL CALCULATOR (OPTIMAL EXPECTATION) (1)

This Actuarial Calculator is a Forward Projection Pro Forma for the performance of 80 Franchises (each costing an average of $250,000) funded via an Underwriting of REVPAC BONDS that are wrapped into a $20 Million Funding Package. Each franchise is funded via a FUND (which owns investment portfolios denominated in REVPAC BONDS) that provides a Full Redemption Guaranty (Risk Insurance coverage) for the Investment Principal ($250,000 each Franchise). The aggregate Risk Insurance Liability for the Underwriters is $250,000 per Franchise. The following Performances of the Franchises within the $20 Million Funding Package are conservative Forward Estimates presented for purposes of Actuarial Evaluation of Risk.

Number of Franchises	% of Total Funding Pkg.	Franchise Revenue Performance Category	Revenue Volume	Projected Risk Policy Value for Rev. Performance Category	Total Value of Risk Category
16	20%	50% LOSS	-0-	($250,000)(2)	($2,000,000)
20	25%	MINIMAL (1)	$2,500/Day	$217,500	$4,350,000
20	25%	MINIMAL (2)	$3,000/Day	286,500	5,730,000
8	10%	MEDIAN (1)	$3,500/Day	343,000	2,744,000
8	10%	MEDIAN (2)	$4,000/Day	399,500	3,196,000
4	5%	OPTIMAL (1)	$4,500/Day	456,000	1,824,000
4	5%	OPTIMAL (2)	$5,000/Day	512,500	2,050,000
80 Franchises	100 %				$17,894,000

Notes: (1) The projection within this 7-Year Actuarial Calculator deploys the formula 2-5-3. The formula's significance is that 2 of 10 Investments will lose money / 5 of 10 Investments will "Breakeven" /and earn "minimal returns" / 3 of 10 Investments will earn significant Returns-on-Investment. ALSO The 2-5-3 formula is marginally "higher in expectation" than the General Rule in Venture Capital Funding for Success-Failure Ratio Calculation — 2-6-2 Rule.

(2) The assumed liability for the Risk Insurer for the $20 Million Investment Package is $39.6 Million. In the event all franchises incurred "Total Loss" - this is the amount that the Insurer is obligated to "pay-out". For purposes of this OPTIMAL EXPECTATION Calculator - the assumption is that the average loss will be 50% of the total assumed liability of the Risk Insurer.

SECTION 7.0

I P E G   I N D E X

INVESTMENT PERFORMANCE - EQUITY _vs_ GROSS INDEX (Calculator)

What is the IPEG INDEX?

The IPEG INDEX measures Investment Performance for Revenue Participation Investors, of a single Business Venture ... or a portfolio of Business Ventures.

IPEG allows the Investor (at a single glance) to gauge the Real-Time Yield Performance of REVPAC BOND Investment Products.

What does "IPEG" signify?

It is the acronym for INVESTMENT PERFORMANCE - EQUITY _vs_ GROSS.

How is the IPEG INDEX Computed?

IPEG is an Index - not unlike the Equity Indices of "Dow Jones Industrial Average (DJIA)" and "Standard & Poors (S&P)"... however, rather than serving as an indicator of equity values within the secondary trading market - the IPEG is an investment performance barometer for Gross Revenue Participation Investors. IPEG represents the "ratio" of Gross Revenues (Sales Receipts) of a Business Venture compared to Gross Investment (funding proceeds) in the Business Venture. In effect: what IPEG measures is the relationship between Sales Revenue Dollars to Investment Dollars.

IPEG is quoted in "basis points" (one-hundredth of one percent - 1/100 of 1%). The basis point quotient of the Index represents the Real-Time Return-on-Investment (ROI) Yield of a Business Venture.

The basis formula deployed to compute the IPEG Index is: $\dfrac{\text{Gross Revenues}}{\text{Equity Investment}} \div \text{Days} \times 10000 = \text{IPEG}$

Step One The Gross Revenue Total is divided by the Equity Investment (Investment Proceeds funding the Business Venture)

Step Two The "resulting" quotient is divided by the Number of Calendar Days for the period that is being computed (and in which the Gross Revenue Total was accumulated)

Step Three The result is multiplied by Ten Thousand (10,000) (Basis Point Converter).

<u>Example:</u> A Burger King Franchise is funded for $250,000.

Daily IPEG	Annual IPEG
One Day Gross Sales Revenue totals $2,500. (250 Hamburger Meals @ $10)	One Year Gross Sales Revenue Totals $1,000,000.
Gross Revenues = $2,500	Gross Revenues = $1,000,000
Equity Investment - $250,000	Equity Investment = $250,000
Days = 1	Days = 365
Step One: $\dfrac{2,500}{250,000}$ = .01	Step One: $\dfrac{1,000,000}{250,000}$ = 4
Step Two: $\dfrac{.01}{1}$ = .01	Step Two: $\dfrac{4}{365}$ = .011
Step Three: .01 x 10,000 * 100 (IPEG)	Step Three: .011 x 10,000 * 110 (IPEG)

Understanding How IPEG works...

All REVPAC BOND funded Business Ventures have their ON-LINE Point-of-Sale (POS) Terminals connected to the REVPAC Comptroller Clearing Server - which means that within milliseconds of a sales receipt being created (sale being confirmed) ... the REVPAC Server digitally streams the Revenue Participation Credits to the digital Smart Card accounts of the REVPAC BOND Holders (electing Real-Time Dividend Yields) /or/ to the Trust Administrators, serving REVPAC BOND Holders that elect a re-investment program.

Simultaneous to - and in tandem with - the digital disbursement of Revenue Participation Credits - the IPEG INDEX server receives and processes the sales data and the IPEG INDEX System ...reports the sale...IN REAL TIME!

The IPEG System provides REVPAC BOND Holders with a QUICK-GLANCE R.O.I. Tracker - computed in "basis points" and based on real-time data from the Points-of-Sale - in addition to varied statistical services, with which to gauge past and future market performance of the underlying Business Ventures of the REVPAC BOND Investment Products.

How Investors can use IPEG to track Investments.

Let's go back to the Burger King Franchise which is being funded for $250,000, from three investors "pooling" their funding dollars through three different REVPAC BOND Investment Products. All three investors are purchasing "Dime-a-Dollar-Dividend-Yield" (DADDY) Entitlements - *10% of all Gross Sales Receipts* - for the next 7 years.

Investor Number One has an appetite for "risk". The Investor invests $50,000 ... purchasing a REVPAC Full-Risk BOND. The REVPAC Full-Risk BOND (no Risk Insurance) entitles the Investor to receive pro-rated yields of 10% of each and every sale. Since Investor #1 owns One-Fifth Interest in the $250,000 Burger King Funding - the Investor will be distributed Twenty-Percent (20%) of the DADDY disbursements - or Two Cents ($0.02) on every Sales Dollar for the next 84 months. The Investment is at "Full Risk"! In the event, Burger King Franchise sales are insufficient to yield Investor #1 full Return-of-Investment (during the 7 year term) - Investor #1 may experience a "loss" on the investment.

Investor Number Two is cautious. The Investor invests $100,000 ... purchasing a REVPAC BOND Interest. The REVPAC BOND is Risk Insured and guarantees the Investor 100% Return-of-Investment at full term - at the end of 7 years. The FUND entitles Investor #2 to receive pro-rated yields of 6.5% on each and every sale. The remaining 3.5% of the DADDY is distributed to the Risk Insurer (as an Insurance Premium Payment) in return for the 100% ROI GUARANTY. Additionally, Investor #2 is entitled to receive an "Equity Divestiture" distribution (at full term) in the amount of the aggregate of the Annual Revenue Yields (DADDYs) for the two highest "yielding" years.

Investor Number Three is the more conservative of the three investors. Investor #3 invests $100,000, purchasing a REVPAC BOND "ANNUITY" Interest. The ANNUITY is Risk Insured - guaranteeing the Investor 100% Return-of-Investment at full term plus a fixed-income yield of 14% per year. In consideration of the Guaranty of the capital investment and annual fixed-income - Investor #3 is required to convey 60% of all future DADDYs to the Insurer (as Insurance Premium Payment). The Investor is "credited" for 40% of ALL future DADDYs ($0.04 on each and every sale) ... and any yields over the 14% Fixed-Income GUARANTY are distributed to Investor #3 at the end of each year. Additionally, Investor #3 receives an "Equity Divestiture" distribution (at full term) - identical to Investor #2. ALSO, Investor #3 receives an Insurance Rebate - equivalent to 10% of the Original Investment Yields" (compounded).

The Grand-Opening Day Arrives!

Let's assume that the Opening Day sales receipts total $3,500...The Point-of-Sale has averaged 35 Hamburger Meals per hour for a 10-hour Day. At the close of business - the IPEG INDEX is at "1400"!

Here's what the IPEG means to each Investor: (See IPEG INDEX Calculator)

Investor Number One   - is "on-track" to realize a 51% R.O.I.

Investor Number Two   - 33% R.O.I.

Investor Number Three - 20.5% R.O.I.

The Return-on-Investment "projections" are for Revenue Yield - to be disbursed to the Investors in Real-Time - over the course of the year.

Now! Let's project a year into the future ...The IPEG INDEX is at "1000" ... each Investor has received Revenue Yield disbursements as follows:

    Investor #1 - $18,259 - 36.5% R.O.I. on $50,000 Investment.

    Investor #2 - $23,500 - 23.5% R.O.I. on $100,000 Investment.

    Investor #3 - $14,500 - 14.5% R.O.I. on $100,000 Investment (Fixed Income Guaranty).

The IPEG "tracking" info for each investor projects the "current" INDEX into the future-for the full 7-year term of the Franchise Investment. This is what each Investor sees:

    Investor #1 - is on track to receive 256% R.O.I. (36.5% p.a.)

    Investor #2 - is on track to receive 312% R.O.I. (44.6% p.a.)

    Investor #3 - is on track to receive 243% R.O.I. (34.7% p.a.)

Each day - *and throughout each day* - Investors can monitor the IPEG Index and "track" the performance of their investment ... simultaneous to confirming receipts of the real-time streaming of the DADDYs to their Smart Card Accounts.

Notes of Interest:

(1) REVPAC BOND Investors will develop their individual select and distinct "benchmarks" at which to associate "Investment Performance" plateaus. These "plateaus" will differ between investors - based on the REVPAC Investment Products that they are "tracking".

    ... For Instance: If the IPEG is "1200" - an ANNUITY Investor is receiving a 17.5% R.O.I. - If the IPEG increases to "1400" - the ANNUITY R.O.I. is 20.5% ...

    ... Whereas, a REVPAC BOND FUND Investor will experience the identical R.O.I.(between 17.5% and 20.5%) when the IPEG INDEX is between "700" and "900".

(2) The IPEG INDEX level of "1000" represents a significant "benchmark" for ANNUITY Investors ... This is the point that ANNUITY Investors "start" to earn Revenue Yields in excess of the Fixed Income GUARANTY of 14%.

IPEG INDEX CALCULATOR

INVESTMENT PERFORMANCE - EQUITY to GROSS INDEX (IPEG INDEX)

		SUB-PAR PERFORMANCE		MINIMAL PERFORMANCE		MEDIAN PERFORMANCE		OPTIMAL PERFORMANCE	
	Avg. Daily Revenues	$1,500	$2,000	$2,500	$3,000	$3,500	$4,000	$4,500	$5,000
	% OF EQUITY Total Investment	0.6%	0.8%	1.0%	1.2%	1.4%	1.6%	1.8%	2.0%
	IPEG INDEX	600	800	1000	1200	1400	1600	1800	2000
REVPAC REVENUE YIELD	Investor #1 Full Risk (REVPAC COMMON)	22% ROI	29% ROI	36.5% ROI	44% ROI	51% ROI	58.5% ROI	66% ROI	73% ROI
	Investor #2 Risk Insured REVPAC BOND FUND	14% ROI	19% ROI	23.5% ROI	28.5% ROI	33% ROI	38% ROI	42.5% ROI	48% ROI
	Investor #3 Risk Insured Fixed Income REVPAC BOND ANNUITY	9% ROI	11.5% ROI	14.5% ROI	17.5% ROI	20.5% ROI	23.5% ROI	26.5% ROI	29.5% ROI
	[MIN. 14% GUARANTY]								

7-YEAR RETURN-ON-INVESTMENT									
	Investor # 1								
	Revenue Yield	154%	203%	256%	308%	357%	410%	462%	511%
	Windfall Yield	0	0	0	0	0	0	0	0
	Total	154% + Equity	203% + Equity	56% + Equity	308% + Equity	357% + Equity	410% + Equity	462% + Equity	511% + Equity
	Investor # 2								
	Revenue Yield	98%	133%	165%	200%	231%	266%	298%	336%
	Windfall Yield Equity	28	38	47	57	66	76	85	96
	Redemption	100	100	100	100	100	100	100	100
	Total	226%	271%	312%	357%	397%	442%	483%	532%
	Investor # 3								
	Revenue Yield	98%	98%	102%	123%	144%	165%	186%	207%
	Windfall Yield Equity	28	28	29	35	41	47	53	59
	Ins. Rebate	12	12	12	14	16	18	20	22
	Redemption	100	100	100	100	100	100	100	100
	Total	238%	238%	243%	272%	301%	330%	359%	388%

7.1 IPEG INDEX CALCULATOR - ANNUITY PERFORMANCE

The IPEG Annuity Calculator measures the performance of a 7-Year Revenue-REVPAC BOND ANNUITY at variable gross revenue volumes - as reflected by the IPEG INDEX. The IPEG converts daily gross revenues (sales receipts) of the Business Venture into an Index (denominated in "Basis Points") which is a computation ratio between "average daily receipts" and "gross proceeds invested in the Venture". The IPEG is a measurement of Investment Performance in "Real-Time" and also serves as the basis to project (a) Annual Rates-of-Return (Revenue Yields derived from "DADDYs") and (b) 7-Year Return-of-Investment (Revenue Yields and Windfall Yields)

IPEG INDEX CALCULATOR - REVPAC BOND ANNUITY PERFORMANCE

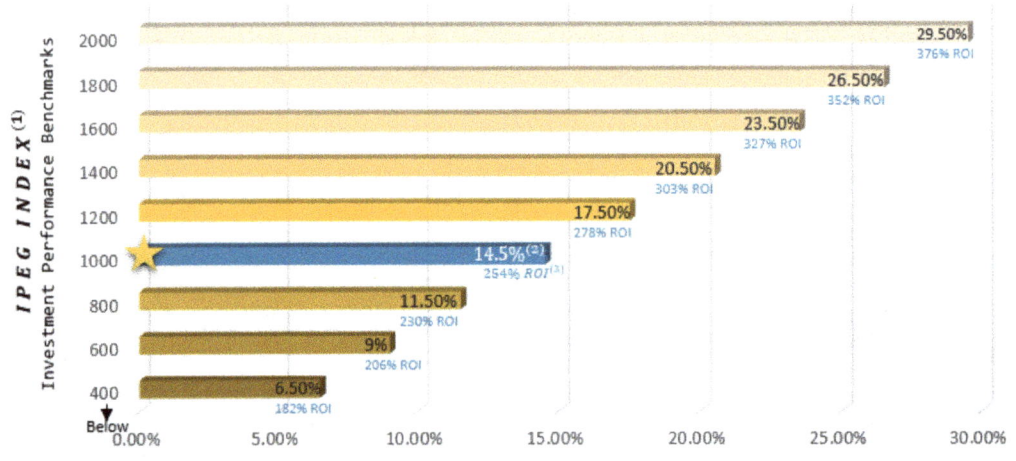

ANNUAL RATES-OF-RETURN
FOR REVPAC BOND ANNUITIES

Notes:

(1) IPEG INDEX Benchmark represents the Daily Average Gross Revenues of the Business Venture, as compared with the Gross Proceeds Invested in the Business Venture. The IPEG is measured (quoted) in Basis Points (1000 points equal 1%). Example: IPEG INDEX Benchmark of "1000" represents Daily Gross Revenues equal to 1% of the Investment Proceeds... If $250,000 is invested in a Venture - and the Daily Average Gross Revenues are $2,500 - the IPEG Benchmark is "1000".

(2) Annual Rates of Return represent the "DADDY" Yield (10% of Gross Revenues) for the corresponding IPEG Benchmark. Example: If the IPEG Benchmark is "1000" - the Business Venture is generating gross revenues equal to 1% of the Gross Proceeds invested into the Venture - the DADDY yields a Rate-of-Return per Year of 14.5% (Annuity) for the Invested Capital. NOTE: The balance of the DADDY yields are distributed to the Risk Insurance Underwriter.

(3) The 7-Year Return-on-Investment is the aggregate of the Revenue Yields and the Windfall Yields for each corresponding IPEG INDEX Benchmark. Example: If IPEG Benchmark is "1000" - the 7-Year Aggregate R.O.I. is 254% (Annuity) for the Invested Capital.

7.2 IPEG INDEX CALCULATOR -
REVPAC BONDS & REVPAC BOND FUND PERFORMANCE

The IPEG REVPAC BOND & REVPAC BOND FUND Calculator measures the performance of a 7-Year Revenue-REVPAC BOND / FUND at variable gross revenue volumes - as reflected by the IPEG INDEX. The IPEG converts daily gross revenues (sales receipts) of the Business Venture into an Index (denominated in "Basis Points") which is a computation ratio between "average daily receipts" and "gross proceeds invested in the Venture". The IPEG is a measurement of Investment Performance in "Real-Time" and also serves as the basis to project Annual Rates-of-Return (Revenue Yields derived from "DADDYs") and (b) 7-Year Return of Investment (Revenue Yields and Windfall Yields)

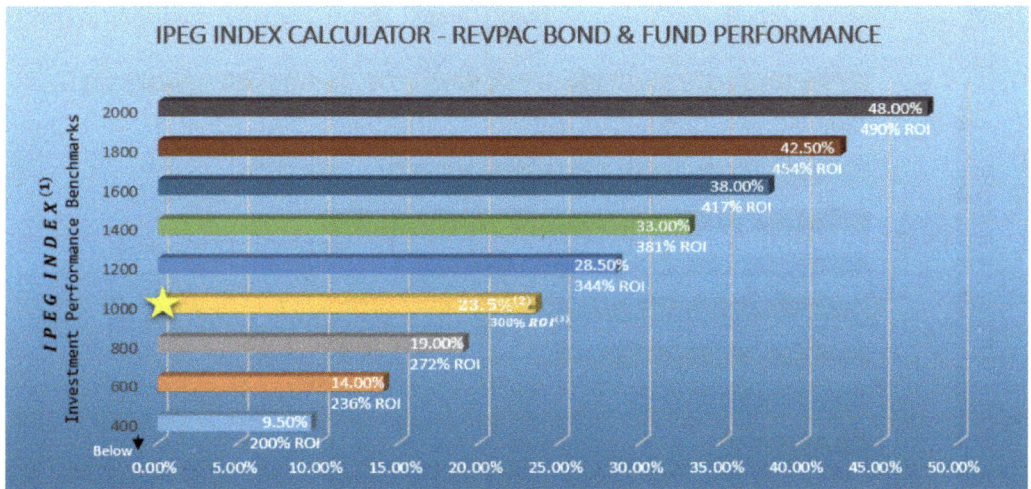

IPEG INDEX CALCULATOR - REVPAC BOND & FUND PERFORMANCE

ANNUAL RATES-OF-RETURN
&
7-YEAR AGGREGATE ROI
FOR REVPAC BONDS & REVPAC BOND FUND

Notes: (1) IPEG INDEX Benchmark represents the Daily Average Gross Revenues c£ the Business Venture, as compared with the Gross Proceeds Invested in the Business Venture. The IPEG is measured (quoted) in Basis Points (1000 points equal 1%). Example: IPEG INDEX Benchmark of "1000" represents Daily Gross Revenues equal to 1% of the Investment Proceeds... If $250,000 is invested in a Venture - and the Daily Average Gross Revenues are $2,500 - the IPEG Benchmark is "1000".

(2) Annual Rates of Return represent the "DADDY" Yield (10% of Gross Revenues) for the corresponding IPEG Benchmark. Example: If the IPEG Benchmark is "1000" - the Business Venture is generating gross revenues equal to 1% of the Gross Proceeds invested into the Venture - the DADDY yields a Rate-of-Return per Year of 23.5% (REVPAC BOND /or/ REVPAC BOND FUND) for the Invested Capital. NOTE: The balance of the DADDY yields are distributed to the Risk Insurance Underwriter.

(3) The 7-Year Return-on-Investment is the aggregate of the Revenue Yields and the Windfall Yields for each corresponding IPEG INDEX Benchmark. Example: If IPEG Benchmark is "1000" - the 7-Year Aggregate R.O.I. is 308% (REVPAC BOND /or/ REVPAC BOND FUND) for the Invested Capital.

7.3 IPEG INDEX CALCULATOR
FOR REVPAC FULL-RISK BOND PERFORMANCE

The IPEG REVPAC Full-Risk BONDs Calculator measures the performance of a 7-Year REVPAC Full-Risk Bond at variable gross revenue volumes - as reflected by the IPEG INDEX. The IPEG converts daily gross revenues (sales receipts) of the Business Venture into an Index (denominated in "Basis Points") which is a computation ratio between "average daily receipts" and "gross proceeds invested in the Venture". The IPEG is a measurement of Investment Performance in "Real-Time" and also serves as the basis to project <u>Annual Rates-of-Return</u> (Revenue Yields derived from "DADDYs") and (b) <u>7-Year Return of Investment</u> (Revenue Yields)

IPEG INDEX CALCULATOR - REVPAC COMMON SHARE PERFORMANCE

IPEG INDEX [1]
Investment Performance Benchmarks

IPEG Benchmark	Rate	ROI
2000	73.00%	511% ROI
1800	66.00%	462% ROI
1600	58.50%	410% ROI
1400	51.00%	330% ROI
1200	44.00%	308% ROI
1000 (★)	36.5% [2]	256% ROI [3]
800	29.00%	203% ROI
600	22.00%	154% ROI
400	14.50%	102% ROI

Below 0.00%   10.00%   20.00%   30.00%   40.00%   50.00%   60.00%   70.00%   80.00%

ANNUAL RATES-OF-RETURN
&
7-YEAR AGGREGATE ROI
FOR REVPAC FULL-RISK BONDS

<u>Notes:</u>

(1) IPEG INDEX Benchmark represents the Daily Average Gross Revenues of the Business Venture, as compared with the Gross Proceeds Invested in the Business Venture. The IPEG is measured (quoted) in Basis Points (1000 points equal 1%). <u>Example:</u> IPEG INDEX Benchmark of "1000" represents Daily Gross Revenues equal to 1% of the Investment Proceeds... If $250,000 is invested in a Venture - and the Daily Average Gross Revenues are $2,500 - the IPEG Benchmark is "1000".

(2) Annual Rates of Return represent the "DADDY" Yield (10% of Gross Revenues) for the corresponding IPEG Benchmark. <u>Example:</u> If the IPEG Benchmark is "1000" - the Business Venture is generating gross revenues equal to 1% of the Gross Proceeds invested into the Venture - the DADDY yields a Rate-of-Return per Year of 23.5% (REVPAC BOND /or/ REVPAC BOND FUND) for the Invested Capital.

(3) The 7-Year Return-on-Investment is the aggregate of the Revenue Yields and the Windfall Yields for each corresponding IPEG INDEX Benchmark. <u>Example:</u> If IPEG Benchmark is "1000" - the 7-Year Aggregate R.O.I. is 308% (REVPAC BOND /or/ REVPAC BOND FUND) for the Invested Capital.

SECTION 8.0
REVPAC BOND CAPITAL THEORY
...FORWARD POTENTIAL IMPACT...

The new and revolutionary Financial Instrument – REVPAC BONDS - is the missing tool sought after by Bankers and Entrepreneurs that have experienced the struggle and anguish of underwriting emerging commercial enterprises - in the face of Today's EQUITY MARKETS' inability to yield "meaningful" funding solutions to worthwhile Venture Capital Opportunities.

The innovative key feature of the new Financial Instrument is the potent combination of "fractionalizing" future gross receipts of commerce and venture enterprises - coupled with an Investment Redemption Guaranty! Combining investment risk-insurance with multiple Return-on-Investment potential creates a cogent capital floodgate opener in the hands of Investment Bankers and Underwriters.

This potential flood of fresh investment capital may well be swift in coming... and 'once arrived' can create the Renaissance that many fund raising managers are seeking.

The REVPAC BOND CAPITAL THEORY offers the Investment-Finance World the opportunity for its first TRUE paradigm shift in recent memory...

The "paradigm shift" redirects the focus onto "fair and reasonable revenue sharing", through which to distribute "meaningful" rewards to risk takers of successful ventures - rather than the expectation of "equity appreciation" (trading stock market values) as is the present-day *practice.*

The REVPAC BOND CAPITAL THEORY "paradigm shift" is a much-needed solution for venture capital underwritings. The integration of investment-risk-insurance coverage brings together insurance-underwriters and investment-bankers into a working relationship - with the potential to foster new methods and products, radically different from anything we have hitherto seen - to fund emerging business ventures and small business enterprises.

Investment Bankers, that embrace the REVPAC BOND CAPITAL THEORY ... in its early stage ... will become the giants of Venture Capital. They will experience phenomenal growth - similar to that experienced by DREXEL BURNHAM and SOLOMON BROTHERS - and their investment syndicates - via their advent of the JUNK BOND and MORTGAGE BACKED GUARANTY - respectfully.

TABLE OF AUTHORITIES

The organic documents for a REVPAC denominated Investment Trust and its public offering is presented in this section. These documents are a real case history of an offering of Revenue Participation Capital Bonds. For the purpose of compliance with jurisdictional securities regulations, the names and contact numbers have been changed so that the publication of the investment materials is not construed as a securities offering solicitation.

The Subordinated Debenture variation, discussed in this book, comprises additional documentation that is not included within the Table of Authorities.

REVPAC Investment Trust Prospectus

MexRx INVESTMENT TRUST

INITIAL PUBLIC OFFERING	PROSPECTUS

NINE HUNDRED THOUSAND (900,000) Revenue Participation Capital Bonds

$4,500,000 USD

MexRx INVESTMENT TRUST (The "Investment Trust" or "Trust") is offering 900,000 Revenue Participation Capital Bonds ("REVPAC Bond Units"). The REVPAC Bond Units are Seven Year Revenue Participation Trust Units. Each Unit consists of one Revenue Share, Full Redemption Guaranty, and one Future Participation Warrant. Each **Revenue Share** entitles the holder to receive a pro-rata share of the gross revenues of the Trust. **Full Redemption Guaranty** entitles the holder to 100% return-on-investment guaranty bond coverage. The Full Redemption Guaranty guarantees that the revenue yields of the Revenue Share will be equivalent to minimum 100% of the offering price of the REVPAC Bond Units purchased in this offering. Each **Future Participation Warrant** entitles the holder to purchase one REVPAC Unit for the subsequent seven year term of the Investment Trust. The REVPAC Bond Units will be fully matured on the seventh anniversary of the completion of this offering. Disbursements of the gross revenue shares will occur at the end of Year Three, Year Four, Year Five, Year Six and Year Seven. Concurrent with the Year Seven Revenue Yield Distribution, all revenue participation rights of the holder will cease, unless the holder has exercised the Future Participation Warrant to purchase a REVPAC Unit for the ensuing Seven Year term of the Trust. **(See "Description of Securities" and "Participation in Costs and Revenues").**

The Investment Trust is organized for the purpose of manufacturing and marketing a proprietary medical-herbal product line and marketing prescription/non-prescription medical products-surgical services for the worldwide marketplace. The Unit Holders will, upon completion of this offering, have the right to share disbursements, as an aggregate, equivalent to 20% of the gross revenues derived from the sales of proprietary Herbal Care Immune System Activator product line and 7.5% of all other medical products-surgical services sold by the Business Manager. **(See "Business of the Trust").**

There is no public market for the REVPAC Bond Units of the Investment Trust however, the Investment Trust anticipates a public trading market to develop following this offering. Upon completion of this offering, the Investment Trust intends to qualify the Units sold in the offering to be listed on select securities trading markets. **(See "Investment Considerations" and "Securities Listings").**

> THE SECURITIES OFFERED HEREBY ARE SPECULATIVE AND THE FUTURE TRADING VALUE WILL DEPEND UPON CERTAIN MARKET CONDITIONS, SEE "INVESTMENT CONSIDERATIONS".

THESE SECURITIES ARE BEING OFFERED TO SELECT
RESIDENTS OF JURISDICTIONS OUTSIDE OF THE UNITED STATES

GENERAL DESCRIPTION OF TRANSACTION	PRICE TO PUBLIC	DISCOUNTS AND COMMISSIONS (1) (2)	PROCEEDS TO THE TRUST (2) (3)
Per Share	$5.00	$0.50	$4.50
Maximum	$4,500,000.00	$450,000.00	$4,050,000.00

UNDERWRITER

Date of this Prospectus is January 10, 20**

163

MexRx Investment Trust

REVPAC The New Revolutionary Financial Instrument

SUMMARY OF THE OFFERING

The following is intended as a brief summary only and should not be relied upon as fully descriptive of this Offering. This Summary is qualified in its entirety by the remainder of this Prospectus.

The Investment Trust:	The Investment Trust, registered in the British Overseas Territory of Gibraltar is organized for the purpose of funding the production and marketing of a proprietary line of medical-herbal products known as "Herbal Care Immune System Activator" and the marketing of prescription/non-prescription medical products and surgical services. The Investment Trust receives disbursements equivalent to 20% of the gross revenues derived from the worldwide sales of the Herbal Care product line and 7.5% of the gross revenues derived from all medical products-surgical services sales.
Business of the Investment Trust:	The prospect of revenues for the Investment Trust is dependent on the actual revenues received by the Business Manager for the proprietary Herbal Care Immune System Activator product line and non-proprietary medical products and surgical services. While the Business Manager for the Investment Trust is of the view that the sales of its products and services via the Internet and through select distributors will be significantly successful within the consumer marketplace, no assurance can be given as to the level of ultimate success of the MexRx marketing programs or the magnitude of the proprietary Herbal Care Immune system Activator product line acceptance.

The Herbal Care Immune System Activator product line, which represents the primary revenue source for the Investment Trust, is a naturopathic substance -manufactured, utilizing proprietary methodology - and centered around a Geraniacie extract resulting a hybrid multi-purpose immune system facilitator that is capable of combating most diseases. In over eight years of laboratory and clinical studies – with thousands of volunteers - conducted in Brazil, Cuba, Mexico and Canada – the reports substantiate a virtual universal remedial effectiveness with absolute absence of ill-effects. The Herbal Care product line is currently registered in Brazil and Hungary and registration is pending within the Republic of Mexico for over-the-counter sales.

The production and marketing of the Herbal Care Immune System Activator product line, with universal remedial applications, including the following: *Rheumatoid Arthritis, Carpal tunnel Syndrome, Herpes zoster, H. genitalis and H. simplex, Seborreic dermatitis, Psoriasis, Tendonitis, Diabetes, Acne and various skin disorders, Cancer and AIDS* – will be funded from the net proceeds of this completed offering. The Business Manager intends to commence production of the manufacturing facility for the Herbal Care Immune System Activator product line upon the completion of this offering; and further intends to complete production thereof within 150 days thereafter, whereupon it will commence to manufacture and market the proprietary product line and market over 1,250 prescription/non-prescription medical products and over 100 surgical procedures via the Internet on a worldwide basis. Future marketing programs of the Herbal Care Immune System Activator product line are scheduled to go on-line via distributors pending the registration of the Herbal Care products in select countries.

The Investment Trust revenue participation entitlement is based on he gross revenues derived from any and all proprietary/non-rietary medical products and surgical services sales by the Business Manager.

SUMMARY OF THE OFFERING *(continued)*

Business Manager of the Investment Trust:	MexRx S.A. de C.V., is the owner of the proprietary Herbal Care product line and is the Business Manager of the Investment Trust. The principal office of the Business Manager is located at the Kirkland Medical Services Hospital, Calle Rufino Tamayo 9910, Esquina Blvd. Cuauhtemoc y Dr. Atl, Zona Rio Tijuana, B.C., Mexico 22320. The e-mail address is _____.
Trust Administrator of the Investment Trust:	PriceWaterhouseCoopers is the Trust Administrator of the Investment Trust. The principal office of the Trust Administrator is located at Tapachula 11550, Chapultepec, CP 22020 Tijuana, Baja California, Mexico. The Telephone/Fax Number is 52.664.615.5000 / 52.664.615.5010,
Total and Type of Offering:	Four Million Five Hundred Thousand ($4,500,000) U.S. Dollars. Registration or exemption to registration filing in select jurisdictions outside the United States.
Securities:	The Investment Trust is offering 900,000 REVPAC Bond Units. There are currently 27,000 Units outstanding. (See "Description of Securities").
Price per Bond Unit:	Five ($5.00) Dollars.
Minimum Purchase:	Subscribers are required to purchase a minimum of one thousand (1,000) Units for an aggregate purchase of Five Thousand ($5,000) Dollars. (See "Plan of Distribution").
Investment Considerations:	There are numerous investment considerations unique to the Investment Trust and its proposed business venture. (The prospective investor should see "Investment Considerations").
Guaranty Offering, Escrow & Proceeds:	The Investment Trust has established an escrow for all proceeds derived from the offering. The escrow provides that all funds received from subscribers to the REVPAC Bond Units be deposited in a subscription escrow account until such time that the certificates evidencing the REVPAC Bond Units purchased are delivered to the subscribers-at which time, the proceeds will be released to the Trust Administrator and Underwriter. Any and all REVPAC Bond Units that remain not sold within the offering period – ending August 25, 20__- will be purchased by the Underwriter for its trading account. All subscription proceeds are immediately available for distribution to the Trust Administrator and Underwriter as the Units are sold and the certificates, evidencing ownership of the REVPAC Bond Units are delivered to the subscribers. Under the terms of the escrow, the Trust Administrator will have available to allocate to the Business Manager of the Trust 87% of the gross proceeds derived from the placement of all Bond Units.

SUMMARY OF THE OFFERING (continued)

Market for REVPAC Bond Units: The REVPAC Bond Units of the Investment Trust offered hereby are offered in reliance upon registration or exemption from registration filing in select jurisdictions outside the United States. Although the units offered hereby, shall not be required to carry a restrictive legend, and that the units are intended to be registered with select trading exchanges, the potential investor should be aware that no market for the REVPAC Bond Units of the Investment Trust presently exists. The Business Manager is scheduled to effect registration and listing of the units within 90 days following completion of this offering.

Use of Proceeds: Assuming all 900,000 REVPAC Bond Units offered hereby are sold, the Administrator for the Invesrust will allocate net cash proceeds of approximately $3,825,000, after deducting applicable costs of this offering. $3,700,000 from the proceeds of this offering will be allocated to the Business Manager - and overseen by the Administrator - to develop and manufacture the proprietary Herbal Care Immune System Activator product line and to implement the marketing and distribution of the various prescription/non-prescription medical products and surgical services. $125,000 from the proceeds will be retained by the Administrator to defray costs of operating the Investment Trust. (See "Use of Proceeds").

Revenue Distribution: The Administrator is entitled to receive a fee of $25,000 p/a for reasonable, ordinary and necessary operating expenses, requisite to the operating expenses of the Trust. The Net Cash Flow of the Investment Trust – which is equivalent to 20% of the gross sales revenues of any and all Herbal Care Immune System Activator products and 7.5% of any and all prescription/non-prescription medical products and surgical services, plus accumulated interest– is to be distributed to the REVPAC Unit holders on a pro-rata basis. The first Revenue Distribution is to occur on the third year anniversary following completion of this offering. An additional Revenue Distribution is to occur for each anniversary thereafter. Upon the fifth Revenue Distribution, on the seventh anniversary following this offering, all Revenue Distribution rights will cease for the REVPAC Unit holder, unless the holder has exercised the Warrant (attached to the instant REVPAC Unit) and purchased a newly issued REVPAC Unit for the ensuing Seven Year term of the Investment Trust.

Full Redemption Guaranty: The Full Redemption Guaranty is a "Zero-Risk" feature that is attached to the REVPAC Bond Units purchased by the subscriber. Subscribers are guaranteed, through the Full Redemption Guaranty coverage, that the accumulated value of their Revenue Yields, distributed over the seven year term of the REVPAC Unit, will equal a minimum $5.00 per REVPAC Unit. In the event, accumulated Revenue Yields do not equal the full amount of the Initial Public Offering Price of $5.00 per REVPAC Unit, the Full Redemption Guaranty will reimburse the difference concurrent with the Revenue Yield distribution payment of Coupon #5.The REVPAC Unit holder may elect to utilize the Full Redemption Guaranty in connection with the exercise of the Future

REVPAC The New Revolutionary Financial Instrument

SUMMARY OF THE OFFERING *(continued)*

Future Participation Warrant:

The REVPAC Unit is a seven year Revenue Participation Trust Unit. At the end of seven years, the holder may elect to exercise the Future Participation Warrant for the ensuing seven year term of the Investment Trust /or/ the holder may elect to sell the REVPAC Unit with the attached Future Participation Warrant through one of the securities trading markets upon which the Investment Trust is listed.

Those REVPAC holders that exercise the Future Participation Warrant receive the identical revenue sharing rights for the ensuing seven year term as that which was effective for the initial seven year term period. In the event, the REVPAC holders have received 500% Return on Investment - at the end of the seven year term - aggregate Revenue Sharing Yields of $25 per REVPAC Unit, allocation of revenues are to continue into the renewal term for an additional four years. In the event the REVPAC holders have received aggregate Revenue Yields of less than $25 per REVPAC Unit, allocation of revenues are to continue for the entire seven years of the renewal term. Additionally, the REVPAC holders that exercise the Future Participation Warrant receive additional revenue sharing rights in a business venture, to be designated by the Business Manager concurrent with the notice to REVPAC holders of the right to exercise the Future Participation Warrant. The cost of purchasing a newly issued REVPAC Unit for the succeeding term is identical to the cost of the REVPAC Unit in the Initial Public Offering - $5.00 per Unit.

In the event the instant MexRx business venture is made part of the ensuing 7-year term, the capital assets – not to exceed $4,500,000, which comprise any and all production facilities, MexRx marketing programs, proprietary Herbal Care Immune System Activator production methodology and applicable Intellectual Property Claims – remain the property of the Investment Trust and its REVPAC holders.

NOTES APPLICABLE TO COVER PAGE

(1)   Units will be sold on a surety guaranty basis by the Underwriter. The Underwriter will receive a ten percent (10%) commission on all Units sold. This does not include additional compensation to Underwriter, in the form of a non-accountable expense allowance of 3% which amounts to a total of $135,000 once all 900,000 Units are sold and one (1) six month warrant to be sold to the Underwriter at a price of $0.10 per warrant for every 33.3 Units offered hereunder and sold. Each of which warrants shall entitle the owner to purchase one "REVPAC" Unit of the Investment Trust at the price of $1.00 per Unit, subject to adjustments under applicable anti-dilution provisions. All units remaining unsold 180 days following commencement of this offering will be purchased by the Underwriter.

(2)   Before deducting expenses estimated at $90,000 relating to the offering payable by the Investment Trust for securities filing, printing, legal, accounting and miscellaneous.

(3)   This offering is being offered on a Surety Guaranty 900,000 Unit basis. In the event the Investment Trust does not realize sales of at least 900,000 Units during the term of this offering, the Underwriter will purchase all unsold Units for its trading account. All funds received by the Investment Trust pursuant to this offering will be made immediately available for allocation by the Administrator to the Business Manager of the Investment Trust.

FORWARD

The Trust Administrator and Business Manager of the Investment Trust have prepared this Offering Memorandum and have provided all the information contained herein, including the financial data.

The Trust Administrator's principal offices are located at Tapachula 11550, Chapultepec, CP 22020 Tijuana, Baja California, Mexico. The Telephone/Fax Number is 52.664.615.5000 / 52.664.615.5010. The Business Manager's principal offices are located at na Blvd. Cuauhtemoc y Dr. Atl, Zona Rio Tijuana, B.C., Mexico 22320. The e-mail address is _____.

Purchasers and their representatives are urged to read this Prospectus carefully. Purchasers desiring additional information concerning the Investment Trust may contact the Trust Administrator and the Business Manager at the address, telephone and FAX number above. Purchasers may pose any reasonable questions to the Trust Administrator and Business Manager and receive answers thereto via any of these mediums during normal business hours after reasonable notice. Copies of all documents and Investment Trust records to which reference is made herein may be made available for inspection upon request.

Purchasers and their representatives, if any, will be asked to acknowledge, in the Subscription Agreement, that they were given the opportunity to obtain such additional information and that they either did so or elected to waive such opportunity.

THIS OFFERING IS AVAILABLE ONLY TO SUBSCRIBERS THAT ARE RESIDENTS OF JURISDICTIONS OUTSIDE THE UNITED STATES OF AMERICA, IN WHICH THIS OFFERING IS VALID PURSUANT TO APPLICABLE SECURITIES REGULATIONS.

INVESTMENT CONSIDERATIONS

Prospective investors should carefully consider the following information relating to the business of the Investment Trust.

Nature of Business Venture - The Investment Trust is entitled to receive disbursements equivalent to 20% of the Gross Sales Revenues derived from the proprietary Herbal Care Immune System Activator product line and 7.5% of the Gross Sales Revenues derived from MexRx prescription/non-prescription medical products and surgical services sold by the Business Manager. Entitlement by the Investment Trust in the potential sales revenues of the proprietary and non-proprietary products and services represents the sole source of future potential revenues and valuation for the REVPAC Bond Units. There are substantial investment considerations involved in the Investment Trust's reliance on future gross sales revenues derived from the MexRx products and services:

(a) **Limited Operations of Business Manager.** MexRx S.A. de C.V., Business Manager for the Investment Trust, is solely responsible for any and all future gross sales revenues of the products and services from which the REVPAC Bond Units can derive future revenues and valuation. The Business Manager has had limited operations to date. The Business Manager has been engaged in the development of and market preparedness for the unique Herbal Care Immune System Activator product line and overall MexRx marketing system since its inception however, the Business Manager must be considered a "start up" operation. Accordingly, it is subject to all the risks inherent in a new business. Since the marketing of the Herbal Care Immune System Activator product line and the MexRx marketing programs are a new venture, it is without any substantial record of earnings or revenues, there can be no assurance that the Business Manager's business activities will result in any significant sales revenues or revenue share disbursements in the future.

(b) **Liquidity and Capital Resources.** The Business Manager is entirely reliant upon the proceeds of this offering to produce and market the Herbal Care Immune System Activator product line and the MexRx marketing programs described in this Prospectus. Any further capital resources required by the Business Manager to market the Herbal Care product line and MexRx products and services may only become available to the Business Manager from net income which may be generated from the Business Manager's operations. Failure by the Business Manager to effectively utilize the proceeds of this offering can cause the production and marketing of the Herbal Care and MexRx products/services, on behalf of the Investment Trust, to no longer be viable or severely restricted in scope. Such an occurrence may result in substantial risk, causing the investors, to rely upon the Full Redemption Guaranty coverage, to realize recovery of a portion or all of their investment.

(c) **Competition.** Competition in the health care industry is intense. The Business Manager faces strong competition from other health care product/service marketing companies that compete for the same revenues as the Herbal Care and MexRx products and services – *however, in the view of the Business Manager, there does not exist an Internet marketing service offering similar products and services at the discounted prices, as offered by MexRx nor does there exist any competitor with all of the features inherent in the proprietary Herbal Care Immune System Activator product line.* The Investment Trust's Business Manager believes that optimum results are obtained from developing assertive marketing and promotional techniques to attract the consumer market place to the MexRx website – which offers health care consumers significant discounts on medical products and surgical services, in addition to MexRx serving as the only portal for the proprietary Herbal Care Immune System Activator product line. The business Manager is resolved in its commitment to schedule a control growth program for its Herbal Care and MexRx products and services – which is a niche market occupied, on an exclusive basis, by the Business Manager. Though many of the competing health care companies have greater financial resources, larger staffs and facilities than the Business Manager, the Business Manager believes that the uniqueness of the Herbal Care Immune System Activator product line will facilitate a significant number of joint venture relationships with competing health care companies that will erode traditional competitor foot-holds within the marketplace.

INVESTMENT CONSIDERATIONS
(continued)

Investment Trust **REVPAC** *Bond* *Units* - An investor purchasing REVPAC Bond Units in the Investment Trust offered herein, is subject to numerous investment considerations which include, but are not limited to:

(a) *Revenue Participation Arrangements.* The Administrator to the Investment Trust will be entitled to receive a fee of $25,000.00 p/a for reasonable ordinary and necessary operating expenses requisite to the operating expenses of the Trust. The Net Cash Flow of the Investment Trust - which is equivalent to 20% of the gross sales revenues of the proprietary Herbal Care Immune System Activator product line and 7.5% of non-proprietary MexRx medical products and surgical services - plus accumulated interest, is to be distributed to the REVPAC Unit holders on a pro-rata basis. The Business Manager is entitled to receive the balance of the gross sales revenues from Herbal Care and MexRx sales, with which the Business Manager is to develop new markets for its health care products and services, defray cost of sales, marketing and general operating expenses. Terms of these revenue sharing arrangements have been established by the Business Manager without arm's length negotiation, however, the Business Manager believes that such terms are fair and reasonable under the circumstances.

(b) *Cash Distributions to the Unit Holders.* The first Revenue Distribution to the holders of REVPAC Bond Units is to occur on the third year anniversary following completion of this offering. An additional Revenue Distribution is to occur for each anniversary thereafter during the term of REVPAC Unit – which is seven years. Upon the fifth Revenue Distribution on the seventh anniversary following completion of this offering, all Revenue Distribution rights cease for the REVPAC Unit holder. The REVPAC Unit holders can anticipate a total of five Revenue Distributions during the seven year term of the REVPAC Unit. The amount of any cash distributions to the REVPAC Unit holders will be dependent upon numerous factors which are beyond the control of the Business Manager. Such factors include but are not limited to the prevailing market acceptance of the Herbal Care Immune System Activator product line by the consumer market that the Investment Trust is relying upon for cash disbursements. Accordingly, there can be no assurances that the Investment Trust will be able to make regular or significant distributions to the REVPAC Unit holders.

(c) *Cessation of Cash Distributions.* The Investment Trust REVPAC Unit limits cash distributions to the REVPAC Unit holders to five distributions. The REVPAC Unit holders can expect to receive their pro-rata disbursements, if any, upon the third, fourth, fifth, sixth and seventh year anniversaries following completion of this offering. Upon the fifth disbursement - on the seventh year anniversary - all revenue participation rights of the REVPAC Unit holders will cease. The REVPAC Unit holder has the option of purchasing one Investment Trust REVPAC Unit for the ensuing seven year period of the Investment Trust via the exercise of the attached warrant. The REVPAC Unit holder, that elects to exercise the warrant, is entitled to purchase the Investment Trust REVPAC Unit for the next seven year period at the identical price as is being offered in this offering - $5.00 per Unit. The REVPAC Unit holder is also entitled to receive the identical pro-rata revenue participation rights during a portion or the entire term of the next seven year period - depending on the amount of aggregate Revenue Yield distributions during the first seven year term **(see "Description of Securities - Future Participation Warrant")**. While the REVPAC Unit holders, purchasing Units in the next seven year period retain their revenue participation entitlements in the proprietary Herbal Care product line and MexRx non-proprietary products and services of the Investment Trust, there can be no assurances that the REVPAC Unit holder will receive the same cash disbursements, if any, during the entitled period of the next seven year period as the REVPAC Unit holder received during the first seven year term.

(d) *Full Redemption Guaranty Distributions.* The Full Redemption Guaranty entitles the REVPAC Unit holder to receive the difference between any and all revenue share disbursements and the IPO price of the REVPAC Unit at full term. The REVPAC Unit holder, electing Full Redemption Guaranty coverage forfeits one-half of any and all future revenue share disbursements – as a premium payment for the 100% return of investment guarantee. The REVPAC Unit holder may realize substantial premium payments and forfeiture of potential revenue share disbursements in return for the 100% return of investment guarantee. However, since the business venture is considered a "start-up", the Business Manager is of the view that the compensation of the Full Redemption Guaranty coverage outweighs the potentially significant premium payment.

INVESTMENT CONSIDERATIONS	*(continued)*

(e) ***Future Participation Warrants and Mandatory Dissolution.*** In the event that over 60% of the REVPAC Unit holders fail to exercise the attached Future Participation Warrants and remit the same to the Trust Administrator, at full term, the Investment Trust will automatically be dissolved. "Dissolution" means that 100% of the capital assets of the Investment Trust will be sold to the highest bidder – with the Business Manager owning the first right of refusal – in accordance with the Collateralized Yield Obligation - that is overseen and administered by the Trust Administrator and the proceeds distributed to the REVPAC Unit holders. Those investors that do not desire dissolution of the Trust – if they represent, in aggregate, less than 40% of the issued and outstanding units – will not be provided an opportunity to be REVPAC Unit holders for the next seven year term of the Investment Trust. Thus, an investor in the Units may be forced into a Mandatory Dissolution though the investor does not desire to effect such action.

(f) ***No Prior Public Market.*** There has been no prior market for the Investment Trust REVPAC Bond Units and though, the Investment Trust is scheduled to be registered and listed on select securities exchanges, there can be no assurance that an active market will develop or be sustained.

(g) ***Revenue Participation Dilution.*** "Dilution" represents the difference between the revenue sharing disbursements to investors of this offering, paying full Offering Price for the REVPAC Bond Units, and the revenue sharing disbursements for purchasers of Investment Trust REVPAC Bond Units paying less then full Offering Price. There are currently 27,000 Investment Trust REVPAC Bond Units issued and outstanding. The REVPAC Bond Units are issued to REVPAC Funding Foundation, as consideration for cash and services rendered in connection with this offering. The REVPAC Bond Units were issued at the price of $1.00 per Unit. Additionally, the Underwriter is entitled to receive one warrant for every 33.3 REVPAC Bond Units sold in this offering. The warrant entitles the holder to purchase one Investment Trust REVPAC Unit, at any time during the sixty month period following completion of this offering, at the price of $1.00 per Unit. Upon the placement by the Underwriter of all 900,000 REVPAC Bond Units in this offering, the Underwriter will receive the right to purchase a total of 27,000 Investment Trust REVPAC Bond Units for an aggregate $27,000. Therefore, the purchaser of the REVPAC Bond Units offered hereby will suffer an immediate dilution of Revenue Participation disbursements, equivalent to 6% of total cash disbursements that would have been effected in the absence of such dilution. In the event the Underwriter exercises all 27,000 warrants the total number of Units issued and outstanding in the Investment Trust will be 954,000 REVPAC Bond Units.

SOURCE AND USES OF PROCEEDS

The net proceeds to the Investment Trust, if the maximum number of Units are sold, are estimated to be $3,825,000 after payment of expenses and commissions. Such proceeds are expected to be used as follows:

SCHEDULE A - SOURCE AND USES OF PROCEEDS

Sources	CAPITAL	% OF TOTAL	
Gross Offering Proceeds	$4,500,000		
Less:			
- Commissions (1)	450,000	10.00 %	
- Underwriter Non-Acct. Expenses (2)	135,000	3.00%	
- Offering Expenses (3)	90,000	2.00%	
Total Expenses		15.00%	
Net Offering Proceeds		100.00%	$3,825,000

Uses	CAPITAL	% OF NET	
Herbal Care/MexRx Marketing Programs (4)	$1,250,000	32.7%	
IMS Common Stock Purchase (5)	725,000	19.6%	
Herbal Care Production Facility (6)	500,000	13.1%	
Administrator Reserve (7)	125,000	3.3%	
Capital Reserve	1,200,000	31.3%	
Total/Net Offering Proceeds	$3,825,000	100.00%	$3,825,000

All amounts above are estimated and approximate within a margin of error of 5%. Trust Administrator and Business Manager reserve the right to reallocate the use of proceeds among the foregoing categories as may, in the judgment of the Trust Administrator and Business Manager and within the margin of 5%, be in the best interests of the Investment Trust.

Footnotes:
1 & 2 The Underwriter receives ten percent (10%) commission and a non-accountable expense allowance of three percent (3%) on all Units sold.

3   Expenses relating to the offering payable by the Investment Trust for filing, printing, legal, accounting and miscellaneous fees.

4 & 6 Investment Trust purchases production equipment to manufacture Herbal Care Immune System Activator product line and all design software for MexRx website. Investment Trust provides all requisite production, sales and marketing funding for the Herbal Care and MexRx products and services. The agreement with the Business Manager requires that the production facility and design software – capital assets of the Investment Trust - be maintained and managed by the Business Manager throughout the term of the Investment Trust. The production facility and design software represent, at all times, the property and capital asset of the Investment Trust.

5   Investment Trust purchases 40% of the issued and outstanding common shares of International Medical Services S.A. de C.V., the holding company of one of the largest private medical facilities and a major Health Maintenance Organization (HMO) in the Republic of Mexico. The facility is located in Tijuana, B.C., Mexico.

7.   Administrator to the Investment Trust receives an operating expense account of $25,000 p/a to defray the costs of administrating the Investment Trust. The interest accrued during the term on the pre-paid five years defrays the Trust Administrator cost for Year-6 and Year-7.

CAPITALIZATION	

GENERAL TRUST INFORMATION	DESCRIPTION	
JURISDICTION, DATE OF FORMATION:	BRITISH OVERSEAS TERRITORY OF GIBRALTAR 20__	
SECURITIES INFORMATION:	**Description**	
CLASSES OF SECURITIES		

A. Investment Trust Units Par value: N/A	**AUTHORIZED**	**ISSUED AND OUTSTANDING**
1. Number of Units authorized	954,000	
2. Number of Units issued and outstanding		27,000
i. Units owned by Business Manager and Administrator		0
ii. Number of "Other Restricted" Units		27,000
iii. Number of Units widely held		0
iv. Number or Unit holders		1
3. Number of Units in treasury		0
B. Warrants/Options:		
1. Warrants Currently Outstanding?		0
2. Warrants (or Options) to be ?		27,000

DESCRIPTION OF WARRENTS (W): /OPTIONS (O):	PRICE	NUMBER BEING REGISTERED	POTENTIAL CAPITAL RECEIVED PER CLASS, WHEN EXERCISED:	ALL EXERCISED
i. Class A (W)	$1.00	27,000		$27,000
Total				$27,000
3. Are these Warrants being registered?				Yes

GENERAL TRUST INFORMATION	Description
1. Intended registration	Select Exchanges
2. Trading now	No
3. Intended exchange	Select Exchanges

(This space intentionally left blank)

REVENUE PARTICIPATION DILUTION

"Revenue Participation Dilution" represents the difference between the revenue sharing disbursements to investors of this offering, paying full Offering Price for the REVPAC Bond Units, and the revenue sharing disbursements for purchasers of REVPAC Bond Units paying less than full Offering Price. In this offering, the level of dilution will be increased as a result of REVPAC Bond Units being issued for more than the 900,000 of this offering and for less than full price of this offering.

The Units of this offering are being sold at $5.00 per Unit. A total of 900,000 Units are offered. There are currently 27,000 Units issued and outstanding, for which the Investment Trust received a price of $1.00 per Unit. Therefore, upon the sale of all 900,000 Units offered herein, the purchasers of the Units will suffer a Revenue participation Dilution of 3% of total cash disbursements that would have been effected in the absence of such dilution.

The following table illustrates the revenue participation dilution of the purchaser of the REVPAC Bond Units.

Units of this Offering	
Number of Units Offered	900,000 Units
Offering Price of Units	$5.00
Units Issued and Outstanding	
Number of Units Issued and Outstanding	27,000 Units
Price of Units Issued prior to Offering	$1.00
Total Number of Units	
Per Unit Revenue Participation Dilution to Purchaser (1)	**3%**

(1) Does not include 27,000 REVPAC Bond Units reserved for possible issuance upon the exercise of the Underwriter Warrants. The Investment Trust has not issued any warrants to date **(See "Underwriter Warrants").**

(This space intentionally left blank)

REVPAC The New Revolutionary Financial Instrument

THE INVESTMENT TRUST

INVESTMENT TRUST

MexRx Investment Trust is an Investment Trust registered in the British Overseas Territory of Gibraltar and organized for the purpose of developing, producing and marketing a unique and proprietary Herbal Care Immune System Activator product line in addition to non-proprietary medical products and surgical services - on an international basis. Marketing emphasis for the MexRx products and services is via the Internet. The Investment Trust has the right to share revenue disbursements equivalent to 20% of the gross sales revenues derived from the proprietary Herbal Care Immune System Activator product line and 7.5% of the gross sales revenues derived from the MexRx non-proprietary medical products and surgical services. The Investment Trust, upon completion of the underwriting, will own the claim of right, title and interest to the production facility for Herbal Care product line, proprietary computer software programming for the "e-commerce marketing website", 40% of the issued and outstanding common shares of Kirkland Medical Services S.A. de C.V., the holding company of the largest private medical facilities in Mexico – as well as a major Health Maintenance Organization (H.M.O.) in Mexico, and all proprietary intellectual property (under chattel) that protect the Herbal Care product line and MexRx products and services - which represent the capital assets of the Trust.

BUSINESS MANAGER OF THE TRUST

MexRx S.A. de C.V., a corporation registered in the Republic of Mexico, based in Tijuana, Mexico, is the Business Manager of the Investment Trust. The company's management has been engaged in the development and market preparedness of the Herbal Care Immune System Activator product line and MexRx medical products and surgical services since 1995. The Business Manager is the owner of all right, title and interest, including the Copyright, Tradename and Patent Pending, in and to the Herbal Care product line – which is scheduled to be conveyed to the Investment Trust (under chattel) and represents one of the capital assets of the Investment Trust. The Business Manager also owns the proprietary Trade name of MexRx and right, title and claim to all software programs and market methodology for the "e-commerce marketing website" which is the company's platform to market the Herbal Care product line and non-proprietary medical products and surgical services – which is scheduled to be conveyed to the Investment Trust upon completion of the offering and which represents a part of the capital assets of the Investment Trust. MexRx S.A. de C.V. is an affiliate of Kirkland Medical Services S. A. de C.V. (hereinafter referred to as "KMS"), of which the Investment Trust will own a 40% capital stock interest, upon completion of this offering. KMS is the holding company of one of the largest private medical facility in the Republic of Mexico with its own facilities hospitals, laboratories, radiology and pharmacies. Additionally, KMS a fully licensed H.M.O. in Mexico, servicing thousands of H.M.O. members on a worldwide basis.

BUSINESS OF THE TRUST

The Business Manager, subsequent to completion of this offering, intends to inaugurate a modern methodology in medical and health care. The Business Manager is scheduled to launch an Internet website, which will market three primary product/service menus: MexRx Alternative Medicine- Herbal Care Immune System Activator: proprietary non-prescription products for immune system enhancement, MexRx Pharmaceuticals: over 1,250 discounted prescription and non-prescription medical products, and MexRx Surgical Services: over 100 various surgical operations at significant discounts.

MexRx Alternative Medicine - Herbal Care Immune System Activator – Proprietary formulation and production methodology processes complex active material from natural herbs-featuring Geraniaceae extract, into transdermal activators which enhance immune systems. The naturopathic substance results in a hybrid multi-purpose immune system facilitator capable of overcoming most infections. Laboratory and clinical studies conducted since 1993 in Brazil, Cuba, Mexico and Canada substantiate virtual universal remedial effectiveness with absolute absence of ill-effects for applications including: Rheumatoid Arthritis, Carpal tunnel syndrome, Herpes zoster, H. genitalis and H. simplex, Seborreic dermatitis, Psoriasis, Ten-

THE INVESTMENT TRUST   *(continued)*

The inaugural Herbal Care Immune System Activator product line is comprised of seven products. Each product is designed to enhance the immune system in varying degrees of respiratory bursts for specific body locations or remedial requisites. The product includes: Transdermal Activator Liquid (5%), Pain Gel (2%), Skin Gel (2%), Immune system Gel (5%), Acne Gel (1%), Face Gel (1%) and Vaginal Gel (1%).

MexRx Pharmaceuticals – Pharmacy prescription drugs, medicines or vitamins approved by the government of the Republic of Mexico are scheduled to be offered to MexRx Pharmacy members for shipment anywhere in the world. Over 1,250 prescription and non-prescription drugs, medicines and vitamins, both brand names as well as generic, are currently being processed for H.M.O. members of the Business Manager's affiliate, Kirkland Medical Services, for shipment to the U.S. and throughout Mexico. Discounts range from 30-60% as compared with U.S. pharmacy prices.

MexRx Surgical Services – Over 100 surgical services are scheduled to be offered by the Business Manager as they are currently availed to H.M.O. members by the Business Manager's affiliate, International Medical Services, at deep discounted rates. All surgeries are performed at the KMS hospital, one of the largest private medical facility or affiliated hospitals in Mexico. All medical services utilize the same designs as in the United States and adheres to all U.S. medical codes and identification for medical billing and central record files. Discounts range from 30-70% as compared with U.S. surgical rates.

The Business Manager is scheduled to market the MexRx products and services, on a primary basis, through its Internet website. Additionally, the Business Manager intends to market the Herbal Care Immune System Activator product line through distributors, as the registration of the proprietary product line allows over-the-counter sales in select countries. Advertising and marketing campaigns are scheduled for target users of the MexRx products and services within 120 days following completion of this offering. Approximately 70% of the advertising and marketing campaigns are targeted for U.S. markets through network marketing companies.

The Business Manager is scheduled to commence fabrication of the manufacturing facility and fulfillment center for the proprietary Herbal Care Immune System Activator product line upon completion of this offering. The facility is to be located in Tijuana, Mexico and will have, upon completion – which is scheduled 150 days thereafter - an immediate production capacity of approximately 10 million retail dollars per day.

Furthermore, the Business Manager intends to develop revenue sharing joint-venture strategic alliances with independent medical and health care providers for the purpose of accessing broad-scale end user participation within the MexRx programs.

Approximately 97% of the net proceeds of this offering are to be utilized to develop, produce and market the MexRx medical and health care programs. The Business Manager intends to integrate the MexRx programs into select markets that provide the Investment Trust with optimal revenue potential. The Business Manager further intends, through its management efforts, to expand the initial H.M.O. marketing efforts – through Internet access and assertive promotional campaigns – and to increase the value of the overall usage of the MexRx medical and health care programs via strategic alliances with independent medical and health care providers – with short term earning capability and long term consumer usage potential. The Business Manager believes that, in the long term, a significant number of medical and health care providers will opt to utilize the Herbal Care Immune System Activator product line on a private-label basis – wherein the providers will distribute the proprietary Herbal Care products under their own trade names – and a lesser number of providers will amalgamate their sales and distribution operations together with MexRx under the MexRx tradename.

The prospect of revenues for the Investment Trust is solely dependent on the gross sales revenues derived by the Business Manager from the MexRx medical and health care programs. While the historical performance record of the expanding medical/health care industry is indicative of successful consumer acceptance and the unique advantages of the Herbal Care Immune system Activator product line – coupled with the pricing discounts of non-proprietary MexRx medical products and surgical services –provides substantial gross revenue potential , no assurance can be given that the Business Manager or its marketing strategies and strategic alliance

THE INVESTMENT TRUST

programs will ultimately succeed in effecting a successful performance for the Investment Trust and its REVPAC Unit holders. Investors are reminded therefore that the Business Manager has integrated the option of Full Redemption Guaranty coverage into this offering in order to ensure subscribers 100% return of their investment at full term.

MexRx MEDICAL AND HEALTH CARE PROGRAMS POTENTIAL/COMPETITION

Medical and health care usage is expanding, in tandem with the population growth within the world marketplace. There are many companies currently providing medical and health care products and services – however, there is no Internet access that provides all products and services within today's marketplace at the deep discounted prices, as offered by the Business Manager. The Herbal Care Immune System Activator, subsequent to extensive laboratory and clinical testing on thousands of volunteers, has proven itself worthy of entering the marketplace. The Herbal Care product line is universal in its application for immune deficiency invaders and in the view of the Business Manager is the only product line that provides a non-toxic remedy for many of the prominent diseases in today's environment. The Business Manager is of the further view that the Herbal Care Immune System Activator product line will experience rapid consumer acceptance. The Business Manager is of the conclusion that there exists no competition within the sphere of the marketplace that the MexRx programs are embarking and the medical and health care services which they facilitate.

MANAGEMENT STRATEGY

Short Term: The Business Manager, upon completion of this offering, intends to focus its resources on the manufacturing of the Herbal Care Immune System Activator product line production facility, finalization of registration of the Herbal Care product line in the Republic of Mexico for over-the-counter sales, expansion of the H.M.O. into the United States market – in which the Investment Trust has a 40% stockholder interest and which will provide a firm foundation for future marketing efforts, launching of the Internet portal for its medical and health care programs and implementation of its assertive advertising and promotional campaigns on behalf of the MexRx Internet portal. Once the Herbal Care production facility is operational and on-line, within 150 days from completion of this offering, the production facility is designed to sustain a daily product-value manufacturing capacity of $10 Million.

Long Term: The Business Manager intends to expand the sales efforts through aggressive public relations campaigns. In addition, the Business Manager intends to effectuate joint-venture alliances with distributors of parallel products and medical/health care providers while augmenting the variety of medical and health care products and services available via the MexRx programs.

MexRx Medical Products and Services

The following is a partial compilation of the non-proprietary medical products and surgical services offered by the Business Manager. The average pharmaceutical price in the U.S. is compared to the **MexRx** price with the resultant percentage of savings to the patient.

MexRx PHARMACY PRESCRIPTION DRUGS

U.S. NAME	FORMULA	MEX. NAME	DOSAGE	AVG. U.S. PHARM. PRICE	MexRx PHARM. PRICE	AVG. % OF SAVINGS
Accolate (Zeneca)	Zafirlukast	Accolate w/28 T.	20 mg. T.	$1.10	$0.88	25.00%
Accupril (Parke-Davis)	Quinapril	Acupril w/16 T.	10 mg. T.	$1.05	$0.76	38.16%
Adalat CC (Beyer Pharm)	Nifedipine	Adalac CC W/10 T.	30 mg. T.	$1.14	$0.75	52.00%
Albuterol Aerosol (Allen & Hanburys)	Albuterol	Ventolin	17 gm.	$34.98	$22.00	59.00%
Alesse 28 (Wyeth-Ayerst)	Levonorgestrel EthinylEstradiol	Mycrogynon 28 W/28	28 mg. W/28	$1.08	$0.70	54.29%
Alprazolam (Green-stone)	Alprazolam	Tafin W/30	.25 mg. T.	$0.58	$0.37	56.76%
		Tafin W/30	.50 mg. T.	$0.72	$0.45	60.00%
		Tafin W/30	1 mg. T.	$0.97	$0.62	56.45%
Altace (Hoechst Marion)	Ramipril	Tritace w/16	2.5 mg. t.	$0.99	$0.78	26.92%
Atenolol (ESI Lederle Generics)	Atenolol	Tenormin w/28 T.	50 mg. T.	$0.79	$0.50	58.00%
		Tenormin w/28 T.	100 mg. T.	$1.12	$0.70	60.00%
Atrovent Inh (Boehr Ingelheim)	Ipratropium	Atrovent Sol.	Solution	$56.57	$35.50	59.35%
		Atrovent Spray	Spray 15 ml.	$32.79	$20.50	59.95%
Augmentin (SK Becham Pharm)	Amoxicilin/ Clauvula-	Augmentin Susp. 60 ml.	125 mg./31 -25 mg.	$18.81	$11.80	59.41%
		Augmentin W/10 T.	250 mg. 125 mg. T.	$2.54	$1.60	58.75%
		Augmentin W/15 T.	500 mg. 125 mg. T.	$3.74	$2.35	59.15%
		Augmentin W/10 T.	875 mg. 125 mg. T.	$4.99	$3.15	58.41%
Axid (Lilly)	Nizatidine	Axid w/20 T.	150 mg. T.	$1.84	$1.15	60.00%
		Axid w/20 T..	300 mg. T.	$3.51	$2.25	56.00%
Azmocort (RPR)	Trimcino-	Nasacort Spray 16.5 ml	Aerosol 20 gr.	$56.25	$36.00	56.25%
Bacotroban (SK Beecham Pharm)	Mupirocin	Bacotroban	Ointment Top. 15 gm.	$20.96	$13.20	58.79%
Biaxin (Abbott Pharm)	Clarithro-	Klaricid Susp.	GFF 125 mg.	$17.08	$16.10	6.09%
		Klaricid Susp.	GFF 250 mg.	$32.51	$21.67	50.02%
Cardizem CD (Hoechst-Marion)	Diltiazem	Angiotrofin-AP W/20 T.	120 mg. T.	$1.35	$0.85	58.82%

MexRx Medical Products and Services   (continued)

U.S. NAME	FORMULA	MEX. NAME	DOSAGE	AVG. U.S. PHARM. PRICE	MexRx PHARM. PRICE	AVG. % OF SAVINGS
Cardizem CD (Hoechst-Marion)	Diltiazem	Angiotrofin-RTD W/10 T.	180 mg. T.	$1.68	$1.05	60.00%
		Angiotrofin-RTD W/20 T.	240 mg. T.	$2.28	$1.45	57.24%
		Angiotrofin-AP W/20 T.	300 gm.	$2.98	$1.74	71.26%
Cerftin (Glaxo)	Cefuroxime	Zinnat Susp.	250 mg. PDR 50 ml.	$29.48	$26.88	9.67%
		Zinnat c/10	250 mg T.	$4.18	$2.60	60.77%
		Zinnat c/10	500 mg. T.	$6.82	$4.30	55.31%
Cefzil	Cefprozil	Procef c/10 T.	250 mg. T.	$3.49	$2.20	58.64%
		Procef c/10 T.	500 mg. T.	$6.82	$4.30	58.60%
Cephalexin (Apoth-econ)	Cephalexin	Ceporex c/20 C.	250 mg. Cap	$0.63	$0.53	18.87%
Cephalexin (Teva)		Ceporex c/20 C.	500 mg. Cap	$1.43	$1.06	34.91%
Cimetidine (Mylan)	Cimetidine	Tagamet c/30 CT.	200 mg. T.	$0.88	$0.55	60.00%
		Cimetase c/30	300 mg. Cap	$0.92	$0.60	53.33%
		Cimetase c/30	400 mg. Cap	$1.54	$1.00	54.00%
		Tagamet c/16	800 mg. Cap	$2.82	$1.70	65.88%
Cipro (Bayer Pharm)	Ciprofloxacion	Suiflox W/12 T.	250 mg. T.	$3.75	$2.35	59.57%
		Suiflox W/8 T.	500mg. T.	$4.40	$2.75	60.00%
Claritin (Schering)	Loratadine	Claritine 60 ml. Sol	Syrup 480 ml.	$16.83	$11.15	50.94%
		Claritine W/10 T.	10 mg. T.	$3.20	$2.00	60.00%
Claritin D 12 Hr. (Shering)	Loratadine/ Pseu-doephedrine	Claritine D W/10 T.	10 mg./240 mg T.	$2.72	$1.70	60.00%

HOSPITALIZATION AND SURGICAL SERVICES

The following is a partial compilation of major **MexRx** surgical services together with applicable fees. All fees are inclusive of hospitalization and surgery payments. The fee schedule is discounted between 40-60% as compared with U.S. prices.

DISEASE AND SURGICAL PROCEDURES	MexRx FEE
SPINAL	
Spinal Procedures	$ 3,800.00
Laminectomy, site	$ 3,800.00
Carpal Tunnel Release	$ 750.00
EYE	
Cataract	$ 1,500.00

MexRx Medical Products and Services *(continued)*

DISEASE AND SURGICAL PROCEDURES	MexRx FEE
SINUS	
Mastoidectomy	$ 750.00
Sinusotomy	$ 850.00
Cleft Lip and Palate Repair	$ 1,200.00
Nasal Septal Repair and Plastic Operation	$ 1,200.00
Septoplasty	$ 1,100.00
Rhinoplasty	$ 1,100.00
Tonsillectomy and/or Adenoidectomy	$ 500.00
Temporomandibular, Arthrosplasty	$ 1,500.00
BREAST	
Breast Reconstruction, plastic surgery	$ 1,500.00
Breast Implant	$ 1,500.00
Breast Implan, removal	$ 500.00
CHEST	
Bronchoscopy	$ 250.00
Excision, lymph node	$ 1,200.00
HEART	
Cardiac Valve Replacement	$ 22,000.00
Cardiac Catheterization	$ 2,800.00
Coronary Bypass	$ 19,000.00
Coronary Angioplasty	$ 5,800.00
Pacemaker Implant	$ 3,000.00
VASCULAR	
Angiogram	$ 1,900.00
Angioplasty	$ 3,500.00
Amputation, lower limb	$ 850.00
Amputation, below knee	$ 850.00
Amputation, foot	$ 650.00
Amputation, toe	$ 350.00
Varicose Vein Removal	$ 5,500.00
Saphenectomy	$ 1,200.00
Sympathectomy	$ 950.00

(This space intentionally left blank)

REVPAC The New Revolutionary Financial Instrument

PARTICIPATION IN COSTS AND REVENUES

MexRx S.A. de C.V., Business Manager for the Investment Trust has entered into a Management Agreement with **MexRx Investment Trust.** Under the terms and conditions of the agreement, the Business Manager is responsible to conduct the day-to-day business operations requisite for the establishment, maintenance, marketing, fulfillment, administration and management of the **MexRx** medical and health care programs owned by the Investment Trust.

Also, under the terms of the Management Agreement, the Investment Trust is responsible to contribute 100% of the capital requirements to develop and market the **MexRx** medical and health care programs. The Investment Trust retains 100% ownership, during the term of the Investment Trust, of the proprietary right, title and interest to the **MexRx** computer software for the Internet marketing website, Herbal Care Immune system Activator product line manufacturing facility, 40% stockholding interest in International Medical Services S.A. de C.V. and (under chattel) Intellectual Property claims for **MexRx** and Herbal Care product line. The Trust Administrator oversees the allocation of 80% of the gross sales revenues of the Herbal Care product line and 92.5% of the gross sales revenues of **MexRx** medical products and surgical services to the Business Manager – from which the Business Manager is to continually replenish and up-date the **MexRx** Investment Trust holdings – which are part of the Investment Trust's capital assets. The maintenance and "replenishment" of the Herbal Care product line manufacturing facility and **MexRx** computer software system continues throughout the term of the Investment Trust. Additionally, as compensation for the capital investment, the Investment Trust is entitled to receive 20% of gross sales revenues derived from the Herbal Care product line and 7.5% of gross sales revenues derived from **MexRx** medical products and surgical services. Acting as Trust Administrator for the Investment Trust is PriceWaterhouseCoopers of Tijuana, B.C., Mexico .*The Administrator is responsible to allocate all proceeds and revenues of the Investment Trust and oversee the business operations.*

All sales revenues derived from Herbal Care Immune System Activator product line and **MexRx** medical products/surgical services are deposited by the Business Manager into an account overseen by the Investment Trust Administrator. The Investment Trust's 20% Revenue Participation share of Herbal Care product line gross sales revenues and 7.5% Revenue Participation share of **MexRx** medical products and surgical services are automatically segregated into an interest bearing Trust Account for the Investment Trust Unit holders administered by the Trust Administrator. The remaining gross sales revenues are allocated to the Business Manager to defray operational/business costs and expenses - including the maintenance and replenishment of the Investment Trust capital assets.

The Trust Administrator is entitled to receive a fee of $25,000.00 per year for reasonable, ordinary and necessary operating expenses of the Trust.

The Net Cash Flow of the Investment Trust – which is equivalent to Investment Trust Revenue Participation portion of gross sales revenues, plus accumulated interest– is distributed to the Investment Trust Unit holders on a pro-rata basis.

DISTRIBUTION OF REVENUES TO UNIT HOLDERS

The first Revenue Distribution occurs on the third year anniversary following completion of this offering. An additional Revenue Distribution occurs on each anniversary thereafter. Upon the fifth Revenue Distribution – on the seventh year anniversary following this offering – all Revenue Distribution rights will cease for the Investment Trust Unit holder, unless the holder has exercised the Future Participation Warrant (attached to the Investment Trust REVPAC Unit) and purchased a newly issued Investment Trust Unit for the ensuing Seven Year term of the Investment Trust.

FULL REDEMPTION GUARANTY COVERAGE

The Full Redemption Guaranty attached to each REVPAC Unit provides the holder a guaranteed 100% return on investment at full term. In effect, the investor is guaranteed that the aggregate Revenue Share disbursements during the seven-year term will equal minimum 100% of the IPO cost for the REVPAC Bond Units of this offering. As a risk insurance premium payment for Full Redemption Guaranty coverage, the holder relinquishes one-half of all future Revenue Share disbursements. In other words, the REVPAC Unit holder forfeits 50% of all future Revenue Share disbursements in return for the guarantee that all Revenue Share disbursements will equal minimum the Initial Public Offering price of the REVPAC Bond Units. The Full Redemption Guaranty provides the unit holder with a zero-risk investment, wherein if the Revenue Share disbursements fail to equal the IPO price of the REVPAC Bond Units, the Full Redemption Guaranty may be redeemed for the difference between the aggregate revenue share disbursements received and the IPO price of the REVPAC Unit. The Business Manager has elected that all subscribers of this offering be afforded Full Redemption Guaranty coverage in order that all subscription proceeds are protected against partial or full loss.

Ninety days prior to the REVPAC Unit reaching "full maturity" and up to the Full Redemption Guaranty redemption date – which is coincident with the "full maturity" date, the REVPAC Unit holder may elect one of two choices. Either:

(a)   The REVPAC Unit holder may submit the Full Redemption Guaranty to the Trust Administrator– in connection with the Futurity Warrant – and purchase a newly issued REVPAC Unit for the ensuing seven year term of the Investment Trust for that portion of the Full Redemption Guaranty redemption that is applicable /or/

(b)   The REVPAC Unit holder may submit the Full Redemption Guaranty for a cash payment that is based on the difference between aggregate Revenue Share disbursements and Unit IPO price.

The Unit holder is required to elect Full Redemption Guaranty coverage at the time that the REVPAC Bond Units are purchased in the Initial Public Offering. Full Redemption Guaranty coverage guarantees the holder that seven years following completion of this offering the REVPAC Bond Units will have yielded an aggregate of $5.00 per Unit in the form of Revenue Share disbursements and Full Redemption Guaranty redemption payments – equal to 100% return on investment.

FUTURE PARTICIPATION WARRANT	*MANDATORY DISSOLUTION OF TRUST*

The REVPAC Unit has a seven-year term. At the end of seven years, following completion of this offering, the REVPAC Unit and all Revenue Participation Rights in connection with Revenue Share disbursements cease. The holder may, 90 days prior to "full maturity" or within 90 days of notice by Business Manager and Trust Administrator of earlier exercise rights, elect to exercise the Future Participation Warrant for the ensuing seven year term of the Investment Trust /or/ the holder may elect to sell the REVPAC Unit with the attached Future Participation Warrant through one of the securities trading markets upon which the Investment Trust is listed.

In the event, at least 60% of the Trust's Revenue Sharing Venture Bond Holders exercise the Future Participation Warrant for an additional term of the Trust.The REVPAC Holders will receive revenue sharing rights in a new Business Venture designated by the Business Manager for an additional 7-Year term. Additionally, in the event, the REVPAC Holders have received at least 500% Return on Investment – aggregate Revenue Sharing Yields of $25 per REVPAC Unit, during the first 7-Year term, Allocation of Revenues, derived from the Capital Assets are to continue for the first four years of the 7-Year renewal term. In the event, the REVPAC Holders have received less than 500% Return on Investment, Allocation of Revenues derived from the Capital Assets are to continue for the entire 7-Years of the renewal term.

All capital assets – comprised of proprietary computer software, manufacturing facility and Intellectual Property rights – remain the property of the Investment Trust and its REVPAC holders from one term to the ensuing term under the conditions of the Collateralized Yield Obligation.

In the event that 60% of the outstanding REVPAC Unit holders fail to submit the attached Future Participation Warrants to the Trust Administrator 90 days prior to "full maturity" and exercise their right to purchase a newly issued REVPAC Unit for the ensuing seven year term, the Investment Trust will be dissolved. In the event of dissolution, all capital assets will be liquidated – with the Business Manager maintaining a first-right-of refusal to purchase the capital assets pursuant to the Collateralized Yield Obligation - and the proceeds distributed to the Unit holders.

THE BUSINESS MANAGER

MexRx S.A. de C.V., is a corporation registered in the Republic of Mexico with its principal office located at Calle Rufino Tamayo 9910, Esquina Blvd. Cuauhtemoc y Dr. Atl, Zona Rio, B.C., Mexico 22320. The Business Manager is responsible to utilize the proceeds of this offering for the purpose of developing, producing, maintaining, marketing, managing and administrating the MexRx medical and health care programs described herein and to oversee and conduct the business development operations pursuant to the Management Agreement between the Company and MexRx Investment Trust.

The officers and directors of the Business Manager conduct the day-to-day business of the Company and bear primary responsibility for ensuring that the business operations of the Investment Trust are conducted in the manner herein described.

The principal Executive Officers of the Business Manager are as follows:

Name	Address	Position
FRANCISCO GARCIA	Calle Rufino Tamayo 9910 Esq. Cuauhtemoc y Dr. Atl Zona Rio Tijuana B.C., Mexico, 22320	President, CEO and Chairman of the Board
RENE PAREDES	Calle Rufino Tamayo 9910 Esq. Cuauhtemoc y Dr. Atl Zona Rio Tijuana B.C., Mexico, 22320	Vice President and Administrator
CARMEN MIRANDA	Calle Rufino Tamayo 9910 Esq. Cuauhtemoc y Dr. Atl Zona Rio Tijuana B.C., Mexico, 22320	Treasurer and Director of Finance
ALFREDO RIVERA	Calle Rufino Tamayo 9910 Esq. Cuauhtemoc y Dr. Atl Zona Rio Tijuana B.C., Mexico, 22320	Secretary
DR. FERNANDO CRUZ	Calle Rufino Tamayo 9910 Esq. Cuauhtemoc y Dr. Atl Zona Rio Tijuana B.C., Mexico, 22320	Advisory Board Member
DR. PEDRO GUTIERREZ	Calle Rufino Tamayo 9910 Esq. Cuauhtemoc y Dr. Atl Zona Rio Tijuana B.C., Mexico, 22320	Advisory Board Member

(This space intentionally left blank)

REVPAC The New Revolutionary Financial Instrument

THE BUSINESS MANAGER *(continued)*

The following information sets forth the principal occupations of the directors, executive officers and advisory board members for the past ten years.

Name		Position
FRANCISCO GARCIA		President, CEO and Chairman of the Board

President of MexRx S.A. de C.V. since 1998. For the Period 1992-1998 - Mr. Garcia directed the activities of government controlled educational and cultural agencies in the northern Sonora area such as *CONACULTA, Casa de la Cultura, Museo de Ciencias* . Prior to 1992 - Mr. Garcia served in upper management with the State of Sonora Commission of Public Services and the National Institute for Adult Education. Mr. Garcia has served as an active member of the Chamber of the Restaurant Industry in Hermosillo , the Office of the State Secretary of Tourism for the State of Sonora, the State Council for Aquaculture Cooperative Society and the National Confederation of Cooperative Societies. Mr. Garcia graduated from the Faculty of Administratrio – Hermosillo Sonora, in 1967, with a Bachelor of Marketing.

Name		Position
RENE PAREDES		Vice President and Administrador

Administrator of MexRx S.A. de C.V. since inception and concurrently the Chief Administrator of *Kirkland Medical Services S.A. de C.V.* – one of the first Health Maintenance Organization (HMO) within the Republic of Mexico since 1990. Prior to 1990 - Mr. Paredes served as Supervisor of Operations in the Cybernetic Department at Bourns de Mexico and as a Collaberating Computer Programming Instructor at the *Windsor Institute* of Mexico. Mr. Paredes graduated from the Centro de Ensenanza Tecnica y Superior, in 1963, with a degree in Technical Systems Analyst Programming.

Name		Position
CARMEN MIRANDA		Treasurer and Director of Finance

Director of Finance of MexRx S.A. de C.V. since inception and concurrently the Treasurer and Director of Finance of *Kirkland Medical Services S.A. de C.V.* since 1997. Prior to 1997 - Ms. Miranda served as an accountant for governmental agencies and commercial enterprises in Northern Sonora . Ms. Miranda graduated from the Universidad Autonoma of Guadalajara in 1966 with a degree in Accounting. Ms. Miranda is Certified Public Accountant since 1967.

Name		Position
ALFREDO RIVERA		Secretary

Secretary of MexRx S.A. de C.V. since inception and concurrently the OIC for pharmaceutical purchasing and accountability of *Kirkland Medical Services S.A. de C.V.* since 1998. Prior to 1998 – Mr. Rivera served as the Purchasing Director and Cost Accountant for *Besser Company* – Mexico City, and Administrator of Multi-National Services for *Articulos Terapeuticos S.A. de C.V.* Mr. Rivera graduated from UNIVERSITY OF

THE BUSINESS MANAGER *(continued)*

Name		Position
DR. FERNANDO CRUZ		Advisory Board Member

Advisory Board Member of MexRx S.A. de C.V. since inception and concurrently – since 1991 – an Internist and General Physician at *Kirkland Medical Services S. A. de C.V.* Prior to 1991 – Dr. Cruz served as a Physician at Hospital General.– Oregon, Sonora, Mexico. He also served as Physician from 1977-83 at *Instituto Mexicano del Seguro Social* - Culiacan and Guasave Sinaloa Mexico. Dr. Cruz graduated from the University of Guadalajara Medical School in 1967 and received postgraduate education in Internal Medicine at Centro Medico Nacional de Occidente in Guadalajara, Jalisco.

Name		Position
DR. PEDRO GUTIERREZ		Advisory Board Member

Advisory Board Member of MexRx S.A. de C.V. since inception and concurrently – since 1991 – the Medical Director at *Kirkland Medical Services S.A. de C.V.* Previously, Dr. Gutierrez served in the Earthquake Medical Relief Corps with the *U.S. Salvation Army* in El Salvador and as the Medical Director of *Alvarado Hospital* in San Diego, CA. Dr. Gutierrez graduated from the University of Guadalajara in 1986 with a medical degree.

(This space intentionally left blank)

UNDERWRITING

The Investment Trust is offering 900,000 REVPAC Bond Units to the public through the Underwriter. The price of each Unit is $5.00. A 1,000 Unit minimum purchase is required. Persons wishing to subscribe for the units should complete the Subscription Agreement attached hereto and forward it together with a check payable to **MexRx Investment Trust Escrow Account**. The Trust has agreed to pay the Underwriter a cash sales commission of $0.50 per share sold. In addition, the Trust has agreed to pay to the Underwriter a non-accounting expense allowance of $0.15 per share sold.

The Trust has established an escrow, in accordance with the Underwriting Agreement and administered by the Trust Administrator of the Investment Trust- for all proceeds derived from the offering. The escrow provides that all funds received for subscriptions will be deposited in a subscription escrow account pending delivery of the certificates evidencing Units purchased to the subscriber. Upon delivery of the certificates to the subscribers, the proceeds will be released to the Trust Administrator for allocation to the Business Manager and the Underwriter. This offering is being offered on a "surety guaranteed" basis – wherein the Underwriter agrees to purchase any and all Units that remain unsold at the end of the offering and as of January 10, 2003. Also, included in the terms of the escrow, an allocation of 10% commission and 3% non-accountable expense allowance on all proceeds derived from the sales efforts of the Underwriter will be paid to the Underwriter. The Investment Trust will receive 87% of all proceeds derived from the Underwriter's sales efforts out of escrow.

Each subscriber hereof shall be required to complete and sign a Subscription Agreement. The Subscription Agreement indicates the number of Units to be purchased by the Subscriber, the aggregate offering price and describes the terms of this Offering. Certificates representing REVPAC Bond Units purchased shall be registered in the name(s) of the beneficial owner(s) as it appears on the Subscription Agreement and forwarded to the address appearing therein.

UNDERWRITER WARRANTS

The Investment Trust has agreed to sell for $0.10 per Warrant to the Underwriter one Warrant for each 33.3 Units sold. Each such Warrant will permit the holder thereof to purchase one REVPAC Unit of the Investment Trust at an exercisable price of $1.00 per Unit. The Warrants will be exercisable for a period of sixty (60) months, commencing from the closing date of this offering. The price payable upon exercise of the Warrants and the number of Units covered by the Warrants are subject to adjustment in certain events to prevent dilution. The Warrants are exercisable to or transferable from the date of issuance to selected dealers and their officers or partners. The Trust will agree, in the event that all of the REVPAC Bond Units offered hereby are sold, at its expense, upon request of an Underwriter, in any one occasion during the sixty month period commencing after the closing date of this offering, to file a notification, Offering Memorandum or Registration Statement and Prospectus if necessary to permit the public offering and sale of such Warrants, and the REVPAC Bond Units underlying such warrants.

DESCRIPTION OF SECURITIES

Investment Trust Unit. The authorized capital of the Investment Trust consists of 954,000 REVPAC Bond Units. 900,000 Units are being offered pursuant to this offering, 27,000 are issued to REVPAC Funding Foundation and 27,000 are reserved for issuance to the Underwriter in connection with this offering. A maximum 954,000 Revenue Participation Capital Bonds (REVPAC Bond Units) will be issued and outstanding subsequent to the successful completion of this offering and the exercise of the Underwriter's warrants. Each REVPAC Unit consists of one <u>Revenue Share</u>, one <u>Full Redemption Guaranty</u> and one <u>Future Participation Warrant</u>.

Revenue Share. Each Revenue Share entitles the holder to receive a pro-rata share of the gross revenues from the business of the Trust, which is defined – during the instant seven year term – as 20% of the gross sales revenues derived from the Herbal Care Immune System Activator product line and 7.5% of the gross sales revenues derived from the MexRx medical products and surgical services. The Revenue Share holder's portion of gross revenues is held in an interest bearing account – administrated by the Administrator – prior

DESCRIPTION OF SECURITIES *(continued)*

to distribution. The holder of one Revenue Share is entitled to receive 1/954,000 part of the gross revenue portion, plus accumulated interest, less applicable Trust Administrator fees.

The seven year Revenue Share has five (5) Revenue Yield Coupons attached to each Revenue Share Certificate. These coupons are redeemable as follows: Coupon #1 – 36 Months following completion of this offering, Coupon #2 – 48 Months following completion of this offering, Coupon #3 – 60 Months following completion of this offering, Coupon #4 – 72 Months following this offering and Coupon #5 – 84 Months following this offering. Upon payment of Coupon #5, the Revenue Share expires and all revenue yield rights of the holder cease.

Full Redemption Guaranty. Each Full Redemption Guaranty entitles the holder to receive a surety bond guarantee that any and all Revenue Share disbursements - *from the five attached Revenue Yield Coupons* – will be equivalent to minimum $5.00 per REVPAC Unit. In the event that the aggregate Revenue Share disbursements, at full term, are not equivalent to $5.00, the Full Redemption Guaranty redemption payment will equal the difference between the aggregate Revenue Share disbursements received and $5.00 per REVPAC Investment Trust Unit. The holder of one Revenue Share is entitled to receive 1/954,000 part of the gross revenue portion, plus accumulated interest. The Full Redemption Guaranty is elected by the Business Manager to be mandatory for all subscribers of this offering. Full Redemption Guaranty coverage requires the investor to pay a premium equivalent to one-half of any and all future Revenue Share disbursements. This 50% relinquishment of future Revenue Share disbursements is the *premium payment* in return for 100% return on investment guarantee. Full Redemption Guaranty holders must submit the Full Redemption Guaranty to the Administrator of the Trust 90 days prior to the full term maturity date of the REVPAC Unit – 81 months following completion of this offering. The value at which the Full Redemption Guaranty is to be redeemed is based on the $5.00 IPO price of the REVPAC Unit less the total accumulated Revenue Yield Coupon disbursements. The holder may elect to exchange the Full Redemption Guaranty, at full term, for a newly issued REVPAC Unit, *if redemption payment is due* -for the ensuing seven year term of the Investment Trust – by submitting the Future Participation Warrant together with the Full Redemption Guaranty and a cash payment equivalent to the difference between the Full Redemption Guaranty redemption payment and $5.00 to the Trust Administrator. In the event the holder elects to exercise the Future Participation Warrant through the exchange of the Full Redemption Guaranty, the exchange basis is one REVPAC Unit for one Full Redemption Guaranty. In the event the holder elects to redeem the Full Redemption Guaranty for cash payment, distribution of redemption payment is made by the Administrator concurrent with the distribution of coupon #5 Revenue Yield payment – on the 84th month following completion of this offering.

Future Participation Warrant. The REVPAC Unit has a seven-year term. At the end of seven years, following completion of this offering, the REVPAC Unit and all Revenue Participation Rights in connection with Revenue Share disbursements cease. The holder may, 90 days prior to "full maturity" or within 90 days of notice by Business Manager and Trust Administrator of earlier exercise rights, elect to exercise the Future Participation Warrant for the ensuing seven year term of the Investment Trust /or/ the holder may elect to sell the REVPAC Unit with the attached Future Participation Warrant through one of the securities trading markets upon which the Investment Trust is listed.

In the event, at least 60% of the Trust's Revenue Sharing Venture Bond Holders exercise the Future Participation Warrant for an additional term of the Trust and the REVPAC Holders have received 500% Return on Investment – aggregate Revenue Sharing Yields of $25 per REVPAC Unit during the first seven year term, allocation of identical revenue yields, derived from the Capital Assets, are to continue for the initial four years of the renewal term. In the event, the REVPAC Holders have received less than 500% Return on Investment, allocation of revenues derived from the Capital Assets are to continue for the full seven years of the Renewal Term. Additionally, the REVPAC Holders that exercise the Warrant receive additional revenue sharing interests in a new business venture to be designated by the Business Manager, concurrent with the notice to REVPAC Holders of the right to exercise the Future Participation Warrant.

All capital assets – comprised of proprietary computer software, manufacturing facility and Intellectual Property rights – remain the property of the Investment Trust and its REVPAC holders from one term to the ensuing term under the conditions of the Collateralized Yield Obligation.

In the event that 60% of the outstanding REVPAC Unit holders fail to submit the attached Future Participation Warrants to the Trust Administrator 90 days prior to "full maturity" and exercise their right to purchase a newly issued REVPAC Unit for the ensuing seven year term, the Investment Trust will be dissolved. In the event of dissolution, all capital assets will be liquidated – with the Business Manager maintaining a first-right-of refusal to purchase the capital assets pursuant to the Collateralized Yield Obligation - and the proceeds distributed to the Unit holders.

DESCRIPTION OF SECURITIES
(continued)

The Holders of REVPAC Bond Units (i) have equal rights to Revenue Yield distributions: (i.i.) are entitled to share ratably in all of the capital assets of the Investment Trust available for distribution; and (i.i.i.) are not entitled to exercise discretion concerning the business operations of the Investment Trust of Business Manager.

The foregoing statement is a summary of the rights and privileges of the holder of the Investment Trust's REVPAC Bond Units. It does not purport to be complete and is subject to the provisions of United Kingdom Law and to the terms of the Investment Trust's Certificate of Origin.

UNDERWRITER

The Company's Underwriter will be serving the Investment Trust in this securities offering. The Underwriter is
_____.

SECURITIES LISTINGS

The Investment Trust intends to make all of the filings required so that the Investment Trust's "REVPAC" Units can be listed . This will allow the Investment Trust's Units to be traded in all jurisdictions in which the Investment Trust meets the standard and requirements for trading in said jurisdictions.

LITIGATION

The Investment Trust nor the Business Manager are not presently a party to any material litigation, nor to the knowledge of the Trust Administrator or Business Manager is litigation threatened against either which may be material.

ESCROW AGENT

Subject to the Trust and Escrow provisions of the Underwriting Agreement, all proceeds received from the sale of the Units of this offering for the full Offering Price shall be transmitted by the Underwriter or its agents to an escrow account substantially entitled "MexRx INVESTMENT TRUST ESCROW ACCOUNT". The account is administered by the Trust and Escrow Agent: PriceWaterhouseCoopers located at Tapachula 11550, Chapultepec, CP 22020 Tijuana, Baja California, Mexico. The Telephone/Fax Number is 52.664.615.5000 / 52.664.615.5010.

SUBCRIPTION AGREEMENT OF
MexRx INVESTMENT TRUST

SUBSCRIPTION PRODEDURES: Persons who desire to subscribe to the REVPAC Bond Units of **MexRx Investment Trust** may do so by executing the Subscription Agreement included herewith.

SUBSCRIPTION AGREEMENT AND REPRESENTATIONS OF SHAREHOLDER

The undersigned hereby acknowledges and warrants as follows:

1. SUBSCRIPTION

Subscribes and purchases at the price of $5.00 per Unit the REVPAC Bond Units of **MexRx Investment Trust** set forth immediately above the signature of the undersigned. It is understood that this subscription may be rejected by the Business Manager and Trust Administrator of the Trust.

2. SECURITIES LAW – REGISTRATION AND EXEMPTION

Stipulates that the undersigned understands that the REVPAC Bond Units described in this Agreement are being offered and sold in compliance with registration requirements or qualification by exemption in select jurisdictions outside the United States where the Units are qualified for sale.

3. REPRESENTATIONS

Certifies, represents and warrants that:

A. The undersigned has received a full copy of the Prospectus dated January 10, 20** as prepared by the Business Manager and Trust Administrator of the Investment Trust;

B. The Units described in this Agreement are being purchased by the undersigned for the account of the undersigned or in a fiduciary capacity for a person or entity that is legal within the jurisdiction where the Units are eligible to be offered.

C. The undersigned has not relied in executing this Agreement and making the purchase herein described on any representations not contained in the Prospectus for the Units described in this Agreement;

D. The undersigned understands that no jurisdictional regulatory agency has passed on the merits or fairness of the Investment Trust Unit offering described in the Agreement for sale to investors;

E. The undersigned is capable of bearing the economic risks and burdens normally associated with the purchase of the REVPAC Bond Investment Trust Units described in the Prospectus including, but not limited to, the possibility of incurring a full return of contributed capital without interest – *in the event the undersigned receives full return of contributed capital from the Full Redemption Guaranty coverage* – and the lack of adequate liquidity within a public market which may cause the REVPAC Bonδ Units to be less readily liquidated than desired;

F. The address set forth in this agreement is the true and correct address of the undersigned and the undersigned has no present intention of becoming a resident of any other jurisdiction;

G. The undersigned has been advised to consult with an attorney of the choosing of the undersigned regarding legal matters concerning an investment in the Trust and the tax and risk consequences of participating in the Investment Trust.

BY SUBSCRIBER

This is to certify that I am a bonafide resident of the jurisdiction designated as my domicile and that I hereby agree to purchase _____ REVPAC Bond Units in MexRx Investment Trust for the total sum of _____ _____ ($_____). The undersigned hereby executes this page as part of the Prospectus dated January 10, 20**.

UNIT HOLDER

The Undersigned requests that the Unit(s) be issued in the name of the Undersigned and delivered to the undersigned at the address below, dated: _____.

I will hold title to my units as follows: (Initial one)

Community Property	Joint tenancy (both must sign)
Tenants in common	Individual ownership
(each must sign)	Trust or Pension Plan
As custodian for Minor	Partnership
As custodian, trustee or agent for:	Corporation
	Other: (please describe)

(Signature of Authorized Representative)	(Signature of Subscriber) (Seal)
(Print Name, Title of Authorized representative)	(Print Name, [Title, if applicable])

Please type or print the following information:

Full name(s) of Subscriber(s) as it (they) should appear on certificates

Street Address	City	Cntry	Zip Code

Telehone			Fax

Passport or Tax I.D. No.		Passport or Tax I.D. No.	
Dated:		Dated:	

Signature	Signature

Title or capacity of signing party if the subscriber is partnership, corporation, trust or other non-individual entity.

Remittance should be payable to:	MexRx INVESTMENT TRUST ESCROW ACCOUNT
Remittance should be sent to Underwriter /or/ Transmitted by wire to Escrow Bank.	

REVPAC The New Revolutionary Financial Instrument

MexRx Investment Trust Brochure

**THE SECURED NEW AND
EXCITING WAY TO INVEST IN THE
HEALTH CARE INDUSTRY**

MexRx Investment Trust

Presents

**Revenue Participation Capital
(REVPAC) Bonds...The New Financial
Instrument for Medicine & Health Care**

**...Stabilizing the economics of
Health Care Development for the next
generation**

MexRx Investment Trust...is the first Investment Trust of its kind – utilizing the new, revolutionary Financial Instrument ... Revenue Participation Capital (REVPAC) Bond.

IMAGINE... RECEIVING YIELDS BASED UPON GROSS REVENUES!

Medical and Health Care investors have long awaited the emergence of a new financial instrument that is revenue-powered...not equity or debt driven.

Now, MexRx Investment Trust unveils its much heralded financial instrument – REVPAC Bond – which allows investors to...

ENJOY THE POWER OF REVENUE YIELDS LINKED TO REAL-TIME PERFORMANCE!

MexRx Investment Trust is a dynamic investment alternative to stocks and limited partnerships. At the heart of this breakthrough is the REVPAC Bond, the ultimate financial instrument for the Medical and Health Care Business that **- for the very first time -** stabilizes the economics of the business of medicine and health care with *meaningful* investor participation.

The REVPAC Bond is like no other financial instrument:

- Extraordinary Short Term Yield Potential

  Investors receive cash disbursements on each and every medical and surgical transaction - worldwide.

- Long Term Revenue Sharing Rights

  Investors receive revenue disbursements on all proprietary medical and health care products owned by the Investment Trust in addition to all new medicines and health care products developed during the term of the Investment Trust.

- Full Redemption Guaranty

  Investors are guaranteed that accumulated cash disbursements - during term of Investment Trust - will be equivalent to *at least* return of their entire investment - at full term.

- Liquidity

  Investors can trade their REVPAC Bond Units on securities markets

REVPAC Bond is destined to become the financial instrument of choice for future generations of health care investors**...and it is available TODAY through MexRx Investment Trust.**

**MexRx
Investment Trust**

Its Time Has Come

REVPAC Bonds:
Changing the
way we invest
in Health Care

1

Introduction to
REVPAC Bonds

**MexRx
Investment Trust...
leading the
Health Care Business
into a new era**

REVPAC Bonds are a leading edge financial instrument designed to optimize revenue opportunities for the fast-expanding markets of the world-wide Health Care Business.

The REVPAC Bond brings together powerful features from traditional financial instruments and bundles them into a single securities unit that provides an easy-to-use Financial Instrument for Health Care Business investors.

Imagine a Revenue Participation Share with Revenue Yield Disbursement Coupons – Full Redemption Guaranty – and Windfall Warrant bundled together into a "user-friendly" Financial Instrument...Voilà!...you have the REVPAC Bond.

The REVPAC Bond embodies three component parts wrapped into an Investment Trust...which provides unerring accountability - "real-time" performance - extraordinary revenue yield potential and a Full Redemption Guaranty - where the investor may be assured of the full return of the investment.

Holder receives yields for seven years based on worldwide gross sales revenues of all MexRx medical products and surgical services.

Revenue Yield Coupons disburse accumulated revenue entitlements on 36, 48 , 60, 72, 84 months following completion of IPO of the Investment Trust

Holder is entitled to recover return of original investment at full term

Holder can purchase new REVPAC Bond Units for ensuing 7 year term of Investment Trust

2

**Introduction to
REVPAC Bonds**

Revenue Bonds allow investors to share in each and every dollar derived from the worldwide sales of all MexRx medical products and surgical services during a seven-year term. No more guesswork about "yields"...the revenues flow directly from the marketplace to the investors...no middle management interference, or deductions.

For instance, if there are only 1,250 patients purchasing the proprietary Herbal Care Immune System Activator product - known as the *Transdermal Activator* - there will result gross sales revenues of $18 Million - the REVPAC Bond Unit holders - receiving 20% share Revenue Participation will have earned $3.6 Million for a single year on a single product.

Revenue Yields are distributed during the 7 year life of the REVPAC Bond Unit. All revenues accumulate in the investor's trust account until distributed. Distribution commences with the redemption of Coupon #1 on the third anniversary of the completion of the IPO. Distribution continues each year thereafter. No fewer than 5 distributions shall be made.

MexRx INVESTMENT TRUST REVENUE YIELD COUPON #1	Coupon No. 1 After 36 months: first distribution of gross revenue yields
MexRx INVESTMENT TRUST REVENUE YIELD COUPON #2	Coupon No. 2 After 48 months: second distribution of gross revenue yields
MexRx INVESTMENT TRUST REVENUE YIELD COUPON #3	Coupon No. 3 After 60 months: third distribution of gross revenue yields
MexRx INVESTMENT TRUST REVENUE YIELD COUPON #4	Coupon No. 4 After 72 months: fourth distribution of gross revenue yields
MexRx INVESTMENT TRUST REVENUE YIELD COUPON #5	Coupon No. 5 After 84 months: fifth distribution of gross revenue yields

Once the Gross Revenue Yield for the final Coupon is distributed, all revenue sharing rights expire.

3

Introduction to
REVPAC Bonds

Full Redemption Guaranty allows investor to redeem the REVPAC Bond Unit for a "cash payment" up to the IPO price paid by the investor - $5.00 per Unit - at the end of the 7 year term. The Full Redemption Guaranty is secured by a Risk Insurance Package Wrap, underwritten through Lloyd's of London and other insurance organizations of equal standing in the world insurance community.

FULL REDEMPTION GUARANTY

This Guaranty entitles the holder to receive a redemption payment - concurrent with the final Revenue Yield Coupon disbursement - equivalent to the difference between the aggregate disbursements of all Revenue Yield Coupons and the IPO price up to a maximum cash payment of $5.00 per unit.

The holder may redeem this Full Redemption Guaranty coupon - in lieu of cash payment - for a newly issued Unit of the Investment Trust, for the ensuing seven year term of the Trust, by submitting this coupon together with the Warrant and applicable payment on the "Redemption Due Date".

FRG Coupon # A-1001 Redemption Date: March 15, 20**

Redemption payments are distributed concurrently with the final revenue yield disbursement to investors with the redemption of Coupon #5.

If investors do not desire to receive a cash payment and elect instead to purchase a new REVPAC Bond Unit for the next seven year term of the Investment Trust, the investor may submit the Full Redemption Guaranty together with the Warrant and receive credit toward the $5.00 per Unit purchase.

The Full Redemption Guaranty provides the investor the security that the REVPAC Bond Unit will have added value at full term in addition to the return on investment received via the five Revenue Yield Coupons.

Future Participation Warrants are attached to each REVPAC Bond Unit. Each Warrant entitles the investor to purchase a new REVPAC Bond Unit for the ensuing Seven Year term of the Investment Trust. The purchase price is $5.00 per Unit. The Revenue Share entitlements for the next seven year term are the identical percentage of worldwide gross sales revenues from the sales of any and all medical products and surgical services plus additional revenue sharing entitlements that the Business Manager (see below) may declare.

In effect, the value of the revenue participation rights may be significantly enhanced by the increased number of patients enrolled in the MexRx medical and health care programs during the ensuing seven year term...thereby providing the investor with a potential "windfall" on investment.

The Warrants ensure that the investor can financially benefit from the "enhanced maturity value" of the overall MexRx System and the expanded MexRx medical and health care distribution network - attributable to the first seven year term of the Investment Trust - funded by the investor.

FUTURE PARTICIPATION WARRANT

This warrant entitles the holder to purchase Units of the Investment Trust for the Seven-Year term commencing March 15, 20** and ending March 15, 20**. The amount of Units that the holder is entitled to purchase is equivalent to the number of Units evidenced by the Certificate to which this Warrant is attached.

To exercise the Warrant, the holder must submit this Warrant and payment of $5.00 per Unit on or before the expiration date. The holder may also surrender the Full Redemption Guaranty Coupon attached hereto as partial or full consideration for the exercise of the Future Participation Warrant.

WARRANT # A-1001   Expiration Date : March 15, 20**

5

Executive Summary

INVESTMENT TRUST OVERVIEW

MexRx Investment Trust is an Investment Trust registered in the British Overseas Territory of Gibraltar and organized for the purpose of developing, producing and marketing a unique and proprietary Herbal Care Immune System Activator product line in addition to non-proprietary medical products and surgical services - on an international basis. Marketing emphasis for the MexRx products and services is via the Internet. The Investment Trust has the right to share revenue disbursements equivalent to 20% of the gross sales revenues derived from the proprietary Herbal Care Immune System Activator product line and 7.5% of the gross sales revenues derived from the MexRx non-proprietary medical products and surgical services. The Investment Trust, upon completion of the underwriting, will own the claim of right, title and interest to the production facility for Herbal Care product line, proprietary internet fulfillment software programming, 40% of the issued and outstanding common shares of International Medical Services S.A. de C.V., the holding company of the largest private medical facility in Mexico – which is also the first Health Maintenance Organization (H.M.O.) in Mexico and awaiting qualification as an H.M.O. in the State of California, and all proprietary intellectual property (under chattel) that protect the Herbal Care product line and MexRx products and services - which represent the capital assets of the Trust.

THE CONCEPT

MexRx S.A. de C.V., the Business Manager of the MexRx Investment Trust, has conceived a logical and conventional business approach to market high quality and affordable health care products and services to residents living in Mexico or working the U.S. Through its stockholding interest in International Medical Services S.A. de C.V. (I.M.S.), the Business Manager is enabled to operate as a staff model, "H.M.O." where its doctors and staff are full time employees. The I.M.S. staff only serves its members and are well trained to provide convenient and sensitive medical care. I.M.S. utilizes a "quality assurance program" and a "preventive medicine philosophy" that has been patterned after U.S. style managed health care. I.M.S. is the only organization in Mexico that has its own facilities Hospitals, laboratories, radiology and pharmacies. I.M.S. offers its services throughout Mexico and also provides emergency coverage worldwide with its optional medical and reinsurance plans. I.M.S. serves thousands of members who are from individual families and employees of companies. I.M.S. is represented by many U.S. insurance agents, who have helped I.M.S. enter into contracts with administrators, unions, associations, maquiladoras, insurance companies and a large variety of service, agriculture and manufacturing industries.

The I.M.S. H.M.O. affords the Business Manager with a platform from which to market its unique Herbal Care Immune System Activator product line and MexRx medical products and surgical services.

6

BUSINESS OF THE INVESTMENT TRUST

The Business Manager, subsequent to completion of this offering, intends to inaugurate its fulfillment platform for medical and health care. The Business Manager's digital platform will market three primary product/service menus: *MexRx Alternative Medicine- Herbal Care Immune System Activator:* proprietary non-prescription products for immune system enhancement, *MexRx Pharmaceuticals:* over 1,250 discounted prescription and non-prescription medical products, and *MexRx Surgical Services:* over 100 various surgical operations at significant discounts.

MexRx Alternative Medicine - Herbal Care Immune System Activator – Proprietary formulation and production methodology processes complex active material from natural herbs-featuring *Geraniaceae extract,* into transdermal activators which enhance immune systems. The naturopathic substance results in a hybrid multi-purpose immune system facilitator capable of overcoming most infections. Laboratory and clinical studies conducted since 1993 in Brazil, Cuba, Mexico and Canada substantiate virtual universal remedial effectiveness with absolute absence of ill-effects for applications including: Rheumatoid Arthritis, Carpal tunnel syndrome, Herpes zoster, H. genitalis and H. simplex, Seborreic dermatitis, Psoriasis, Tendonitis, Diabetes, Acne and various skin disorders, Cancer and AIDS. The MexRx Herbal Care Immune System Activator is currently registered for over-the-counter availability in Brazil and Hungary. Registraion is pending within the Republic of Mexico.

The inaugural Herbal Care Immune System Activator product line is comprised of seven products. Each product is designed to enhance the immune system in varying degrees of *respiratory bursts* for specific body locations or remedial requisites. The product includes: Transdermal Activator Liquid (5%), Pain Gel (2%), Skin Gel (2%), Immune system Gel (5%), Acne Gel (1%), Face Gel (1%) and Vaginal Gel (1%).

MexRx Pharmaceuticals – Pharmacy prescription drugs, medicines or vitamins approved by the government of the Republic of Mexco are scheduled to be offered to *MexRx Pharmacy* members for shipment anywhere in the world. Over 1,250 prescription and non-prescription drugs, medicines and vitamins, both brand names as well as generic, are currently being processed for H.M.O. members of the Business Manager's affiliate, International Medical Services, for shipment to the U.S. and throughout Mexico. Discounts range from 30-60% as compared with U.S. pharmacy prices.

Executive Summary

MexRx Surgical Services – Over 100 surgical services are scheduled to be offered by the Business Manager as they are currently availed to H.M.O. members by the Business Manager's affiliate, International Medical Services, at deep discounted rates . All surgeries are performed at the IMS hospital, the largest private medical facility in Mexico. All medical services utilize the same designs as in the United States and adheres to all U.S. medical codes and identification for medical billing and central record files. Discounts range from 30-70% as compared with U.S. surgical rates.

The Business Manager is scheduled to market the MexRx products and services, on a primary basis, through its sales fulfillment platform. Additionally, the Business Manager intends to market the Herbal Care Immune System Activator product line through distributors, as the registration of the proprietary product line allows over-the-counter sales in select countries. Advertising and marketing campaigns are scheduled for target users of the MexRx products and services within 120 days following completion of this offering. Approximately 70% of the advertising and marketing campaigns are targeted for U.S. markets. network marketing companies.

The Business Manager is scheduled to commence fabrication of the manufacturing facility and fulfillment center for the proprietary Herbal Care Immune System Activator product line upon completion of this offering. The facility is to be located in Tijuana, Mexico and will have, upon completion – which is scheduled 150 days thereafter - an immediate production capacity of approximately 10 million retail dollars per day.

Furthermore, the Business Manager intends to develop revenue sharing joint-venture strategic alliances with independent medical and health care providers for the purpose of accessing broad-scale end user participation within the MexRx programs.

8

Executive Summary

THE MARKET

Medical and health care usage is expanding, in tandem with the population growth within the world marketplace. There are many companies currently providing medical and health care products and services – however, there is no Internet access that provides all products and services within today's marketplace at the deep discounted prices, as offered by the Business Manager. The Herbal Care Immune System Activator, subsequent to extensive laboratory and clinical testing on thousands of volunteers, has proven itself worthy of entering the marketplace. The Herbal Care product line is universal in its application for immune deficiency invaders and in the view of the Business Manager is the only product line that provides a non-toxic remedy for many of the prominent diseases in today's environment. The Business Manager is of the further view that the Herbal Care Immune system Activator product line will experience rapid consumer acceptance. The Business Manager is of the conclusion that there exists no competition within the sphere of the marketplace that the MexRx programs are embarking and the medical and health care services which they facilitate.

BUSINESS STRATEGY

Short Term: The Business Manager, upon completion of this offering, intends to focus its resources on the manufacturing of the Herbal Care Immune System Activator product line production facility, finalization of registration of the Herbal Care product line in the Republic of Mexico for over-the-counter sales, completion of the H.M.O. licensing process of International Medical Services in the State of California – _in which the Investment Trust has a 40% stockholder interest and which will provide a firm foundation for future marketing efforts,_ launching of the Internet portal for its medical and health care programs and implementation of its assertive advertising and promotional campaigns on behalf of the MexRx Internet portal. Once the Herbal Care production facility is operational and on-line, within 150 days from completion of this offering, the production facility is designed to sustain a daily product-value manufacturing capacity of $10 Million.

Long Term: The Business Manager intends to expand the sales efforts through aggressive public relations campaigns. In addition, the Business Manager intends to effectuate joint-venture alliances with distributors of parallel products and medical/health care providers while augmenting the variety of medical and health care products and services available via the MexRx programs.

Executive Summary

BUSINESS MANAGER OF THE TRUST

MexRx S.A. de C.V., a corporation registered in the Republic of Mexico, based in Tijuana, Mexico, is the Business Manager of the Investment Trust. The company's management has been engaged in the development and market preparedness of the Herbal Care Immune System Activator product line and MexRx medical products and surgical services since 1995. The Business Manager is the owner of all right, title and interest, including the Copyright, Tradename and Patent Pending, in and to the Herbal Care product line – which is scheduled to be conveyed to the Investment Trust (under chattel) and represents one of the capital assets of the Investment Trust. The Business Manager also owns the proprietary Tradename of *MexRx* and right, title and claim to all software programs and market methodology for the company's fulfillment platform to market the Herbal Care product line and non-proprietary medical products and surgical services – which is scheduled to be conveyed to the Investment Trust upon completion of the offering and which represents a part of the capital assets of the Investment Trust. MexRx S.A. de C.V. is an affiliate of International Medical Services S. A. de C.V. (hereinafter referred to as "IMS"), of which the Investment Trust will own a 40% capital stock interest, upon completion of this offering. IMS is the holding company of the largest private medical facility in the Republic of Mexico with its own facilities hospitals, laboratories, radiology and pharmacies. Additionally, IMS a fully licensed H.M.O. in Mexico, servicing thousands of H.M.O. members on a worldwide basis.

ADMINISTRATOR OF THE TRUST

PriceWaterhouseCoopers (PWC) is the Trust Administrator of the Investment Trust. The principal office of the Trust Administrator is located at Tapachula 11550, Chapultepec, C.P. 22020, Tijuana, Baja California Mexico. The Telephone/Fax Number is: 52.664.615.5000 / 52.664.615.2010.

CAPITALIZATION OF THE TRUST

The authorized capital of the Investment Trust is denominated in REVPAC Bond Units. REVPAC Bond Units are the cutting-edge new financial instruments for today's modern investor in the lucrative Health Care Business. Now, for the first time ever, investors can purchase meaningful shares in Medical and Health Care ventures that offer extraordinary Revenue Yields and that trade in the Securities trading markets.

10

Executive Summary

The Administrator is entitled to receive a fee of 0.25% of the Revenues of the Investment Trust, plus reimbursements for reasonable, ordinary and necessary operating expenses, requisite to the operating expenses of the Trust – not to exceed $25,000 p/a. After payment of the Trust Administrator fees, the Net Cash Flow of the Investment Trust – which is equivalent to 20% of the gross sales revenues of any and all Herbal Care Immune System Activator products and 7.5% of any and all prescription/non-prescription medical products and surgical services, plus accumulated interest, less applicable Administrator fees – is to be distributed to the REVPAC Bond Unit holders on a pro-rata basis. The first Revenue Distribution is to occur on the third year anniversary following completion of this offering. An additional Revenue Distribution is to occur for each anniversary thereafter. Upon the fifth Revenue Distribution, on the seventh anniversary following this offering, all Revenue Distribution rights will cease for the REVPAC Bond Unit holder, unless the holder has exercised the Warrant (attached to the instant REVPAC Bond Unit) and purchased a newly issued REVPAC Bond Unit for the ensuing Seven Year term of the Investment Trust.

REVENUE DISTRIBUTION

11

MexRx Investment Trust

Revenue and Secondary Market Projections for Revenue Sharing Term

Date of Offering 15-Jan-20**

RevPaC term - 7 Years

Amount to be raised	$4,500,000.00	Investment Trust Revenue Sectors			
Units Issued at $5.00	900,000	Herbal Care		Medicine/Surgery	
Units Issued at $1.00	54,000	Revenue Sharing %	20.0%	Revenue Sharing %	7.5%
		Net Margin	40.0%	Net Margin	42.5%
Total Units Issued	954,000	Cost of Sales	40.0%	Cost of Sales	50.0%

Revenues	Year One	Year Two	Year Three	Year Four	Year Five	Year Six	Year Seven	Total	%'s
Gross Sales	$19,620,000	$44,025,000	$79,140,000	$111,855,000	$164,550,000	##########	$271,350,000		
Cost of Sales	$7,911,000	$17,754,000	$31,932,000	$45,150,000	$66,372,000	$87,624,000	$109,380,000	$366,123,000	40.33%
To RevPaC Holders	$3,845,250	$8,625,000	$15,483,000	$21,861,000	$32,220,000	$42,594,000	$53,220,000	$177,848,250	19.59%
MexRx S.A. C.V. Net	$7,863,750	$17,646,000	$31,725,000	$44,844,000	$65,958,000	$87,102,000	$108,750,000	$363,888,750	40.08%
Accumulated Sales	$19,620,000	$63,645,000	$142,785,000	$254,640,000	$419,190,000	##########	$907,860,000	$907,860,000	100.00%

RevPaC Yields	Y1	Y2	Y3	Y4	Y5	Y6	Y7	Total	ROI
Full Risk	$4.03	$9.04	$16.23	$22.92	$33.77	$44.85	$55.79	$186.42	3726.47%
Zero Risk	$2.02	$4.52	$8.11	$11.46	$16.89	$22.32	$27.89	$93.21	1864.24%

Projected Secondary Market Performance during REVPAC term							
			1st Yield	2nd Yield	3rd Yield	4th Yield	Final Yield
	Y1	Y2	Y3	Y4	Y5	Y6	Y7
Trading Full Risk	$35.00	$40.00	$50.00	$60.00	$65.00	$70.00	$75.00
Trading Zero-Risk	$17.50	$20.00	$25.00	$30.00	$32.50	$35.00	$37.50

Please note: Future Participation Warrant may effect secondary market performance
($) Amounts in US Dollars

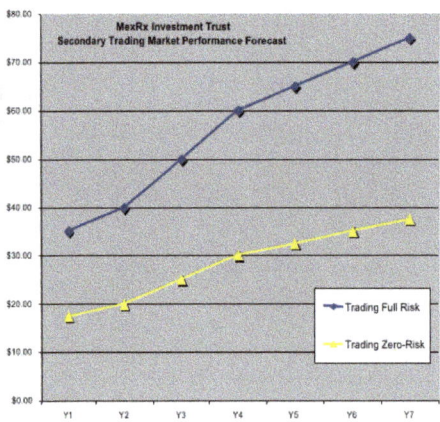

MexRx Investment Trust
Secondary Trading Market Performance Forecast

Trading Full Risk
Trading Zero-Risk

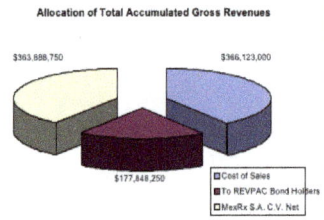

Allocation of Total Accumulated Gross Revenues

$363,888,750 $366,123,000

$177,848,250

Cost of Sales
To REVPAC Bond Holders
MexRx S.A. C.V. Net

12

Here's How MexRx Investment Trust Works

MEXRX MEDICAL AND HEALTH CARE PROGRAMS

Investment Trust owns revenue share interest in worldwide sales revenues of any and all MexRx medical products and surgical services. Every time that a medical or health care product or service is sold, the investor earns a revenue share.

BUSINESS OF THE TRUST

The high quality-low cost MexRx medical products and surgical services are marketed via the Internet and through network marketing distributors. The marquee product line of MexRx is the unique Herbal Care Immune System Activator products - which have the potential of realizing significant sales revenues.

CAPITALIZATION

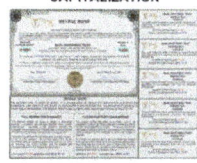

Investment Trust capital is denominated in REVPAC Bond Units - the new and revolutionary Financial Instrument for the Health Care Industry. The REVPAC Bond Units are sold to investors and the proceeds used to develop the proprietary MexRx medical and health care programs and the MexRx distribution network.

BUSINESS MANAGER

The Investment Trust is managed by MexRx S.A. de C.V. with the objective of earning uninterrupted maximum yields for the investors from the the proprietary Herbal Care Immune System Activator product line and non-proprietary medical MexRx products and surgical services sold - around the world.

13

Here's How MexRx Investment Trust Works

INVESTOR EARNINGS ACCUMULATE

20% of all gross sales revenues from the worldwide sales of the proprietary Herbal Care Immune System Activator product line and 7.5% of all gross sales revenues of the MexRx medical products and surgical services are distributed to the Investment Trust and accumulate in investors' trust accounts.

If the Business Manager of the Trust realizes sales of the Herbal Care Immune System Activator product known as *Transdermal Activator* to only 1,250 patients per year - then the Investment Trust is designed to distribute extraordinary Return on Investment yields of over 1,200% to investors.

REVENUE YIELDS

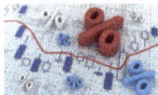

Accumulated "Revenue Share" percentage of gross sales revenues of the proprietary Herbal Care Immune System Activator product line and MexRx medical products and surgical services are distributed as "Revenue Share Yields" to the investors upon the 36, 48, 60, 72 and 84 month anniversary following completion of the Investment Trust Initial Public Offering (IPO).

REAL-TIME REPORTING

"Full-disclosure" Investment Trust reporting services provide the investors with "real-time" updates on the performance of MexRx Business (sales results, investor earnings, future program projects, scheduled marketing and promotion campaigns, etc.) and is disseminated via the Administrator for the Investment Trust.

INVESTOR SERVICES

Investment Trust provides "Full-Frill" MexRx Investor Service package to all investors: Discounted MexRx products and services, Meet the Business Manager luncheons,
- RSVP Invitations to special events.
- Discounted MexRx Medical Insurance programs.

14

Here's How MexRx Investment Trust Works

FULL REDEMPTION GUARANTY

Investors may redeem the REVPAC Bond Unit for a cash payment up to IPO price paid by Investors - $5.00 per Unit - at the end of the 7 year term. The Investors may use the Full Redemption Guaranty to purchase a new REVPAC Bond Unit for the ensuing 7 year term of the Trust by exercising the Warrant.

LIQUIDITY

The Investment Trust is listed and publicly traded on securities markets - allowing investors to liquidate their ownership interests at any time while availing speculators the opportunity to purchase REVPAC Bond Units of the Investment Trust as its MexRx Business matures and revenue yields accumulate.

WARRANT

REVPAC Bond Warrant guarantees investor the opportunity to purchase (at full term) the identical revenue sharing rights (at the same price as the instant Investment Trust IPO) for the ensuing 7 year term of the Investment Trust. This provides the investor the potential to realize "Windfall" value - as the MexRx patient base increases in size and the overall MexRx program increases in value as the unique universal Herbal Care Immune System Activator product line matures in the marketplace.

15

What You Might Be Asking...

What does REVPAC Bond stand for?

The REVPAC Bond is the capital trade name for the "Revenue Participation Capital" Investment Trust Bond Unit.

Can I buy REVPAC Bonds for my retirement plan portfolio?

Yes! REVPAC Bond Units - protected by the Full Redemption Guaranty coverage - are highly desirable financial instruments that provide security of investment capital and hedges against down-turn economic trends and significant yield potential. REVPAC Bonds qualify for most retirement-pension plans and programs.

How do I keep track of my investment?

The Trust Administrator for the Investment Trust issues quarterly and annual reports to all investors, can access "real-time" Revenue Yields, Buy/Sell Trading Quotes, status of Herbal Care Immune System Activator product line and MexRx medical products/surgical Services sales in the consumer market place (including revenue performance and earnings for each distribution outlet), scheduled marketing campaigns plus other pertinent data and information, updated daily, via accessing the Business Manager's reporting service website.

Can I borrow against my REVPAC Bond?

Yes! REVPAC Bond Units qualify as highly desirable collateral security instruments for lending institutions. REVPAC Bond s that are secured by Full Redemption Guaranty coverage or those that have accumulated (undistributed) revenue yields are especially desirable.

When can I expect to receive Revenue Yields?

Revenue Yields are distributed after thirty six months (36) following the completion of the public offering of the REVPAC Bond Units for the Investment Trust. To receive payment, the investor remits coupon #1 from the REVPAC Bond Unit to the Administrator for the Investment Trust. Additional revenue yield distributions occur each year thereafter, on the 48th month (coupon #2), the 60th month (coupon #3), the 72nd month (coupon #4) and the 84th month (coupon #5). The coupon #5 revenue yield distribution is the final revenue yield payment.

Who keeps track of my money?

The Investment Trust Administrator, monitors, administers and distributes all financial transactions conducted by the Investment Trust on behalf of the REVPAC Bond Unit holders. Full disclosure reporting on all financial matters, including accumulated revenue yields, is sent to all investors (quarterly) and is also available via the "real-time" reporting service of the business manager.

16

**What You Might Be
Asking...**

Yes! REVPAC Bond Trust Units with Full Redemption Guaranty coverage provide excellent investment security for potential short term - high yield/long term - significant growth. The REVPAC Bond unit is a "low-risk" - revenue share with the potential of out-performing most "secured" financial instruments in today's marketplace.

**Would REVPAC Bonds
make a good investment
for my child's college
trust?**

REVPAC Bond Units are fully "matured" on the 84th month anniversary following completion of the public offering of the MexRx Investment Trust. Before the accumulated revenue yield for year seven (coupon #5) is paid, the investor may elect to exercise the "revenue sharing" term in the Investment Trust. The investor may purchase the ensuing seven year REVPAC Bond Trust Units by applying the accumulated (undistributed) Revenue Yields toward the exercise of the Warrant by redeeming the Full Redemption Guarantee for the new REVPAC Bond Unit. The investor may also elect to sell the REVPAC Bond Unit via the securities trading markets (together with the accumulated Revenue Yields and Warrants) in order to realize potential windfall trading return.

**What happens to my
investment when my
REVPAC Bond reaches
full maturity?**

17

Collateralized Yield Obligation

MexRx Investment Trust

COLLATERALIZED YIELD OBLIGATION

THIS COLLATERALIZED YIELD OBLIGATION (hereinafter **"Agreement"**) is made effective upon execution at Tijuana, B.C., Mexico by and between **MexRx S.A. de C.V.**, herein referred to "Business Manager" and **MexRx Investment Trust**, herein referred to as "Trust".

SECTION 1
Property Subject to this Agreement

1.01. Property Described. Business Manager agrees to transfer, convey and assign, and the Trust agrees it shall hold as security assurance, for the consideration hereinafter provided, the following assets (collectively referred to as the "Capital Assets"):

(a) Business Manager's rights, title and interest in and to all that certain proprietary property described as construction designs, research material, operational and marketing methodology , production equipment and all contracts between the Business Manager – present and future – for the development of any and all proprietary and non-proprietary products as described in the Offering Prospectus of the Investment Trust and known as Herbal Care Immune System Activator and MexRx medical products/surgical services, wherein the funding, in part or whole, has been allocated from the Trust. The proprietary property is further described in Exhibit 1 attached hereto and incorporated herein by reference and hereafter referred to as "MexRx business venture; and

(b) All of Business Manager's right, title and interest, if any, to any and all copyrights, trademarks, trade names and service marks relating to and/or used in connection with the development of the proprietary and non-proprietary properties referred to above (collectively referred to as the "Marks").

(c) Except as herein elsewhere specifically provided, the Trust accepts – as security assurance – the Proprietary Property and Marks "as is" without warranty, expressed, implied or statutory, including, without limitation, any warranty of merchantability for a particular purpose and is relying on its Trust Administrator's previously conducted due diligence and inspection of the Proprietary Property. The Proprietary Property and Marks shall be converted to the Trust free and clear of all liabilities, obligations, liens and encumbrances in the event the Business Manager Agreement, executed between the Business Manager and the Trust is terminated, for cause, by the Trust Administrator.

SECTION 2
Consideration from the Trust

2.01. Consideration. In consideration of the security assurance of the Proprietary Property, Marks and revenue participation rights, the Trust shall allocate $3,700,000 from a public offering of Trust securities to the Business Manager for purposes of acquiring a capital asset base of an Herbal Care Immune System Activator product line production facility, MexRx computer software program and a 40% stockholding interest in International Medical Services S.A..

2.02. Payment. The Consideration shall be paid to the Business Manager from the Trust Administrator following the completion of the public offering. The schedule of payment is as follows:

(a) The Trust Administrator shall allocate to the Business Manager $500,000.00 within 10 business days following the accumulation of net offering proceeds of that amount as provided for in the Underwriting Agreement executed between the Trust and the Underwriter. These funds are to be utilized by the Business Manager for operating and sub-contractual expenses directly related to the development of the Herbal Care and MexRx properties.

(b) The Trust Administrator shall allocate to the Business Manager $1,000,000.00 within 10 business days following the accumulation of net offering proceeds of that amount as provided for in the Underwriting Agreement. These funds are to be utilized by the Business Manager in the first phase acquisition of capital assets.

(c)   Upon acquisition completion, by the Business Manager and inspection by the Trust Administrator of the first phase of capital assets- which is designated in Exhibit 2, the Trust Administrator shall allocate to the Business Manager $1,000,000.00 within 10 business days following Trust Administrator's inspection or following the accumulation of net offering proceeds of that amount – whichever occurs earlier. These funds are to be utilized by the Business Manager in the second phase acquisition of initial capital assets.

(d)   Upon acquisition completion by the Business Manager and inspection by the Trust Administrator of the second phase of capital assets- which is designated in Exhibit 2, the Trust Administrator shall pay to the Business Manager $500,000.00 within 10 business days following Trust Administrator's inspection or following the accumulation of net offering proceeds of that amount – whichever occurs earlier. These funds are to be utilized by the Business Manager in the third phase acquisition of capital assets.

(e)   Upon acquisition completion by the Business Manager and inspection by the Trust Administrator of the third phase of capital assets – which is designated in Exhibit 2, the Trust Administrator shall pay to the Business Manager $700,000.00 within 10 business days following Trust Administrator's inspection or following the accumulation of net offering proceeds of that amount – whichever occurs earlier;

(f)   The Business Manager shall be allowed to utilize the net offering proceeds for purposes of marketing and general overhead that will be overseen by Trust Administrator.

2.03. Selection of Capital Asset Acquisitions. The select capital assets to be acquired and the method, terms and conditions of acquisition shall be unilaterally determined by the Business Manager. This schedule, once determined, shall be drafted into Exhibit 3 of this Agreement and attached hereto.

SECTION 3
Title to Capital Accets

3.01. Capital Assets. The Herbal Care Immune System Activator production facility, MexRx computer software program and 40% stockholding interest in International Medical Services S.A. shall represent and be designated as part of the capital assets. Ownership of the capital assets shall belong exclusively to the Trust.

3.02. Maintenance, Refurbishment, Replenishment and Replacement of Capital Assets. The Business Manager shall cause to be maintained –in good working condition – all capital assets. In the event that capital assets require refurbishment, replenishment or replacement, the Business Manager shall cause said action to be effectuated. Funds to pay for said maintenance, refurbishment, replenishment and replacement of the capital assets, once funding of the MexRx business venture is completed, as provided in Section 2 of this Agreement shall be forthcoming as a disbursement, overseen by the Trust Administrator and derived from the Business Manager's portion of the sales revenues resulting from the MexRx business venture Operations.

3.03. Ownership of Replenishment, Refurbished or Replaced Capital Assets. Title to the replenishment refurbished or replaced capital assets shall at all times belong exclusively to the Trust.

3.04. First Right of Refusal to Purchase the Capital Assets. The Business Manager shall maintain the first right of refusal to purchase the capital assets – upon termination of the Trust. In order to exercise the first right of refusal, the Business Manager shall be required pay an amount in accordance with the following schedule:

REVPAC Holders Accumulated Yields (1)	Capital Asset Purchase Price (2)
Less than 100% ROI	100% Replacement Value
101% to 150%	90%
151% to 200%	75%
201% to 250%	60%
251% to 300%	50%
351% to 400%	40%
401% to 450%	30%
451% to 500%	20%
501% to 550%	10%
Over 550%	0%

(1)   Based on IPO price

(2)   Based on replacement cost for capital assets owned by Investment Trust

In the event, the Business Manager does not exercise the first right of refusal to purchase the capital assets, the capital assets of the Trust will be sold by auction, unless otherwise provided for in the contracts with the communities, serviced by the digital communications systems. Such auction or bid is to be conducted by the Trust Administrator. In the event the Business Manager does not exercise the first right of refusal – within 15 business day from receipt of notice to exercise issued by the Trust Administrator, the capital assets are to be sold to the highest bidder. 100% of the proceeds from the sale of the Capital Assets are to be remitted to the Trust for distribution to the Trust's REVPAC Holders.

3.05 Ownership of Capital Assets in the event Renewal for Additional Term of Trust Occurs. In the event, at least 60% of the Trust's Revenue Sharing Venture Bond Holders exercise the Future Participation Warrant for an additional term of the Trust and the REVPAC Holders have received 500% Return on Investment – aggregate Revenue Sharing Yields of $25 per REVPAC Unit, the Capital Assets are to remain the property of the Trust during the first four years of the additional term at which time the Capital Assets are to revert to the Bussines Manager and the Trust's claim to the Capital Assets will cease. In the event, the REVPAC Holders have received less than 500% Return on Investment, the Capital Assets are to remain the property of the Trust for the 7-Years of Additional Term – until expiration– at which time the Capital Assets are to revert to the Business Manager.

SECTION 4
Distribution of Revenues

4.01. Administration of Revenues. The Trust Administrator shall oversee all revenues derived from the Herbal Care Immune System Activator product line and MexRx non-proprietary medical products/surgical services sales. The Business Manager shall deposit any and all sales receipts into the bank account designated and overseen by the Trust Administrator.

4.02. Allocation of Revenues. The Trust Administrator shall assure the allocation and payment of any and all sales revenues as follows:

(a)   Investment Trust is to receive 20% of gross revenues derived from the sale of any and all Herbal Care Immune System Activator products and 7.5% of gross revenues derived from the sale of any and all MexRx non-proprietary medical products/surgical services;

(b)   Business Manager is to receive 80% of gross revenues derived from the sale of Herbal Care Immune System Activator products and 92.5% of gross revenues derived from the sale of MexRx non-proprietary medical products/surgical services.

4.03. Accounting Form for Allocations. The Trust Administrator shall account for all allocation payments as follows:

(a)   Investment Trust receipt of proportionate gross revenues, derived from product/service sales, up to and including aggregate yields amounting to $5 per REVPAC Unit is accounted for as **"Return of Capital"**.

(b)   Investment Trust receipt of proportionate gross revenues above and beyond $5 per REVPAC Unit is accounted for as a **"Premium" Payment**.

4.04. Allocation of Revenues in the event Renewal for Additional Term of Trust Occurs. In the event, at least 60% of the Trust's Revenue Sharing Venture Bond Warrant for an additional term of the Trust and the REVPAC Holders have received 500% Return on Investment – aggregate Revenue Sharing Yields of $25 per REVPAC Unit, allocation of revenues, derived from the Capital Assets are to continue into the renewal term and cease at the end of the fourth year of the 7-Year Term. In the event, the REVPAC Holders have received less than 500% Return on Investment, Allocation of Revenues derived from the Capital Assets are to continue for the entire 7-Years of Additional Term – until such time that the REVPAC Holders have been allocated $25 per REVPAC Unit – at which time Allocation of Revenues derived from the Capital Assets are to cease.

4.05. Allocation of Gross Sales Proceeds in the event of Business Manager Sale of Corporate Divisions. In the event, the Business Manager divests a corporate division, through a sale, the Business Manager shall allocate the Revenue Sharing percentage of 12% of any and all sales proceeds to the Investment Trust. Prior to said divestiture, the Business Manager is to receive written notification from the Trust Administrator authorizing the sale. Trust Administrator is to appraise the value of the divestiture and determine fair-market-value of the transaction in an expeditious time period.

4.06. <u>Allocation of Gross Sales Proceeds in the event of Business Manager Sale of Equity Ownership Interest in Business Manager Itself.</u> In the event, the Business Manager divests any or all of the equity ownership interest\in MexRx S.A. de C.V., through a sale – other than a public offering of its equity – wherein the terms of said divestiture designate the termination of Revenue Sharing allocations from the MexRx business venture operations, the Business Manager shall allocate the Revenue Sharing percentage of 20% of any and all sales proceeds to the Investment Trust. In the event the Revenue Sharing percentage allocation of 20%, derived from the divestiture, to the Investment Trust and the aggregate Revenue Sharing percentage derived from MexRx business venture operations results in less than 500% Return on Investment for Investment Trust Revenue Sharing Venture Bond Holders, the Revenue Sharing percent age is to be increased up to and including that percentage that provides a 500% Return on Investment to the Investment Trust Revenue Sharing Venture Bond Holders. Prior to said divestiture, the Business Manager is to receive written notification from the Trust Administrator authorizing the sale. Trust Administrator is to appraise the value of the divestiture and determine fair-market-value of the transaction in an expeditious time period.

SECTION 5
Forfeiture of Security Collateral

5.01. <u>Condition of Forfeiture</u>. In the event that the Business Manager Agreement is in default and without remedy after 15 days of receipt by the Business Manager of written notice thereof /or/ if Business Manager is in a condition as described in Business Manager Agreement-Par. 11(c)- the Trust Administrator shall take necessary action to transfer, convey and assign the Capital Assets Proprietary Property and Marks to the benefit of the Trust.

5.02. <u>Purpose of Forfeiture.</u> The Trust's sole reliance on deriving its royalties and return of capital investment rests upon the good will and performance of the Business Manager. In the event the Business Manager is unable, unwilling, incapable or for any reason fails to perform its duties as provided for by the Business Manager Agreement, the Trust Administrator will have no recourse but to terminate the Business Manager and to seek another Business Manager to assume the day-to-day operations of the business.

5.03. <u>Waiver of Rights to Security Collateral</u>. The Business Manager agrees to waive all right, title and interest to the Proprietary Property and Marks that comprise the Security Collateral in the event the Business Management Agreement is terminated by the Trust Administrator.

SECTION 6
Miscellaneous

6.01. <u>Legal Provenance.</u> The laws of the United Kingdom, applicable to Collateral Pledge Agreements and contracts made and wholly performed therein shall govern the validity, construction, performance and effect of this Collateralized Yield Obligation.

6.02. <u>Venue.</u> London, Great Britain shall be the primary exclusive venue, unless both parties mutually agree on another jurisdiction that practices English Common Law for any action brought by the parties in any way related to this Collateralized Yield Obligation.

6.03. <u>Increment</u>. This Collateralized Yield Obligation shall inure to the benefits of and be binding upon the parties hereto and their respective successors and assignees.

6.04 <u>Term.</u> This Agreement is to remain in force and effect for the entire term of the Investment Trust and sixty days thereafter, unless the Trust is terminated by dissolution.

IN WITNESS WHEREOF, The Business Manager and the Trust have executed this Agreement as of the day and year first above written.

TRUST ADMINISTRATOR ON BEHALF OF
MexRx INVESTMENT TRUST ("Trust")   Date:_____

MexRx S.A. DE C.V. ("Business Manager")   Date:_____

4 of 4

Business Manager Agreement

MexRx Investment Trust
BUSINESS MANAGER AGREEMENT

BETWEEN: MexRx INVESTMENT TRUST (hereinafter referred to as the "Trust") and **MexRx S.A. de C.V.** (hereinafter referred to as the "Business Manager");

WHEREAS: the Trust, organized to finance the development and marketing of proprietary and non-proprietary medical/health care products and services from Tijuana B.C., Mexico ("MexRx Operation");

AND WHEREAS: the Business Manager, a Corporation domiciled in the Republic of Mexico possesses the Intellectual Property rights to a proprietary medical/health care product line and the expertise and management resources requisite to develop and manage the medical/health care product line in addition to other non-proprietary medical/health care products and services;

NOW THEREFORE: it is mutually agreed that the Trust and the Business Manager will form a working relationship for the purpose of developing, manufacturing and marketing medical/health care products and services from the medical facilities of International Medical Services S.A. within Tijuana B.C., Mexico (hereinafter referred to as the "Business Venture") and in consideration of the mutual promises, covenants and other agreements contained herein, the parties hereto further agree as follows:

1. **Business Manager.** MexRx S.A. de C.V., with offices located at calle Rufino Tamayo 9910, esquina Blvd. Cuauhtemoc y Dr. Atl Zona Rio, Tijuana B.C. Mexico, owns proprietary Intellectual Property claims and operational methodology rights to manufacture and market a medical/health care product line known as Herbal Care Immune System Activator. The Business Manager also owns the rights to market non-proprietary medical/health care products and surgical services primarily originating from Tijuana B.C., Mexico. Additionally the Business Manager owns the first right of refusal to purchase a 40% stockholding interest in International Medical Systems S.A., the holding company of one of the largest privately owned medical clinic in Mexico and a Health Maintenance Organization (H.M.O.) in Mexico (see Business Plan-Exhibit 1).

2. **Investment Trust.** MexRx Investment Trust, with registered domicile in the Republic of Mexico is effecting a public offering of its securities for the purpose of financing the Business Venture (See Prospectus – Exhibit 2).

3. **Investment Trust Offering.** The Trust is offering 900,000 REVPAC Bond Units at $5.00 per Unit for an aggregate $4,500,000. Subsequent to the offering, the Trust is to realize net cash proceeds of approximately $3,700,000. The proceeds are to be allocated by the Trust Administrator to the Business Manager for the purpose of effecting the Business Venture and defraying the costs requisite to the operation and administration of the Investment Trust.

4. **Business Venture.** The Business Venture's objective is to manufacture and market the proprietary Herbal Care Immune System Activator product line; marketing non-proprietary medical/health care products and surgical services designated in Exhibit 2 of this Agreement. The Business Manager is responsible for overseeing all phases of the development, manufacturing and marketing of the products and services. The Business Manager also intends to purchase a 40% stockholding interest in International Medical Services S.A.

    Subsequent to the Investment Trust Offering, the Business Manager will cause to be acquired-by purchase – a manufacturing facility as specified in Exhibit 2 and to be located within the Northern Baja California, Mexico area. The Business Manager will be responsible for the marketing and fulfillment of the medial/health care products and services.

    The products and services enumerated and described in Exhibit 2 are considered as the preliminary development stage of a complete line of medical/health care products and services to be developed and marketed throughout the term of the Investment Trust. As revenues are realized from the Business

Venture, the Business Manager will cause to be acquired or developed additional medical/health care products and services on behalf of the Investment Trust.

5. **Terms of the Business Venture**. The Business Manager and the Trust agree to the following obligations and participation in costs and revenues in connection with the Business Venture:

   (a) **Obligations of the Trust:** The Trust is responsible to contribute 100% of the capital requirements to acquire the manufacturing facility for the proprietary Herbal Care Immune System Activator product line; acquire the computer software program to market non-proprietary medical products and surgical services and; to purchase a 40% stockholding interest in International Medical Services S.A.. It is the understanding of the Trust that approximately 95% of the net cash proceeds from the offering of Trust securities, the amount of which is $3,700,000, is adequate for the Business Manager to acquire the required capital assets requisite to effect the development of the Business Venture. It is also the understanding of the Trust that the Business Manager, subsequent to requisite costs incurred in acquiring the required capital assets, is to allocate the net balance toward marketing costs and working capital for operations of the Business Venture.

   (b) **Obligations of the Business Manager:**

      (i) The Business Manager is responsible to conduct the day-to-day business operations requisite for the development, manufacturing and marketing of the proprietary and non-proprietary medical/health care products and services.

      (ii) The Business Manager is further responsible to maintain the capital assets and to replace, replenish or refurbish any capital assets that become damaged or inadequate to meet the market demand. Cost for the maintenance, replacement, replenishment or refurbishment of capital assets is to be borne by the Business Manager.

      (iii) The Business Manager administer all revenues from license or sales and any and all other revenue - each and every occurence that MexRx operations derive revenues and to deposit all revenues into an account administered by the Business Manager and overseen by the Trust Administrator.

   (c) **Participation in Costs and Revenues:**

      Investment Trust is to receive 20% of gross sales revenues derived from the Herbal Care Immune System Activator product line sales and 7.5% of gross sales revenues derived from non-proprietary medical products/surgical services sales.

      Business Manager is to receive 80% of gross sales revenues derived from the Herbal Care Immune System Activator product line sales and 92.5% of gross sales revenues derived from non-proprietary medical products/surgical services sales.

6. **Ownership and Control of Capital Assets.** The acquisition of the manufacturing facility, computer software program and stockholding interest in International Medical Services S.A., is at all times the property and capital asset of the Trust.

   The Business Manager, at all times, is considered as the custodian of the capital assets on behalf of the Trust. It is the responsibility of the Business Manager to maintain adequate insurance and bonding coverage for the capital assets.

   The Business Manager is required to maintain the capital assets in good condition and inform the Trust Administrator, as requested by the Trust Administrator, the location of each asset.

   In the event of dissolution of the Trust – in whole or in part – which is provided for in the Charter of the Trust, no earlier than 81 months following completion of the Trust securities offering, the Business Manager may be required, at the request of the Trust Administrator, to deliver the capital assets for liquidation purposes in accordance with the written instructions of the Trust Administrator.

Should this occur, the Business Manager is to comply with said instructions, no later than 10 days following receipt of such notice from the Trust Administrator.

7. **Indemnification of Trust.** The Business Manager agrees to indemnify the Trust, and to hold the Investment Trust harmless, against any and all, fees, expenses, claims, suits, actions, proceedings, investigations judgments, arbitration decisions, deficiencies, damages, awards, settlements, reasonable legal fees and expenses of attorney(s) chosen by the Trust Administrator, liabilities and expenses incurred based upon, but not limited to, a mistake of fact or law, act, performance, non-performance, alleged act, alleged omission, actual omission, act or omission based upon the advice of counsel or any other cause committed while performing any and all duties in compliance with and according to this Agreement.

8. **Access to Books and Records.** The Business Manager is to maintain accurate status and financial records concerning the development, manufacturing, inventory, marketing, sales and capital assets for the Business Venture. The Business Manager agrees, upon receipt of notice from the Trust Administrator, to provide access to the books and records of the Business Manager and Business Venture for inspection by the Trust Administrator. Said inspection is to occur at the offices of the Business Manager or such other place as designated by the Trust Administrator during normal business hours. Such inspection is to occur not earlier than 30 days following receipt of notice by the Business Manager.

9. **Reporting Procedures.** The Business Manager is to issue to the Trust Administrator monthly manufacturing, inventory, marketing, sales and capital assets reports in the manner and method requested by the Trust Administrator.

10. **Banking Procedures for Sales Revenues.** The Business Manager is not to deposit any other revenues derived from the Business Venture in any bank other than the banking institution and account as agreed upon in writing by the Trust Administrator and Business Manager. All revenues are to be deposited to the credit of the Business Manager or its nominee. The Business Manager shall execute an irrevocable Letter of Instruction to the banking institution providing for immediate transfer of Investment Trust portion of received revenues to the Trust Administrator on behalf of the Investment Trust for all funds that have cleared.

11. **Duration and Termination.**

    (a) Unless otherwise terminated as hereinafter set forth, this Agreement shall continue in full force and effect for a seven-year period following completion of the Trust securities offering.

    (b) If Business Manager shall at any time default in rendering any of the statements required herein, in the deposit of any sales revenues due herein, or in fulfilling any of the other obligations hereof, and such default shall not be cured within 30 days after written notice thereof is given by Trust Administrator to Business Manager, Trust Administrator shall have the right to terminate this Agreement by giving written notice of termination to Business Manager; this Agreement thereby being terminated 30 days after such notice of termination is mailed or delivered by Trust Administrator. Business Manager shall have the right to cure any such default up to, but not after, the giving of such notice of termination.

    (c) Trust Administrator shall have the right to terminate this Agreement by giving written notice of termination to Business Manager in the event of any one of the following, such termination being effective upon receipt of such notice or five days after such notice is mailed or delivered, whichever is earlier:

    > (1) Liquidation of Business Manager;
    > (2) Insolvency or bankruptcy of Business Manager, whether voluntary or involuntary;
    > (3) Inability of Business Manager to meet its obligations herein;
    > (4) Failure of Business Manager to satisfy any judgment against it;
    > (5) Appointment of a trustee or receiver for Business Manager;
    > (6) Any assignment by Business Manager for the benefit of creditors; or
    > (7) Failure of Business Manager to submit the reports, remit sales revenues as herein provided for or permit the inspection/copying of books of account in the manner and extent set forth in this Agreement.

(d) The waiver of any default under this Agreement by Trust Administrator shall not constitute a waiver of the right to terminate this Agreement for any subsequent or like default, and the exercise of the right of termination shall not have the effect of waiving any damages to which the Trust might otherwise be entitled.

(e) Termination of this Agreement, for any cause whatsoever, shall in no manner interfere with, affect or prevent the collection by the Trust of any and all sums of money due to the Trust.

12. **Penalty upon Termination.** In the event of termination, for any cause whatsoever, the Trust Administrator may, at Trust Administrator option, transfer title, right and interest to the property included in the Collateralized Yield Obligation (See Exhibit 3) executed by the Business Manager to the benefit of the Trust. The transference of the property included in the Collateralized Yield Obligation does not preclude the Trust Administrator to seek other financial relief, damages and penalties in a court of law that the Trust Administrator deems are due the Trust.

13. **Notices.** Any and all notices and demands by either party hereto to any other party, shall be given either (i) by delivery in person to the address(es) herein set forth, (ii) by deposit in the mail in a sealed envelope or container, either registered or certified mail, return receipt requested, (iii) by delivery to such address by any courier service keeping records of deliveries and attempted deliveries or (iv) by telecopy to the number herein set forth. Service by mail or courier service shall be conclusively deemed made on the first business day delivery is attempted or upon receipt, which is sooner. Service by telecopy shall be deemed made upon confirmed transmission. The parties may change their address for the purpose of receiving notices or demands as herein provided by a written notice given in the manner aforesaid to the other, which notice of change of address shall not become effective, however, until the actual receipt thereof by the other party.

14. **Miscellaneous.**

(a) The laws of the the United Kingdom, applicable to contracts made and wholly performed therein, shall govern the validity, construction, performance and effect of this Agreement.

(b) The venue of London, Great Britain, shall be the primary exclusive venue, unless both parties mutually agree on another jurisdiction that practices English Common Law for any such action brought by the parties in any way related to this Agreement.

(c) This Agreement shall inure to the benefits of and be binding upon the parties hereto and their respective successors and assignees.

(d) If any term, provision, covenant or condition of this Agreement, or any application thereof, should be held by a court of competent jurisdiction to be invalid, void or unenforceable, all provisions, and conditions of this Agreement and all applications thereof, not held invalid, void or unenforceable shall continue in full force and effect and shall in no way be affected, impaired or invalidated thereby. No addition to or modification of this Agreement shall be binding unless executed in writing by both the Business Manager and the Investment Trust or their assignees.

(e) Time is of the essence of this Agreement and all of the terms, provisions, covenants and conditions hereof.

IN WITNESS WHEREOF, The Business Manager and the Trust have executed this Agreement as of the day and year first above written.

TRUST ADMINISTRATOR ON BEHALF OF
MexRx INVESTMENT TRUST ("Trust")   Date:_____

MexRx S.A. de C.V. ("Business Manager")   Date:_____

Trust Administrator Agreement

MexRx Investment Trust

TRUST ADMINISTRATOR AGREEMENT

THIS TRUST ADMINISTRATOR AGREEMENT ("Agreement") is made and entered into by and between **MexRx Investment Trust** (hereinafter referred to as "Trust"), **MexRx S.A. de C.V.** (hereinafter referred to as "Business Manager") and **PriceWaterhouseCoopers** (hereinafter referred to as "Trust Administrator").

WITNESSETH:

WHEREAS, the Trust intends to offer by means of a Prospectus (a copy of which shall be delivered to the Trust Administrator and attached to this Agreement as Exhibit l), to sell up to 900,000 REVPAC Units at a purchase price of $5.00 per Unit for an aggregate offering of $4,500,000; and

WHEREAS, pending the receipt of net cash proceeds from the offering, the Trust desires to deposit the funds with the Trust Administrator for further allocation to the Business Manager in accordance with the Use of Proceeds appearing in the Prospectus and pursuant to the allocation schedule appearing in an agreement executed by the Business Manager and the Trust (hereinafter referred to as "Business Manager Allocation of Proceeds" attached hereto as Exhibit 2); and

WHEREAS, the Business Manager is to utilize the funds received from the offering for the purpose of acquiring and developing a manufacturing facility for production of a proprietary Herbal Care Immune System Activator product line, developing and implementing a marketing program for the proprietary product line and other non-proprietary medical products/surgical services and acquiring a stockholding interest in International Medical Services S.A. (hereinafter referred to as "Capital Assets"); and

WHEREAS, Business Manager is to operate and market the manufacturing facility and marketing programs under the trade name "MexRx" and deposit all resultant revenues in a banking institution designated and overseen by the Trust Administrator for further allocation to the Business Manager and the Trust in accordance with the Prospectus, Business Manager Agreement and Collateralized Yield Obligation (attached hereto as Exhibit 3); and

WHEREAS, the Business Manager is to maintain and replenish the capital assets as required to meet market demand for the proprietary and non-proprietary MexRx products and services in accordance with the Prospectus, Business Manager Agreement and Collateralized Yield Obligation; and

WHEREAS, the Trust Administrator is willing to serve in such capacity upon the terms and conditions set forth below.

NOW, THEREFORE, in consideration of the mutual promises, covenants and other agreements contained herein, the parties hereto agree as follows:

Article l – Duties of Trust Administrator

1.1   All funds received from the offering of Trust securities shall be promptly deposited with the Trust Administrator in accordance with the instructions from the Trust Administrator, to be allocated in accordance with the Use of Proceeds contained in the Prospectus and in accordance with the allocation schedule appearing in the Collateralized Yield Obligation.

1.2   The Subscription Funds shall be invested by the Trust Administrator in an account at the designated banking institution. The Trust Administrator makes no guarantee as to the rate of return to be earned by such funds prior to allocation.

1.3   The Trust Administrator shall verify the acquisition of capital assets by the Business Manager against the allocation of proceeds pursuant to the allocation schedule appearing in the Collateralized Yield Obligation.

1.4   All MexRx Operations revenues shall be invested by the Business Manager in the aforestated banking institution. The Trust Administrator shall oversee the prompt allocation of that portion of the revenues belonging to the Business Manager in accordance with the Business Manager Agreement and Collateral Yield Obligation. The Trust Administrator shall also oversee the allocation of that portion of the revenues belonging to the Trust to a segregated Trust account.

1.5   The Trust Administrator shall distribute the funds in the Trust segregated account to the REVPAC Unit holders of the Trust on the third through seventh anniversary dates following completion of the offering by the Trust pursuant to the Prospectus, Charter of the Trust and this Agreement.

1.6   The Trust Administrator shall verify that the capital assets are being maintained at the required location and condition by the Business Manager, as provided for in the Business Manager Agreement, Prospectus and Collateralized Yield Obligation.

1.7   The Trust Administrator shall verify that all conditions of the Business Manager Agreement and Collateralized Yield Obligation are being satisfied by the Business Manager. In the event that any material condition causes the Business Manager Agreement to be in default, the Trust Administrator shall promptly notice the Business Manager of said default. In the event that a noticed default is not remedied by the Business Manager, the Trust Administrator shall take such necessary action as provided in the Business Manager Agreement and Collateralized Yield Obligation.

1.8   The Trust Administrator shall issue an accounting of the financial condition of the Trust and the business of the Trust to REVPAC Unit holders of the Trust each quarter year, commencing with the 10th day of the month following the first quarter calendar year subsequent to the completion of the offering by the Trust. Included in the report issued by the Trust Administrator, will be the financial status of each REVPAC holder account.

Article 2 – Duties of the Business Manager

2.1   The Business Manager shall provide the Trust Administrator full access to its books and records concerning the development and management of the MexRx marketing programs, Herbal Care Immune System Activator production facility and other Investment Trust properties, production, marketing, sales and inventory of the MexRx products/services. The Business Manager shall upon receipt of notice from the Trust Administrator, provide the Trust Administrator access to the books and records of the Business Manager for inspection. Said inspection is to occur at the offices of the Business Manager or other place designated by the Trust Administrator during normal working hours, not earlier than 30 days following receipt of notice by the Business Manager.

2.2   The Business Manager is to issue to the Trust Administrator, development, construction, marketing, sales, inventory and capital assets reports in the manner and method requested by the Trust Administrator.

2.3   The Business Manager shall maintain the capital assets at acceptable levels as per Business Manager Agreement and Collateralized Yield Obligation.

2.4   The Business Manager is to deposit all sales revenues into the bank and account designated by the Trust Administrator. The Business Manager is not to accept any sales revenues other than those to be deposited in the Trust Administrator designated bank account.

2.5   The Business Manager is to, at all times, adhere and comply with all terms, conditions and covenants of the Business Manager Agreement and Collateralized Yield Obligation.

Article 3 – Indemnification

3.1   The Business Manager and the Trust hereby agree to indemnify the Trust Administrator for, and to hold Trust Administrator harmless, against any and all, fees, expenses, claims, suits, actions, proceedings, investigations judgments, arbitration decisions, deficiencies, damages, awards, settlements, reasonable legal fees and expenses of attorney(s) chosen by Trust Administrator, liabilities and expenses incurred based upon, but not limited to, a mistake of fact or law, act, performance, non-performance, alleged act, alleged omission, actual omission, act or omission based upon the advice of counsel or any other cause committed while performing any and all duties in connection with and under this Agreement. In addition, the Trust Administrator shall receive full indemnification protection when relying upon any certificate, instruction statement, request, notice, advice, direction, agreement, instrument, document, signature believed by the Trust Administrator to be genuine, or any assumption by the Trust Administrator that any person purporting to give the Trust Administrator any of the foregoing in accordance with the provisions herein has been duly authorized to do so. However, no indemnity for the Trust Administrator under section 3.1 will be provided in situations based upon the errors, willful misconduct or negligence of the Trust Administrator.

3.2   The Trust Administrator shall be under no duty to institute or defend any type of proceeding which may arise regarding this Agreement. However, the Trust Administrator may, in utilizing the Trust Administrator's discretion and at the expense of the parties herein, institute or defend such proceedings.

3.3   The rights of the Trust Administrator and the obligations of and indemnification provided by the Business Manager and Trust pursuant to this Agreement shall survive the termination of this Agreement.

Article 4 – Resignation and Successor of Trust Administrator

4.1   The Trust Administrator may resign or be removed by the Trust and be discharged from duties and obligations under this Agreement at any time or not less than fifteen (15) days written notice of such resignation to the parties herein, specifying the date when such resignation shall take effect. Thereafter, the Trust Administrator shall have no further obligation. In the event of such resignation or removal, the parties to this Agreement agree that they will jointly appoint a banking corporation, trust company, attorney, accounting firm or other qualified person as Successor Trust Administrator within fifteen (15) days of notice of such resignation. The Trust Administrator shall refrain from taking any action until such Trust Administrator has received written instructions from the Trust, designating the Successor Trust Administrator. Upon receipt of such instruction, the Trust Administrator shall, as soon as all fees are received in full, promptly deliver all of the trust funds, books and records, and any other material that is relevant to the administration of the Trust to such Successor Trust Administrator in accordance with such instructions. Upon receipt of the aforestated property of the Trust, the Successor Trust Administrator shall be bound by all the provisions herein and shall promptly deliver a written instrument to each of the parties detailing the terms in which the Successor Trust Administrator agrees to be bound.

Article 5 – Fees to Trust Administrator

5.1   The Trust Administrator shall be entitled to compensation from the Trust for its services under this Trust Administrator Agreement in accordance with the following schedule:

Administration Fee.................................$25,000 per annum

This fee is intended to be full compensation for the Trust Administrator's services as contemplated by this Agreement.

Article 6 – Term of this Agreement

6.1   Unless otherwise terminated as provided herein, this Agreement shall continue in full force and effect for and entire term of Investment Trust and sixty days thereafter, unless otherwise extended.

Article 7 – Dispute Remedy

7.1   In the event there is a dispute between the Trust Administrator and the Trust concerning the terms of this Agreement, the parties shall attempt to resolve their difference. If they cannot, their disagreement shall be resolved by arbitration. The arbitrators are to be selected in the following manner.

3 of 4

The Trust Administrator shall obtain a list of arbitrators from the designated body. The list shall consist of five arbitrators, and the Trust Administrator shall determine by a coin flip whether the Trust Administrator or the Trust shall have the right to remove the first name from the list. The Trust-represented by a committee of minimum three REVPAC holders representing at least, an aggregate, 2.5% ownership of all REVPAC Bond Units issued and outstanding shall act on behalf of the Trust. In the event three REVPAC holders owning minimum 2.5% ownership are not available, the three major holders of REVPAC Bond Units in the Trust that are available are to represent the committee for the Trust. The Trust and Trust Administrator shall meet within seven (7) calendar days of receipt of the list and determine the arbitrator by alternately striking a name. The person whose name remains shall be the arbitrator.

The Arbitrator shall confer with the parties or their representatives and shall hold a hearing promptly, and shall issue a binding decision not later than fifteen (15) calendar days from the date of the close of the hearing. The Arbitrator's decision shall be in writing and shall set forth his findings of facts, reasoning, and conclusions on the issues submitted. The Arbitrator shall be without power or authority to recommend any decision which requires the commission of an act prohibited by law of which violates, modifies or alters the terms of the Trust Administrator Agreement. The decision of the arbitrator shall be binding on each of the parties and shall be communicated to each of them.

The parties agree that this procedure is the exclusive remedy to contest issues relating to the terms of this Agreement.

Article 8 – Miscellaneous

8.1 The laws of United Kingdom, are applicable to contracts made and wholly performed therein shall govern the validity, construction, performance and effect of this Agreement.

8.2 London, Great Britain shall shall be the primary exclusive venue, unless both parties mutually agree on another jurisdiction that practices English Common Law for any such action brought by the parties hereto and their respective successors and assigns.

8.3 This Agreement shall inure to the benefits of and be binding upon the parties hereto and their respective successors and assignees.

8.4 If any term, provision, covenant or condition of this of this Agreement, or any application thereof, should be held by a court of competent jurisdiction to be invalid, void or unenforceable, all provisions, and conditions of this Agreement and all applications thereof, not held invalid, void or unenforceable shall continue in full force and effect and shall in no way be affected, impaired or invalidated thereby. No addition to or modification of this Agreement shall be binding unless executed in writing by the Business Manager, the Trust Administrator and the Trust or their assigns.

8.5 Time is of the essence of this Agreement and all of the terms, provisions, covenants and conditions hereof.

IN WITNESS WHEREOF, the Trust, Business Manager and Trust Administrator have executed this Agreement as of the day and year first above written.

Date: _____   TRUST ADMINISTRATOR ON BEHALF OF
                             MexRx INVESTMENT TRUST (Trust)

Date _____   MexRx S.A. DE C.V. (Business Manager)

Date: _____   PriceWaterhouseCoopers (Trust Administrator)

REVPAC BOND
Investment Trust Certificate

MexRx INVESTMENT TRUST
REVENUE YIELD
COUPON #1
This coupon entitles the holder to receive the first Revenue Share disbursement of the Investment Trust upon the designated distribution date.
Registered Certificate Number A-1001
Revenue Yield Distribution Date: March 15, 20**

MexRx INVESTMENT TRUST
REVENUE YIELD
COUPON #2
This coupon entitles the holder to receive the second Revenue Share disbursement of the Investment Trust upon the designated distribution date.
Registered Certificate Number A-1001
Revenue Yield Distribution Date: March 15, 20**

MexRx INVESTMENT TRUST
REVENUE YIELD
COUPON #3
This coupon entitles the holder to receive the third Revenue Share disbursement of the Investment Trust upon the designated distribution date.
Registered Certificate Number A-1001
Revenue Yield Distribution Date: March 15, 20**

MexRx INVESTMENT TRUST
REVENUE YIELD
COUPON #4
This coupon entitles the holder to receive the fourth Revenue Share disbursement of the Investment Trust upon the designated distribution date.
Registered Certificate Number A-1001
Revenue Yield Distribution Date: March 15, 20**

MexRx INVESTMENT TRUST
REVENUE YIELD
COUPON #5
This coupon entitles the holder to receive the fifth Revenue Share disbursement of the Investment Trust upon the designated distribution date.
Registered Certificate Number A-1001
Revenue Yield Distribution Date: March 15, 20**

REVPAC BOND

REVENUE PARTICIPATION CAPITAL BOND

This is a "Unit" denominated certificate. Each of the Units represented by the certificate is comprised of One Revenue Share with five Revenue Yield Coupons, One Full Redemption Guaranty and One Future Participation Warrant. The Revenue Yield Coupons, Full Redemption Guaranty and Warrant may only be detached from this certificate for the purpose of exercising entitlements on the designated entitlement dates. The Unit certificate is to be transferred intact and without detachments prior to entitlement dates.

MexRx INVESTMENT TRUST
Authorized Capital – 954,000 REVPAC Bond Units
Registered under the Laws of the British Oversees Territory of Gibraltar.

This Certifies that ***"The Bank of New York"*** is the owner of ***1,000*** Revenue Participation Capital Bond Units of MexRx Investment Trust registered in the British Oversees Territory of Gibraltar.

This Certificate is transferable on the books of the Investment Trust by the holder in person or by Attorney upon surrender of this Certificate properly endorsed.

IN WITNESS WHEREOF, the said Administrator and Business Manager of the Investment Trust have caused this Certificate to be signed by their duly authorized officers and the Investment Trust Seal to be hereunto affixed.

Number of Units
1,000

Registered
Certificate Number
A-1001

This Fifteenth
Oscar Rivera
Investment Trust Administrator

day of **March A.D., 20**
Ross Hanbu
Investment Trust Business Manager

Seal — MexRx INVESTMENT TRUST

REVENUE SHARE

The registered holder is entitled to receive, on a pro-rata basis, all revenue yield disbursements as provided in the Collateralized Yield Obligation and Articles of Incorporation of the Investment Trust - the terms of which appear on the reverse side of this Certificate. This Revenue Share is valid for Seven Years and will reach full term on March 15, 20**

FULL REDEMPTION GUARANTY

This Guaranty entitles the holder to receive a redemption payment - concurrent with the final Revenue Yield Coupon disbursement - equivalent to the difference between the aggregate disbursements of all Revenue Yield Coupons and the IPO price up to a maximum cash payment of $5.00 per unit.

The holder may redeem this Full Redemption Guaranty coupon - in lieu of cash payment - for a newly issued Unit of the Investment Trust, for the ensuing seven year term of the Trust, by submitting this coupon together with the Warrant and applicable payment on the "Redemption Due Date".

FRG Coupon # A-1001 Redemption Date: March 15, 20**

FUTURE PARTICIPATION WARRANT

This warrant entitles the holder to purchase Units of the Investment Trust for the Seven-Year term commencing March 15, 20** and ending March 15, 20**. The amount of Units that the holder is entitled to purchase is equivalent to the number of Units evidenced by the Certificate to which this Warrant is attached.

To exercise the Warrant, the holder must submit this Warrant and payment of $5.00 per Unit on or before the expiration date. The holder may also surrender the Full Redemption Guaranty Coupon attached hereto as partial or full consideration for the exercise of the Future Participation Warrant.

WARRANT # A-1001   Expiration Date : March 15, 20**

REVENUE YIELD COUPON #1

Remit this coupon to the Administrator of the Investment Trust no later than10 days prior to the distribution date appearing on the face of this coupon.

Name of holder (Print) _____

Signature Guarantee

Signature (Signature must be guaranteed by banking or accredited financial institution.)

REVENUE YIELD COUPON #2

Remit this coupon to the Administrator of the Investment Trust no later than10 days prior to the distribution date appearing on the face of this coupon.

Name of holder (Print) _____

Signature Guarantee

Signature (Signature must be guaranteed by banking or accredited financial institution.)

REVENUE YIELD COUPON #3

Remit this coupon to the Administrator of the Investment Trust no later than10 days prior to the distribution date appearing on the face of this coupon.

Name of holder (Print) _____

Signature Guarantee

Signature (Signature must be guaranteed by banking or accredited financial institution.)

REVENUE YIELD COUPON #4

Remit this coupon to the Administrator of the Investment Trust no later than10 days prior to the distribution date appearing on the face of this coupon.

Name of holder (Print) _____

Signature Guarantee

Signature (Signature must be guaranteed by banking or accredited financial institution.)

REVENUE YIELD COUPON #5

Remit this coupon to the Administrator of the Investment Trust no later than10 days prior to the distribution date appearing on the face of this coupon.

Name of holder (Print) _____

Signature Guarantee

Signature (Signature must be guaranteed by banking or accredited financial institution.)

Future Participation Warrant

Remit this Future Participation Warrant to the Administrator of the Investment Trust - upon notification of the exercise date - and no later than 10 days prior to the Expiration Date appearing on the face of the Future Participation Warrant.

The holder demands exercise of the Warrant for a newly- issued Unit for ensuing term of Investment Trust.

Name of holder (Print) _____

Signature _____

Signature Guarantee

Signature must be guaranteed by banking or accredited financial institution.

Full Redemption Guaranty

Remit this Full Redemption Guaranty coupon to the Administrator of the Investment Trust - up to 90 days prior - and no later than the Redemption Date appearing on the face of the Full Redemption Guaranty coupon.

The holder demands redemption of:

Cash Payment ☐

Newly issued RevPac™ Unit for ensuing term of Investment Trust ☐

Name of holder (Print) _____

Signature _____

Signature Guarantee

Signature must be guaranteed by banking or accredited financial institution.

ENTITLEMENTS OF REVPAC BOND HOLDERS

The authorized REVPAC Bond Unit capitalization of the Investment Trust is Nine Hundred and Fifty Four Thousand (954,000) Units. In the event all REVPAC Bond Units are issued and outstanding, each REVPAC Bond Unit represents 1/954,000 full portion of the entitlements set forth below:

The Investment Trust REVPAC Bond Unit holders, as a group, are entitled to the following revenue participation, claim to ownership and redemption rights as provided in the Collateralized Yield Obligation and Articles of Incorporation of the Investment Trust.

• One Hundred Percent (100%) claim to ownership in title and interest in capital assets purchased from subscription proceeds of the Initial Public Offering of the Investment Trust and certain other Intellectual Property and License Rights as appearing in the Offering Prospectus.

• Twenty Percent (20%) of the gross sales revenues from proprietary medical/herbal products; Seven and One-half Percent (7.5%) of the gross sales revenues from non-proprietary over-the-counter/prescription medical products and all medical/surgical services derived by the Business Manager.

• In the event the Full Redemption Guaranty is attached to this certificate and effective, the REVPAC Bond Unit holder is entitled to receive one-half of the revenue participation and claim to ownership entitlements appearing herein. Maximum Full Redemption Payment to be distributed to REVPAC Bond holders is Five Dollars ($5.00) per REVPAC Bond Unit.

Investment Trust portion of all sales revenues by Business Manager accumulate in an interest bearing account for the holders of Investment Trust REVPAC Bond Units until disbursement by the Administrator of the Investment Trust. Revenue Yield distributions are due on Coupon #1-15/03/**; Coupon #2-15/03/**; Coupon #3-15/03/**; Coupon #4-15/03/** and Coupon #5-15/03/**.

TRANSFER OF CERTIFICATE

For Value Received, the registered holder hereby sells, assigns and transfers unto _____ Units of the Investment Trust represented by the within Certificate and does hereby irrevocably constitute and appoints _____ TO TRANSFER THE SAID Units on the books of the within named Investment Trust with full power of substitution in the premises.

Dated _____ 20____ In presence of _____

_____
Signature of registered holder

Signature Guarantee

Signature of holder must be guaranteed by banking or accredited financial institution.

Glossary

Most Commonly Used Terms

Affinity programs	Optional programs and incentives provided by the Business Manager to REVPAC Bond holders to encourage investing.
Built-In Risk Insurance Package Wrap	The Venture is wrapped with a complete Surety Risk Insurance Package of Policies. This "package" entails Ten (10) insurance, bond, guaranty, surety and warranty "wraps" that guarantee the performance of the Business Manager to get the Commercial Venture to the marketplace and ensure fiduciary accountability for all revenues.
Business Manager	The company, primary executive officer, or director of a venture. The Business Manager is responsible for the development and emergence of the venture into the marketplace. The Business Manager is performance-bonded to ensure that the venture is not compromised by any substantial failure on its part.
Collateralized Yield Obligation	Contract by which the Business Manager assigns to the Investment Trust all capital and Intellectual Property assets as collateral to secure the pledge to pay gross revenue yields to holders of Investment Trust REVPAC Bond Units.
Full Redemption Guaranty	A "unified" Investment Risk Insurance coverage – comprised of a composite of risk-insurance policies – guaranteeing the original investment price of the REVPAC Bond. The GUARANTY – SURETY Coverage guarantees that future Revenue Yields – disbursed through the Revenue Yield Coupons – will equal to /or/ be greater than the Initial Offering price of the REVPAC Bond.
Future Participation Warrant	The guaranteed opportunity to participate in a future venture inherent in each REVPAC issued at the IPO stage.

Incubating REVPAC Bonds

Investment Trust	The legal entity through which REVPAC Bond proceeds are passed to the Business Manager to fund the venture and to which gross revenue-sharing income passes for revenue yield distributions to REVPAC holders. The Investment Trust is assigned the rights, title, and interest to the capital assets purchased from the IPO proceeds and the proprietary rights to the venture during the term of the REVPAC Bond.
Revenue Participation Share	The entitlement of the investor to the revenue sharing rights of the venture — *usually a percentage of the gross revenues.*
Subordinated Debenture Wraps	REVPAC Variation - for select capital markets, laden with multiple tax levels, to provide a pass-through of revenue share yields to the investor.
Trust Administrator	The legal entity through which REVPAC proceeds are passed to the Business Manager to fund the venture and to which gross revenue sharing income passes for revenue yield distributions to REVPAC holders.
Trust Arbitration Association	A Trust Arbitration Association maintains the ultimate authority to ensure that the fiduciary responsibility of the Trust Administrator is met, and is tasked with arbitrating any disputes stemming from the administration of the REVPAC venture or the investment trust.
Underwriter	The entity that sponsors the REVPAC Bond IPO into the investment community and registers the REVPAC Bond for trading in secondary markets.
Venture	Any enterprise undertaken with the goal of revenue generation.

About the Author

Eminem L'Économiste is a Risk Management Actuarial Advisor to several Hedge and Pension Funds, commissioned to coordinate the fiduciary structuring of Venture Capital Programs and development of investment pipelines for SME and incubation financing of entrepreneurial ventures. Eminem has previously specialized as a securities analyst and underwriting syndicator for the entertainment business sector and served as one of the primary financial syndicators of the investment vehicles that developed Touchstone Pictures – *the American film distribution label of Walt Disney Studios Motion Pictures.*

REVPAC BONDS is Eminem's first hardback publication and he has his sights set on the acceptance of the book, into collegiate educational studies for business and economic development /and/ on-going post-graduate programs for professional service providers to the financial and investment communities.

Eminem resides with his family in London and New York.

NOTES

NOTES

NOTES

www.ingramcontent.com/pod-product-compliance
Lightning Source LLC
Chambersburg PA
CBHW061407210326
41598CB00035B/6123